WHAT DRIVES
FINANCIAL MARKETS

WHAT DRIVES FINANCIAL MARKETS

BRIAN KETTELL

PEARSON EDUCATION LIMITED

Head Office: ^R
Edinburgh Gate
Harlow, CM20 2JE

London Office:
128 Long Acre, London WC2E 9AN
Tel: +44 (0)171 447 2000
Fax: +44 (0)171 240 5771

First published in Great Britain in 1999

ISBN 0 273 63070 9

British Library Cataloguing in Publication Data
A CIP catalogue record for this book can be obtained from the British Library.

10 9 8 7 6 5 4 3

Typeset by Northern Phototypesetting Co. Ltd, Bolton.
Printed and bound in Great Britain by Redwood Books, Trowbridge.

The Publishers' policy is to use paper manufactured from sustainable forests.

ABOUT THE AUTHOR

Brian Kettell (MSc, BSc Econ) has many years experience working in financial markets and banking. A graduate of the London School of Economics, he has worked for Citibank, American Express, Arab Banking Corporation (Vice President) and Shearson Lehman (Vice President). This experience has since been applied in providing training courses on international financial markets. He has delivered training courses on the markets for a variety of organizations including Chase Manhattan Bank, Nomura, Morgan Stanley, Kleinwort Benson, Banque Indosuez and The Euromoney Institute of Finance. He is now Senior Lecturer at London University and a visiting Professor of Finance at several French Business Schools.

He has published widely (over 80 articles) in numerous journals including *Central Banking*, *The Banker*, and *The Securities Journal*, and his previous books include, *The International Debt Game* (with George Magnus, Chief Economist Warburg, Dillon, Read), *Businessman's Guide to the Foreign Exchange Market*, *Monetary Economics*, *The Finance of International Business*, *Gold*, and *The Foreign Exchange Handbook* (with Steve Bell, Chief Economist Deutsche Morgan Grenfell). In addition he has published a large number of case studies on financial markets.

The author would like to dedicate this book to his wife Nadia without whose support it would not have been written; and to the memory of his late parents Alan and Rosina.

CONTENTS

ACKNOWLEDGEMENTS

The author would like to acknowledge drawing on the insights from several excellent texts on US economic indicators. These include *The Business One Irwin Guide to Using The Wall Street Journal*, by Michael B. Lehman, *The Atlas of Economic Indicators*, by W. S. Carnes and S. D. Slifer, and *Using Economic Indicators To Improve Investment Analysis*, by E. M. Tainer.

INTRODUCTION

To say that the global financial markets were subject to information overload would be a major understatement. Indeed the news and data streaming endlessly from computer terminals providing the information that lubricates the workings of the financial world appear limitless. The four main information vendors had total sales of $4.4 billion in 1997.

The sheer volume of words and numbers is amazing. Reuters alone prints out the equivalent of 27,000 pages of data each second. A bond trader with a Bloomberg machine and a Bridge screen on one side, a Dow Jones screen on the other side, and a pair of Reuters terminals in front, plus a television set, an 80 button phone and a computer with company electronic mail on has a problem. How can traders distill this quantity of information into a coherent strategy from which they can endeavor to make money? The aim of writing this book is to provide answers to this problem.

In interpreting these data traders have to know which information they need to follow and which they can reliably ignore. Which indicators are worth paying attention to and which are not? How do the indicators relate to each other in order to build up a meaningful picture of the economy? How can you interpret this stream of information in order to make sensible investment decisions in the financial markets? These are the basic questions that this book addresses.

Many of the factors affecting financial markets are driven by the actions of the US Federal Reserve, the subject of a companion book *Fed-Watching*. Due to the fact that the behavior of financial markets and the actions of the Fed are inextricably connected readers should be aware that Chapters 3 and 4 of this book are also reproduced in *Fed-Watching*.

CHAPTER 1

The role of information in financial markets

INTRODUCTION

In 1980 the world wide market capitalization of all tradable financial assets was $5 trillion. At the end of 1998 it was $65 trillion – an astonishing average annual growth of 12 percent.

The creation of much of this tradable financial wealth has three main causes.

1. The successful and ongoing restructuring of major global corporations that keep driving down costs.
2. New forms of entrepreneurship that take advantage of information technology to exploit skills around the world.
3. The securitization of hitherto unsecuritized future income streams made possible by the revolution in financial risk management techniques that origi- -nated in US financial markets.

The extent to which communication methods and the impact of technology have speeded up over time was neatly illustrated by Alvin Toffler in *Future Shock* (1970), which highlights the rate and magnitude of change.

Man's existence has been estimated at 50,000 years and, using an average lifetime of 62 years this gives us a total of 800 lifetimes. As Toffler shows, of those 800 lifetimes:

- 650 were spent in caves;
- only in the last 70 have we had written communication;
- only in the last 6 have we had mass printing capability;
- only in the last 4 have we been able to measure time accurately;
- only in the last 2 have we had electricity;
- most material goods we use in daily life have been developed in this, the 800th lifetime.

This speeding up of information is clearly highlighted in its impact on financial markets. Indeed the news and data streaming endlessly from computer terminals providing the information that lubricates the workings of the financial world appear limitless.

Economic and financial indicators, like people, are rather diverse and not equally good at accomplishing every objective. As such, they are more helpful when studied individually. Getting to know the particular strengths and weaknesses of each indicator will better protect the decision maker from hasty interpretations of the latest statistics.

MAKING SENSE OF THE DATA

Imagine the first person on earth noticing what have become known as night and day. As the steady pattern of days and nights repeated, this first person became certain that day and night would occur. This certainty was a result of continued observations. The experience of the first days and weeks was probably one of terror and uncertainty. Certainty would not come until the pattern repeated many times.

Since the beginning of time people have desired to predict the future. Astrology, palm reading, tarot cards and the effect of sun spots and lunar cycles all have disciples, whose interest is future-oriented. Predictions of wars, political behavior, personal relationships, and business decisions are just a few areas addressed by the astute astrologer. The astrologer pays attention to the location of the planets, the palm reader to the length of the lifeline, and the tarot reader to the cards. All are observing what is taking place in the present with reference to the past. Based on what has happened in the past, a significant sign is looked for in the current observation, event or happening. This significant sign provides the basis for a forecast.

Opinions and/or decisions are flavored by experience based upon the store of observations. A larger number of observations increases the ability to arrive at a correct conclusion. Here the conclusion is intuitive, where intuition is defined as knowing without the use of rational processes.

On analyzing the thought processes by which intuitive decisions are made, the interpretation of information proceeds through several different stages before arriving at a decision. As more information is received, the probability of an event occurring can be categorized as:

- remote
- possible
- probable
- certain.

One of the toughest challenges facing the analyst working within financial markets is how to move through this sequence in order to keep on top of developments in the economy and then to relate them to investment decisions. Fortunately, the US government is a prodigious producer of indicators of the state of the economy, the alphabet soup of GNP, M2, CPI, etc. Little is done, however, by the US government nor by the financial media to put these indicators into a meaningful perspective for the analyst.

How can you interpret these indicators to understand better what is going on in the economy? Which indicators are worth paying attention to and which are not? How do they relate to each other to make up a meaningful picture of the economy? How do they relate to the investment decision in the financial markets? These are the basic questions this book addresses.

It is more essential than ever to know which economic and investment indicators are the most important and why. This book emphasizes understanding the economic environment using indicators that are announced in the media. It is not an encyclopedia or compendium of every statistic known to economists. No one can make intelligent use of the reams of numbers that government and private agencies produce. To try to understand the economy by looking at all the indicators would be like trying to understand astronomy by looking up at the night sky. The array is dazzling but completely overwhelming. What we need is a simple star chart that points out the key features.

To make sense of the volume of information available on the behavior of the financial markets we need some form of model around which we can incorporate new information as and when it occurs. Without a model we have no coherent way of incorporating new information. The appropriate model for analyzing financial markets is provided by an understanding of the "business cycle."

The National Bureau of Economic Research definition of a business cycle, namely:

> recurrent sequences of cumulative expansions and contractions in various economic processes which are both sufficiently diffused and sufficiently synchronized to show up as major fluctuations in comprehensive measures of employment, production, income and sales

is the one employed in this text.

The definition of a business cycle includes a requirement that expansions and contractions be diffused throughout the economy. Indicators are categorized by the particular economic process (or stage of the business cycle) to which they apply, so that the extent of diffusion and impact on financial markets can be analyzed. We will continually return to the stages of the business cycle and analyze its impact on financial markets throughout this book.

At this point it is useful to set out the broad reaction of the bond, equity and currency markets to these "recurrent sequences of cumulative expansions and contractions in economic processes which characterize the business cycle." The bond market reacts broadly to rising economic activity but positively welcomes falling economic activity. The equity market favors economic activity as long as it does not provoke a rise in interest rates. A depressed economy would send shivers through the equity market. A boom in economic activity with expectations of a rise in interest rates would be good news for the currency markets. However, rising economic activity combined with rising unemployment, which would prevent interest rates being forced up would be viewed unfavorably by currency markets.

The plethora of economic indicators

Economic measures that help to provide a reading on the economy's position are:

- *multidimensional* (production, prices, interest rates, employment, and so on);
- *varied in timing* (daily, weekly, monthly, annual);
- *collected from various sources* (shipping ladings, census, tax returns, sample surveys and so on);
- *reported by many different agencies* (Bureau of Economic Analysis (BEA), Bureau of Labor Statistics (BLS), Federal Reserve, United Nations, Organization for Economic Co-operation and Development (OECD), business associations and labor unions, corporations, among others).

In exercising economic indicators, numerous questions have to be asked.

- What are they? A definition is essential.
- What do they cover? What is and what is not included?
- What is their significance?
- Where and when are they publicized?
- How reliable are they?
- Will they be revised, or are the first-reported figures set in stone? If they are revised, how will financial markets react to the revisions?
- How do they affect financial markets?

As mentioned earlier, using the business cycle model gives us a framework to work from, enabling new information to be analyzed around a model which we broadly understand. With no model to work from, we cannot sensibly analyze new information.

How should we choose between all the information available to us?
Primary qualities and ingredients

The *primary* qualities that information should possess are those of *relevance* and *reliability*.

Relevance means that information must pertain to decision making, and the particular information must be necessary in that it makes a difference. Its primary ingredients in terms of information are outlined below.

● **Predictive value.** Should have some ability to help in making decisions that are future oriented and not historical.

● **Feedback value.** Should provide a basis for comparisons, such as comparing an actual with a forecasted value.

● **Timeliness.** Information must be available upon which to base decisions.

Reliability suggests different things to different people, but a desirable framework would include the following characteristics.

● **Verifiability.** An ability to replicate information by using defined procedures.

● **Neutrality.** Freedom from bias.

● **Representational faithfulness.** Information must represent that which it purports to represent, e.g., an item included in gross national product (*gnp*) belongs in it so that *gnp* is not understated and that the stated total of *gnp* is correct.

So economic indicators must be both relevant and reliable for them to be of value in the financial market place.

THE ROLE OF EXPECTATIONS IN FINANCIAL MARKETS

The critical judgement to be made when analyzing market behavior is on what the market is expecting and why. In financial market language, this is called knowing what has been "discounted" by the market.

For example, if it is widely believed that the Federal Reserve is likely to cut the *discount rate* over the next several weeks, then bond prices will reflect that belief. When the discount rate is actually cut, bond prices may not move very much, because the expectation that was discounted into the market was realized. On the other hand, if for some reason the Federal Reserve chooses not to cut the discount rate, when everyone thought it was going to, then bond prices may react quite negatively, because the expectation of a discount rate cut proved to be incorrect.

What this example shows is the important function that expectations play in the timing of a price movement. Major events that are widely anticipated may have absolutely no effect on prices at the time they occur. Other, equally major, events can have profound impacts on prices if they were not anticipated. The first lesson, then, of market dynamics and expectations is that one must know what future events have already been discounted by the market.

In this book we will be concentrating on examining market dynamics and expectations as to how financial markets react to the flood of economic statistics provided by the US government about the US economy. Market reactions to releases of economic data have often been quite swift and sometimes even violent, only to be reversed a few weeks later as other pieces of data are released. Indeed, the sensitivity of interest rates and stock prices to the release of economic data is an incredible phenomenon. It is incredible because most of the data are eventually revised, many of them are conflicting, and it takes a long time to put together a reasonable picture of what is happening to the economy. But the costs of missing the next move in stock prices or interest rates have become so large that even one more piece of information has taken on added importance. This can be most obviously seen when the markets await the data on non-farm payroll employment data, to which we will return.

EXPECTED VERSUS UNEXPECTED NEWS

The relationship between financial markets and news is straightforward. Expected news does not move markets. Unexpected news does move markets, particularly if it could provoke a policy response on the part of the authorities. An example of unexpected news is provided below, showing the text of a BridgeNews screen concerning the exchange rate at which the pound sterling could have rejoined the exchange rate mechanism.

BridgeNews broke an exclusive story on 7 May 1997 quoting a senior Labor source as saying the UK might rejoin EMU, though only if sterling was below its current levels. Immediately after, sterling fell 5 pfennigs against the Deutschmark and 3 cents against the US dollar. The UK currency remained under pressure throughout the following day as the story was picked up by major news-reporting services and acted upon by traders and economists, thereby becoming a worldwide event.

News can be both qualitative and quantitative. Qualitativeness is measuring by consumer confidence and consumer sentiment indicators. Quantitative news is provided from a wealth of regularly reported hard economic statistics. The basic principle is that if the news is potentially market sensitive then it must be monitored on a regular basis.

Not surprisingly it is also important to know why the news is market sensitive, as well as what the news is. So knowing what has been built into the market helps to analyze market movements when those expectations are or are not satisfied. Knowing why those expectations are in the market helps to analyze how those expectations will change as future economic data are released or government announcements on policy are made.

London – May 7 – 1997. The new Labour Government may join the European Union's Exchange-Rate Mechanism, although the current strength of sterling weighs against imminent entry. A senior Labour economic source told BridgeNews that UK membership might prove attractive if sterling had an entry rate of around 2.5 Deutschmarks rather than the current rate of 2.815 marks.

Sterling would have to fall from its current levels if the government were to take rejoining the ERM seriously, given the impracticality of having an entry rate that is far out of line with the current market rate, he said. The source said that the 'bad vibes' that followed the UK's ignominious exit from the ERM in 1992 had faded, making membership less politically awkward. Labour also has the bonus of being spared the historical ERM baggage that made it impossible for the Conservatives to even contemplate rejoining the system.

Unlike the Tories, Labour has not expressed an objection in principle to joining the ERM. Its concerns are likely to be of a practical nature – the strength of sterling and the width of the fluctuation bands.

Source: *BridgeNews*

Expected news is best measured by the numerous surveys of what the major market participants expect it to be. This is available from the provision of consensus or median numbers provided by the information vendors. It is then a simple exercise to compare the outcome with the consensus. An example of how this would be displayed on a computer screen is provided in Table 1.1.

Table 1.1

			Indicator/event	Previous	Consensus
Tue	14	Mar	CPI (8:30)	0.1%(1.4%)	0.1%(1.5%)
		Mar	CPI ex-food & energy (8:30)	0.3%(2.3%)	0.2%(2.3%)
		Mar	Retail sales (8:30)	0.5%(2.4%)	0.2%(2.9%)
		Mar	Retail sales ex-auto (8:30)	0.6%(2.9%)	0.1%(3.0%)
Wed	15	Feb	Inventories (8:30)	0.0%(4.0%)	0.3%(3.9%)
Thu	16	Mar	Housing starts (8:30)	1.44m (5%)	1.58m(7.0%)
		Apr	Philadelphia Fed survey (10:00)	16.1	17
Fri	17	Feb	International Trade (8:30)	–$12.0bn	–$11.6bn
		Mar	Industrial Production (8:30)	0.1%(4.9%)	+0.4%(5.0%)

There is a well known City of London joke regarding the impact of expectations: A chemist, an engineer and a City economist are marooned on a desert island. They have a can of baked beans but no can opener. The chemist suggests they heat up the can to such a temperature that it bursts. The engineer suggests they make a spear and throw it at the can. The economist taps his calculator and says not having a can opener is in line with market expectations.

HOW CAN YOU FOLLOW THE ECONOMY WHEN THEY KEEP CHANGING THE NUMBERS?

The challenge of charting the direction of the economy for the near future requires careful examination of the latest indicators. One reason for this is a challenge is that indicators often give conflicting signals. Another challenge is that they are frequently revised (*see* Table 1.2).

An example of these revisions was provided by data on total non-farm payroll employment, released on 5 May 1995, which indicated a pattern of slowing employment growth after February. The increase in employment in March was about half that of February, and the small employment decline in April was the first monthly decline since March 1993.

Table 1.2 ● Changes in non-farm payroll employment (in thousands, seasonally adjusted) 1995

Release as of	Jan	Feb	March	April	May	June
5 May	169	355	177	–9		
2 June	186	313	179	–7	–101	
7 July	186	313	179	8	–46	215

The June employment report provided even stronger evidence of a slowdown in economic activity. The May decline in payroll employment was the largest since April 1991. The July release however, changed the pattern substantially. Not only was there healthy growth in June payroll employment (+215), but the May decline was revised to less than half that reported one month earlier (–46).

Given the size of these revisions, how can you use an indicator like payroll employment to gauge trends in the economy? One principle is to use each series in conjunction with others, searching for an overall picture of the pace of economic activity. Another principle is to avoid basing your outlook only on the latest numbers. The latest data on payroll employment (and most other data) are based on incomplete information. The general direction of employment growth may look very different after adding an observation for another month and revisions to the prior data that reflect more complete information on the number of jobs.

In many instances the quality of reported statistics is very poor. Many of the figures which are closely watched represent aggregates of a number of spending components, each of which is subject to error. In some cases the errors tend to average out. However some figures, such as the trade balance or fiscal balance, represent differences between some very large quantities. Small revisions in one of the components can lead to major changes in the net result, a factor seasoned traders are very familiar with.

CHALLENGES TO OFFICIAL STATISTICS

In recent years, governments have made big efforts to improve the accuracy, timeliness and integrity of the statistics they collect. But are the numbers they collect relevant? Far too many statisticians are still trying to measure the output of the 19th century rather than the wizardry of the 21st. Three powerful forces pose special challenges to the traditional statistics.

Globalization

A growing proportion of trade and investment reflects internal decisions made by multinational corporations. This makes it harder to define national economic performance. Is Germany's economy measured best by including Volkswagen's production abroad, but excluding Ford's output in Germany? Some economists would argue that it is, but this would change the economic picture dramatically, and would instantly give the US a trade surplus instead of a chronic deficit.

Invisibility

Conventional statistics were originally devised for tracking the production of physical goods. A growing slice of output consists not of material things, but the production and manipulation of ideas. Output has become less visible, and hence less measurable. The number-crunchers have failed to keep pace. They still churn out masses of figures on the beef population, steel output or sales of "rubber and miscellaneous plastic products," yet fast-growing sectors such as software, telecommunications, entertainment, health care and financial services are barely tracked. In fields such as education and finance, government statistics often assume that output simply rises in line with the number of hours worked. Thus, by definition, productivity never rises.

Technology

New goods, shorter product cycles and rapid quality improvements make it harder to measure changes in output and prices over time. Isn't it great that faster recovery times from operations mean patients spend less time in hospital? Not from a statistician's point of view: if measured by occupancy of hospital beds, output would show a decline. A road-haulage firm might improve its service by using computer navigation to run its lorries more efficiently. But productivity as measured by tonne-miles would drop if lorries reach their destinations more directly.

SUMMARY

Economic indicators are among the most valuable tools that analysts have, as long as they know how to use them. For an economic indicator to be useful to the analyst it must satisfy four basic criteria. The first and most important is *relevance*. Which are the most important economic indicators for making investment decisions? What do they tell us about trends in the economy and how does that trend affect the financial markets? Indicators providing information about the trend in nominal GNP, i.e., real GNP and/or inflationary trends provide the most rewarding predictors of forthcoming policy changes.

A second important criterion is *timely release*. An indicator has to be announced soon enough to be of use. Some of the most widely publicized indicators are amongst the least satisfactory in this respect. Fortunately, other more timely indicators are available, if you know what they are.

A third key criterion is *availability*. The most useful indicators are those published in the financial press or on the screen in dealing rooms as soon as they are released. Other indicators of potential use to investors appear in government publications that take a couple of months to reach subscribers.

The fourth criterion is *stability*. An indicator that wiggles all over the place is of limited value. There is little point, for example, in losing sleep over the significance of the weekly money supply numbers announced by the Federal Reserve. Whether M2 is up or down depends too much on special circumstances in a given week and tells us little, if anything, about the direction of Federal Reserve policy. It makes much more sense to monitor indicators on a monthly basis, particularly looking to see what the trend has been over the past year.

CHAPTER 2

How do you value financial assets?

- The time value of money
- Future values: the role of compounding
- Present values: the role of discounting
- Bond and stock valuation
- Valuation of financial assets – an overview

THE TIME VALUE OF MONEY

The time value of money is a critical consideration in financial and investment decisions. For example, *compound interest* calculations are needed to determine future sums of money resulting from an investment. Discounting, or the calculation of *present values*, which is inversely related to compounding, is the normal method used to evaluate the cash flow associated with the valuation of financial assets.

FUTURE VALUES: THE ROLE OF COMPOUNDING

A dollar in hand today is worth more than a dollar to be received tomorrow because of the interest it could earn from putting it in a savings account. Compounding interest means that interest earns interest. In order to appreciate the concepts of compounding and time value we need some definitions. Let us define:

F_n = future value = the amount of money at the end of year n
P = principal
i = annual interest rate
n = number of years

Then,

F_1 = the amount of money at the end of year 1
= principal and interest = $P + iP = P(1 + i)$
F_2 = the amount of money at the end of year 2
= $F_1(1 + i) = P(1 + i)(1 + i) = P(1 + i)^2$

The future value of an investment compounded annually at rate i for n years is

$$F_n = P(1 + i)^n = P \cdot FVIF_{i,n}$$

where $FVIF_{i,n}$ is the future value interest factor for $1. This can be found in Table 2.1.

EXAMPLE 1

Nadia placed $1,000 in a savings account earning 8 percent interest compounded annually. How much money will she have in the account at the end of 4 years?

$$F_n = P(1 + i)^n$$
$$F_4 = \$1,000(1 + 0.08)^4 = \$1,000 \cdot FVIF_{8,4}$$

From Table 2.1 the FVIF for 4 years at 8 percent can be found to be 1.360. Therefore

$$F_4 = \$1,000(1.360) = \$1,360.$$

Table 2.1 ● Compounded future value of $1 (FVIF)

Years hence	1%	2%	3%	4%	5%	6%	7%	8%	9%
1	1.010	1.020	1.030	1.040	1.050	1.060	1.070	1.080	1.090
2	1.020	1.040	1.061	1.082	1.102	1.124	1.145	1.166	1.188
3	1.030	1.061	1.093	1.125	1.158	1.191	1.225	1.260	1.295
4	1.041	1.082	1.126	1.170	1.216	1.262	1.311	1.360	1.412
5	1.051	1.104	1.159	1.217	1.276	1.338	1.403	1.469	1.539
6	1.062	1.126	1.194	1.265	1.340	1.419	1.501	1.587	1.677
7	1.072	1.149	1.230	1.316	1.407	1.504	1.605	1.714	1.828
8	1.083	1.172	1.267	1.369	1.477	1.594	1.718	1.851	1.993
9	1.094	1.195	1.305	1.423	1.551	1.689	1.838	1.999	2.172
10	1.105	1.219	1.344	1.480	1.629	1.791	1.967	2.159	2.367

As can be seen from Table 2.1, the higher are interest rates, the higher are future values (and vice versa).

PRESENT VALUES: THE ROLE OF DISCOUNTING

Present value is the present worth of future sums of money. The process of calculating present values, or *discounting*, is actually the opposite of finding the compounded future value. In connection with present value calculations, the interest rate *i* is called the *discount rate*.

Recall that $F_n = P(1 + i)^n$

Therefore $$P = \frac{F_n}{(1 + i)^n} = F\left[\frac{1}{(1 + i)^n}\right] = F_n \cdot PVIF_{i,n}$$

Where $PVIF_{i,n}$ represents the present value interest factor for $1. This can be found in Table 2.2.

Nadia has been given an opportunity to receive $20,000 six years from now. If she can earn 10 percent on her investments, what is the most she should pay for this opportunity? To answer this question, one must compute the present value of $20,000 to be received 6 years from now at a 10 percent rate of discount. F_6 is $20,000, i is 10 percent, which equals 0.1, and n is 6 years. The $PVIF_{10,6}$ which can be found from Table 2.2 is 0.564.

$$P = \$20,000 \left[\frac{1}{(1+0.1)^6} \right] = \$20,000(PVIF_{10,6}) = \$20,000(0.564) = \$11,280$$

This means that Nadia, who can earn 10 percent on her investment, should be indifferent to the choice between receiving $11,280 now or $20,000 6 years from now since the amounts are time equivalent. In other words she could invest $11,280 today at 10 percent and have $20,000 in 6 years.

Table 2.2 ● Present value of $1 (PVIF)

Years hence	1%	2%	4%	5%	6%	8%	10%	12%	15%
1	.990	.980	.962	.952	.943	.926	.909	.893	.870
2	.980	.961	.925	.907	.890	.857	.826	.797	.756
3	.971	.942	.889	.864	.840	.794	.751	.712	.658
4	.961	.924	.855	.823	.792	.735	.683	.636	.572
5	.951	.906	.822	.784	.747	.681	.621	.567	.497
6	.942	.888	.790	.746	.705	.630	.564	.501	.432
7	.933	.871	.760	.711	.665	.583	.513	.452	.376
8	.923	.853	.731	.677	.627	.540	.467	.404	.327
9	.914	.837	.703	.645	.592	.500	.424	.361	.284
10	.905	.820	.676	.614	.558	.463	.386	.322	.247

As can be seen from Table 2.2, the higher are interest rates, the lower are present values (and vice versa).

BOND AND STOCK VALUATION

The process of determining the valuation of financial assets involves finding the present value of an asset's expected future cash flows using the investor's required rate of return. The basic security valuation model can be defined mathematically as follows:

$$V = \sum_{t=1}^{n} \frac{C_t}{(1 + r)^t}$$

Where V = intrinsic value or present value of an asset
C_t = expected future cash flows in period $t = 1,....,n$
r = investor's required rate of return.

Bond valuation

The valuation process for a bond requires a knowledge of three basic elements:

- the amount of the cash flows to be received by the investor, which is equal to the periodic interest to be received and the par value to be paid at maturity;
- the maturity date of the loan;
- the investor's required rate of return.

The periodic interest can be received annually or semi-annually. The value of a bond is simply the present value of these cash flows.

If the interest payments are made annually then

$$V = \sum_{t=1}^{n} \frac{I}{(1 + r)^t} + \frac{M}{(1 + r)^n} = I(\text{PVIFA}_{r,n}) + M(\text{PVIF}_{r,n})$$

where I = interest payment each year = coupon interest rate $\times$ par value
M = par value, or maturity value, typically \$1,000
r = investor's required rate of return
n = number of years to maturity
PVIFA = present value interest factor of an annuity of \$1 (which can be found in Table 2.3)
PVIF = present value interest factor of \$1 (which can be found in Table 2.2).

EXAMPLE

Consider a bond, maturing in 10 years and having a coupon rate of 8 percent. The par value is $1,000. Investors consider 10 percent to be an appropriate required rate of return in view of the risk level associated with this bond. The annual interest payment is $80 (8% × $1,000). The present value of this bond is

$$V = \sum_{t=1}^{n} \frac{I}{(1 + r)^t} + \frac{M}{(1 + r)^n} = I(PVIFA_{r,n}) + M(PVIF_{r,n})$$

$$= \sum_{t=1}^{10} \frac{\$80}{(1 + 0.1)^t} + \frac{\$1,000}{(1 + 0.1)^{10}} = \$80(PVIFA_{10\%,10}) + \$1,000(PVIF_{10\%,10})$$

$$= \$80(6.145) + \$1,000(0.386) = \$491.60 + \$386.00 = \$877.60$$

As can be seen from Tables 2.2 and 2.3, if the interest rate was higher both the PVIF and the PVIFA would be lower (and vice versa) for whatever time period we choose.

Table 2.3 ● Present value of an annuity of $1 (PVIFA)

Years	1%	2%	4%	5%	6%	8%	10%
1	0.990	0.980	0.962	0.952	0.943	0.926	0.909
2	1.970	1.942	1.886	1.859	1.833	1.783	1.736
3	2.941	2.884	2.775	2.723	2.673	2.577	2.487
4	3.902	3.808	3.630	3.546	3.465	3.312	3.170
5	4.853	4.713	4.452	4.329	4.212	3.993	3.791
6	5.795	5.601	5.242	5.076	4.917	4.623	4.355
7	6.728	6.472	6.002	5.786	5.582	5.206	4.868
8	7.652	7.325	6.733	6.463	6.210	5.747	5.335
9	8.566	8.162	7.435	7.108	6.802	6.247	5.759
10	9.471	8.983	8.111	7.722	7.360	6.710	6.145

Common stock valuation

Like bonds, the value of a common stock is the present value of all future cash inflows expected to be received by the investor. The cash inflows expected to be received are dividends and the future price at the time of the sale of the stock. For an investor holding a common stock for only one year, the value of the stock would be the present value of both the expected cash dividend to be received in one year (D_1) and the expected market price per share of the stock at year-end

(P_1). If r represents an investor's required rate of return, the value of the common stock (P_0) would be

$$P_0 = \frac{D_1}{(1 + r)^1} + \frac{P_1}{(1 + r)^1}$$

EXAMPLE

Assume an investor is considering the purchase of stock A at the beginning of the year. The dividend at year-end is expected to be $1.50, and the market price by the end of the year is expected to be $40. If the investor's required rate of return is 15 percent, and consulting Table 2.2, the value of the stock would be

$$P_0 = \frac{D_1}{(1 + r)^1} + \frac{P_1}{(1 + r)^1} = \frac{\$1.50}{(1 + 0.15)} + \frac{\$40}{(1 + 0.15)}$$

$$= \$1.50(0.870) + \$40(0.870) = \$1.31 + \$34.80 = \$36.11$$

Since common stock has no maturity date and is held for many years, a more general, multi-period model is needed. The general common stock valuation model is defined as

$$P_0 = \sum_{t=1}^{\infty} \frac{D_t}{(1 + r)^t}$$

There are three cases of growth in dividends.

1. Zero growth
2. Constant growth
3. Supernormal growth.

In the case of *zero growth*, if

$$D_0 = D_1 = ... = D\infty$$

then the valuation model

$$P_0 = \sum_{t=1}^{\infty} \frac{D_t}{(1 + r)^t}$$

reduces to the formula

$$P_0 = \frac{D_1}{r}$$

EXAMPLE

Assuming D equals $2.50 and r equals 10 percent, then the value of the stock is

$$P_0 = \frac{\$2.50}{0.1} = \$25$$

In the case of *constant growth*, if we assume that dividends grow at a constant rate of g every year, i.e., $D_t = D_0(1 + g)^t$, then the above model is simplified to

$$P_0 = \frac{D_1}{r - g}$$

This formula is known as the *Gordon growth model*.

EXAMPLE

Consider a common stock that paid a $3 dividend per share at the end of last year and is expected to pay a cash dividend every year at a growth rate of 10 percent. Assume that the investor's required rate of return is 12 percent. The value of the stock would be

$$D_1 = D_0(1 + g) = \$3(1 + 0.10) = \$3.30$$

$$P_0 = \frac{D_1}{r - g} = \frac{\$3.30}{0.12 - 0.10} = \$165$$

Finally, consider the case of *supernormal growth*. Firms typically go through life cycles, during part of which their growth is faster than that of the economy and then falls sharply. The value of stock during such supernormal growth can be found by taking the following steps:

● compute the dividends during the period of supernormal growth and find their present value;

● find the price of the stock at the end of the supernormal growth period and compute its present value;

● add these two present value figures to find the value (P_0) of the common stock.

EXAMPLE

Consider a common stock whose dividends are expected to grow at a 25 percent rate for 2 years, after which the growth rate is expected to fall to 5 percent. The dividend paid last period was $2. The investor desires a 12 percent return. To find the value of this stock, take the following steps:

1. Compute the dividends during the supernormal growth period and find their present value. Assuming D_0 is $2, g is 15 percent and r is 12 percent:

$$D_1 = D_0(1 + g) = \$2(1 + 0.25) = \$2.50$$
$$D_2 = D_0(1 + g)^2 = \$2(1.563) = \$3.125$$
or $$D_2 = D_1(1 + g) = \$2.50(1.25) = \$3.125$$

$$\text{PV of dividends} = \frac{D}{(1 + r)^1} + \frac{D_2}{(1 + r)^2} = \frac{\$2.50}{(1 + 0.12)} + \frac{\$3.125}{(1 + 0.12)^2}$$

$$= \$2.50(\text{PVIF}_{12\%,1}) + \$3.125(\text{PVIF}_{12\%,2})$$

From Table 2.2:
$$= \$2.50(0.893) + \$3.125(0.797) = \$2.23 + \$2.49 = \$4.72$$

2. Find the price of stock at the end of the supernormal growth period. The dividend for the third year is:

$$D_3 = D_2(1 + g'), \text{ where } g' = 5\%$$
$$= \$3.125(1 + 0.05) = \$3.28$$

The price of the stock is therefore:

$$P_2 = \frac{D_3}{r - g'} = \frac{\$3.28}{0.12 - 0.05} = \$46.86$$

PV of stock price = $46.86(\text{PVIF}_{12\%,2}) = \$46.86(0.797) = \$37.35$

3. Add the two PV figures obtained in steps 1 and 2 to find the value of the stock.

$$P_0 = \$4.72 + \$37.36 = \$42.08$$

VALUATION OF FINANCIAL ASSETS – AN OVERVIEW

Applying the simple valuation models outlined above provides us with a clear view of the impact of changes in interest rates on financial asset prices, particularly bonds and stocks. This principle is summarized in Figure 2.1. As will be evident we are assuming here that other factors are being held constant. Figure 2.2 illustrates that there are in fact many other factors which need to be taken into account when valuing stock prices.

	Bond price	Stock price
Interest rate rises	Falls	Falls
Interest rate falls	Rises	Rises

Fig 2.1 ● The impact on bonds and equities of changes in interest rates

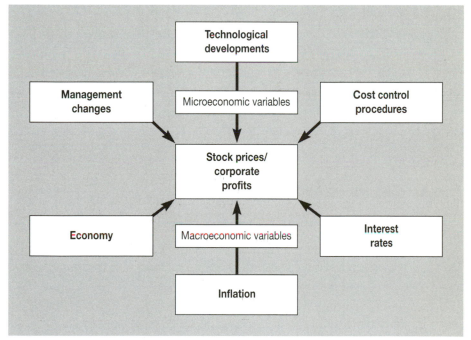

Fig 2.2 ● Factors affecting the stock market

Figure 2.3 summarizes the major factors that drive asset prices. It is important to note the key role of the discount rate and expected future cash flows, used to value financial assets.

It is here that the role of news needs to be stressed. As already detailed, expected news does not change asset prices. It is on the effect of unexpected news that it is essential to concentrate. Unexpected news can result in either a drastic reassessment of future cash flows, a drastic reassessment of the discount rate at which future cash flows are capitalized or changes in both.

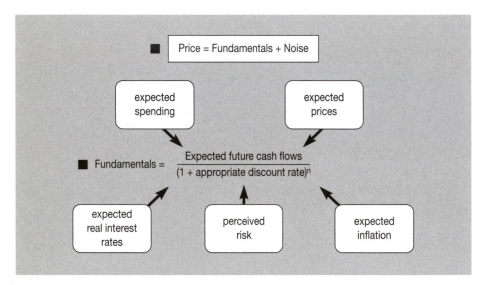

Fig 2.3 ● Asset prices and economic expectations

Present values and discount rates

The impact of changes in interest rates on present values is more dramatic when it is seen diagrammatically rather than using the statistical tables. The impact of a change in the discount rate on the present values of $1 is illustrated in Figures 2.4–2.7. The message that the higher the discount rate the lower the present value, and vice versa, comes out loud and clear.

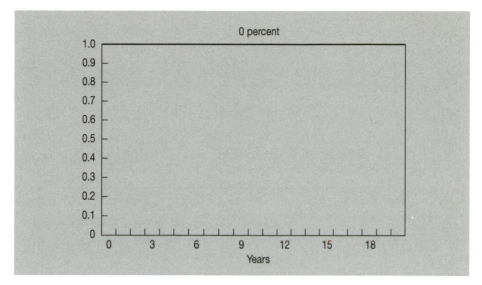

Fig 2.4 ● **$1 discounted at 0 percent after 20 years is still worth $1**

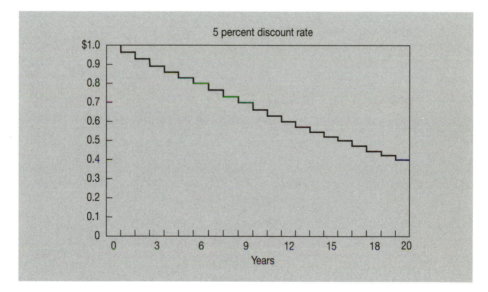

Fig 2.5 ● **$1 discounted at 5 percent after 20 years is worth around 40 cents**

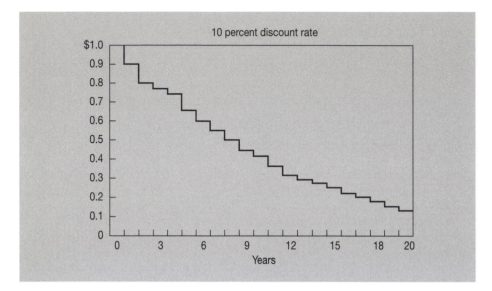

Fig 2.6 ● $1 discounted at 10 percent after 20 years is worth around 20 cents

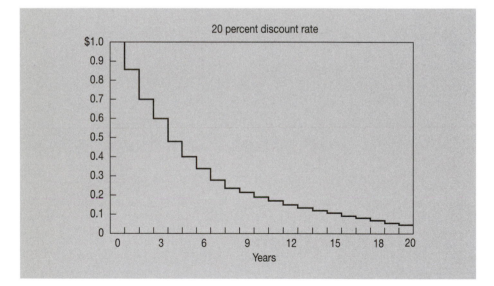

Fig 2.7 ● $1 discounted at 20 percent after 20 years is worth around 5 cents

It is the effect of these changes in discount rates which cause present values of financial assets to be so volatile when interest rates change.

Under the relentless pressures of compound interest, the value of future profits is ground to nothing as the years go by. Suppose, for example, that you had a choice between making the following two gifts to a charity – you could either write a cheque for $10,000 today, or give $1,000 a year for the next 100 years. The latter donation might seem the more generous one, but at a 10 percent interest rate, they are worth the same amount. By the time compound discounting had finished with it, that final $1,000 payment would be worth only 7 cents today (*see* Figure 2.8).

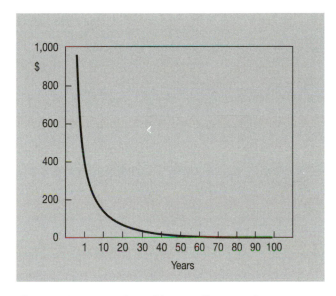

Fig 2.8 ● **Present value of $1,000 discounted at 10 percent**

Company shares adhere to a similar logic. Their value derives ultimately from the never-ending stream of dividends they are expected to pay out. But for a typical blue-chip stock, around a third of its value derives from dividends during the first decade.

The sensitivity of bond prices to interest rates is illustrated in Figure 2.9. This example shows how a 10 percent coupon bond with different maturities varies as interest rates change. The inverse relationship between bond prices and interest rates is clear. In addition, longer dated maturities can be seen to be more volatile than shorter dated maturities.

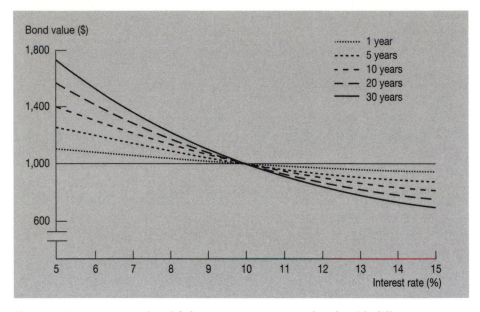

Fig 2.9 ● Interest rate price risk for 10 percent coupon bonds with different maturities

CHAPTER **3**

The business cycle and financial markets

HOW DOES THE BUSINESS CYCLE AFFECT FINANCIAL MARKETS?

The "business cycle" refers to the phenomenon whereby there are ups and downs in the level of economic activity over time and to the fact that these ups and downs invariably recur. It is the latter fact which means that an understanding of the business cycle provides a forecasting framework which can confidently be used to analyze the way financial markets are expected to behave, given that we know at which stage of the business cycle the economy currently is. This forecasting framework is the subject matter of this chapter. Appendix 3.3 discusses the much-debated question as to whether the business cycle remains alive and kicking despite the duration of the US economic upswing which commenced in 1991.

The exact response of financial markets to different stages of the business cycle will be analyzed later in the chapter, but at this stage it is useful to summarize some of the conclusions for the bond, equity, and foreign exchange markets.

- **Bonds** Too much economic activity is bad news, as it may force up interest rates. Too little economic activity is good news, as it could result in falling interest.
- **Equities** Economic activity is good news as long as there is no rise in interest rates. Economic activity increases the likelihood of higher earnings and subsequently dividends. An economic slowdown would have the opposite effect.
- **Foreign exchange** If interest rates rise this is normally good news for the currency, increasing, as it does, the returns from holding the currency. However if there are domestic reasons to prevent rising interest rates, such as high unemployment and there is simultaneously bad news on the inflation side then this is bad news for the currency market. Falling interest rates normally cause the currency to weaken.

Business activity historically goes through waves of expansion followed by waves of contraction. At one stage of the cycle production, employment and profits rise which is then followed by another phase when profits, prices, and output fall resulting in rising unemployment. Then the entire cycle repeats itself. During the expansion phase, demand, production, income, and wealth all grow. Houses and factories are constructed, and investment in machinery and equipment takes place. House prices, share prices, and other assets grow in value. But then comes the inevitable contraction and the forces that caused wealth to rise go into reverse. Demand, production, and incomes fall. The amount of house-building and investment in factories are drastically reduced. Assets fall in value as house prices and share prices fall.

Although no two business cycles are identical, all (or most) cycles have features in common. This point has been made strongly by a leading business cycle theorist and recent Nobel prize winner, Robert E. Lucas, Jr, of the University of Chicago:

> Though there is absolutely no theoretical reason to anticipate it, one is led by the facts to conclude that, with respect to the qualitative behaviour of comovement among economic variables, that *business cycles are all alike*. To theoretically inclined economists, this conclusion should be attractive and challenging, for it suggests the possibility of a unified explanation of business cycles, grounded in the *general* laws governing market economies rather than in political or institutional characteristics specific to particular countries or periods.[1]

Lucas's statement that business cycles are all alike (or more accurately that they have many features in common) is based on examinations of comovement among economic variables over the business cycle.

KEY FEATURES OF THE BUSINESS CYCLE

That business cycles occur and repeat themselves is not in dispute. The causes of regularity and the length and duration of the phases of the cycle have not been completely satisfactorily explained, although Figure 3.1 sets out what seems to be the most plausible explanation. The only certain factor is that the business cycle is created by internal forces from within the economic system. Certain key features of the cycle do recur and it is to these that we now turn. Figure 3.1 provides a summary of many of these characteristics.

1. Forces of supply and demand condition every cycle. Supply creates its own demand. By producing goods incomes are thereby increased which enables employees to buy more goods and services.

2. Neither businesses nor consumers are constrained in their spending pattern to rely solely upon the income they have generated in the process of production. Credit is available.

3. Every expansion carries with it the inevitability of over-expansion and subsequent contraction. Over-borrowing takes place. This need to repay as interest rates rise stretches the ability of individuals to keep spending, forcing a reduction in spending.

4. During contractions production and incomes recede to a sustainable level (i.e., a level not reliant upon a continuous growth in credit).

5. Every contraction sows the seed of the subsequent recovery. As interest rates fall borrowing becomes cheaper, investment and spending rise, and the cycle starts over again.

Fig 3.1 ● Key features of the business cycle

Source: Adapted from Chapter 2, *The Business One Guide to Using the Wall Street Journal*, M. B. Lehman.

It is useful to examine these features in more detail.[2]

- **First, the forces of supply and demand condition every cycle.** In order to enjoy increasing income we must supply or create increased production or output. The level of demand, and the expenditures made in purchasing this output, must justify the level of production. In other words, we must sell what we produce in order to earn an income. With sufficient demand, the level of production will be sustained and will grow, and incomes will increase. If demand is insufficient, the reverse will occur. During the expansionary phase of the cycle, demand and supply interact permitting the growth of production and incomes; during the contractionary phase, their relationship forces a decrease in production and incomes.

- **Second, consumers and businesses are not constrained to rely solely on income generated in the process of production.** They can borrow money and spend more than they earn. Spending borrowed funds permits demand to be higher than current income. This gives rise to the expansionary phase of the cycle. Eventually, the growth in production becomes dependent on the continued availability of credit, which sustains the growth in demand. But once buyers can no longer rely on borrowed funds (because of market saturation, the exhaustion of profitable investment opportunities, or tight credit), demand falls and, with it, the bloated level of production and income. The contractionary phase has begun.

- **Third, every expansion carries with it the inevitability of "overexpansion" and the subsequent contraction is inevitable.** Overexpansion may be caused by businesses that invest too heavily in new plant and equipment in order to take advantage of a seemingly profitable opportunity, or by consumers who borrow too heavily in order to buy homes, autos, or other goods. But when businesses realize that the expected level of sales will not support additional plant and equipment, and when consumers realize that they will have difficulty paying for that new home or auto, then businesses and consumers will curtail their borrowing and expenditure. Since production and income have risen to meet the growth in demand, they fall when the inevitable contraction in demand takes place.

- **Fourth, during contractions, production and incomes recede to a sustainable level, that is, to a level not reliant on a continuous growth in credit.** The contraction returns the economy to a more efficient level of operation.

- **Fifth, every contraction sows the seeds of the subsequent recovery.** Income earned in the productive process rather than the stretched levels of borrowing, maintains the level of demand. Consumers and businesses repay their debts. Eventually, lower debt burdens and interest rates encourage consumer and business borrowing and demand. The economy begins expanding once more.

The cyclical behavior of economic variables: direction and timing

Two characteristics of the cyclical behavior of macroeconomic variables are important to the discussion of the business cycle facts. The first is the *direction* in which a macroeconomic variable moves, relative to the direction of aggregate economic activity. An economic variable that moves in the same direction as aggregate economic activity (up in expansions, down in contractions) is "pro-cyclical." A variable that moves oppositely to aggregate economic activity (up in contractions, down in expansions) is "countercyclical." Variables that do not display a clear pattern over the business cycle are "acyclical."

The second characteristic is the timing of the variable's turning points (peaks and troughs) relative to the turning points of the business cycle. An economic variable is a "leading variable" if it tends to move in advance of aggregate economic activity. In other words, the peaks and troughs in a leading variable occur before the corresponding peaks and troughs in the business cycle. A "coincident variable" is one whose peaks and troughs occur at about the same time as the corresponding business cycle peaks and troughs. Finally, a "lagging variable" is one whose peaks and troughs tend to occur later than the corresponding peaks and troughs in the business cycle.

The fact that some economic variables consistently lead the business cycle suggests that they might be used to forecast the future course of the economy. In some cases the cyclical timing of a variable is obvious from a graph of its behavior over the course of several business cycles; in other cases elaborate statistical techniques are needed to determine timing. Conveniently, the Statistical Indicators Branch of the Bureau of Economic Analysis (BEA) has analyzed the timing of dozens of economic variables. This information is published monthly in the *Survey of Current Business*, along with the most recent data for these variables (*see* Figure 3.2).

Variable	Direction	Timing
Production		
Industrial production	Procyclical	Coincident
Durable goods industries are more volatile than non-durable goods and services		
Expenditure		
Consumption	Procyclical	Coincident
Business fixed investment	Procyclical	Coincident
Residential investment	Procyclical	Leading
Inventory investment	Procyclical	Leading
Government purchases	Procyclical	___[a]
Investment is more volatile than consumption		
Labour Market Variables		
Employment	Procyclical	Coincident
Unemployment	Countercyclical	Unclassified[b]
Average labor productivity	Procyclical	Leading[a]
Real wage	Procyclical	___[a]
Money Growth and Inflation		
Money growth	Procyclical	Leading[c]
Inflation	Procyclical	Lagging
Financial Variables		
Stock prices	Procyclical	Leading
Nominal interest rates	Procyclical	Lagging
Real interest rates	Acyclical	___[a]

[a] Timing is not officially designated by Bureau of Economic Analysis.

[b] Officially designated as "unclassified" by the Bureau of Economic Analysis

[c] M1 money growth is a leading variable; M2 money growth leads the cycle at peaks but is coincident at troughs and is officially "unclassified" overall

Fig 3.2 ● The cyclical behavior of key macroeconomic variables

Source: Survey of Current Business, May 1993. Industrial production: series 47 (total industrial production); consumption: series 57 (manufacturing and trade sales, 1987 dollars); business fixed investment: series 86 (gross private non-residential fixed investment); residential investment: series 89 (gross private residential fixed investment); inventory investment: series 30 (change in business inventories); employment: series 41 (employees on agricultural payrolls); unemployment: series 43 (civilian unemployment rate); money supply: series 85 (percent change in money supply, M1) and series 102 (percent change in money supply, M2); inflation: series 120 (CPI for services, change from previous month, smoothed); stock prices: series 19 (index of stock prices, 500 common stocks); nominal interest rates: series 119 (Federal funds rate), series 114 (discount rate on new issues of 91-day Treasury bills), series 109 (average prime rate charged by banks)

THE STAGES OF THE BUSINESS CYCLE[3]

From the point of view of analyzing financial market behavior during the business cycle, it is useful to break down the cycle into four phases:

- **Phase One:** Trough to recovery
- **Phase Two:** Recovery to expansion
- **Phase Three:** Expansion to peak
- **Phase Four:** Peak to contraction.

The phases are summarized in Figure 3.3.

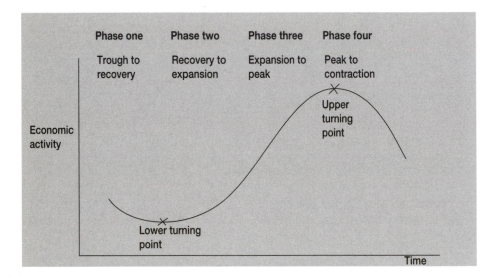

Fig 3.3 ● **The phases of the business cycle**

Phase one: from trough to recovery

During this phase, GNP and industrial production are falling and capacity utilization is declining. This leads to an increase in labor productivity and a fall in unit labor costs, driving down the rate of inflation, as measured by producer prices. Pressures for a fall in interest rates build up. The central bank, seeing rising unemployment, will be actively stimulating the economy with an easing of monetary policy. Figure 3.4 summarizes this phase, and Figure 3.5 illustrates the yield curve implications.

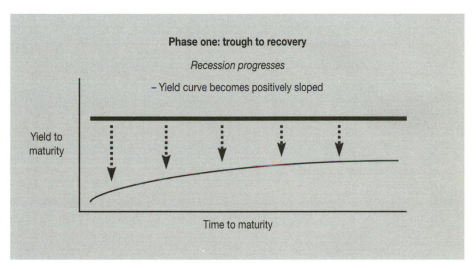

GNP	↓
Industrial production	↓
Capacity utilization	↓
Labor productivity	↑
Unit labor costs	↓
Producer prices	↓
Interest rate trend	↘

Fig 3.4 ● Phase one (Trough to recovery)

Phase one: trough to recovery

Recession progresses

– Yield curve becomes positively sloped

Yield to maturity

Time to maturity

Fig 3.5 ● Yield curve in Phase one

Phase two: from recovery to expansion

At this stage economic activity starts to pick up, reinforced by cheap credit and low inflation. Fluctuations in consumer prices are a key determinant of consumer real income, so a fall in inflation is a boost to real income. This leads to improved consumer sentiment and demand which in turn drives economic expansion. This is evidenced by increased demand in the economy fueled by a rise in consumer credit and increased spending on autos, a rise in retail sales and a rise in the demand for housing (*see* Figure 3.6). The trend in interest rates is one in which pressures are starting to build for rising rates. Figure 3.7 illustrates the yield curve implications.

Consumer price index ↓

Consumer real income ↑

Consumer sentiment ↑

Consumer demand ↑

| Auto sales ↑ | Consumer credit ↑ | Retail sales ↑ | Housing starts ↑ |

Interest rate trend ⇄

Fig 3.6 ● Phase two (Recovery to expansion)

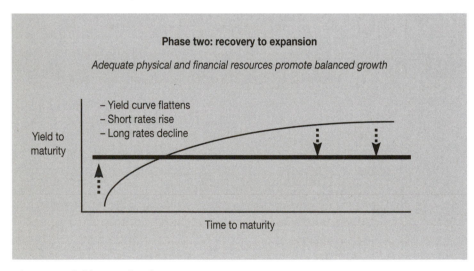

Phase two: recovery to expansion

Adequate physical and financial resources promote balanced growth

– Yield curve flattens
– Short rates rise
– Long rates decline

Yield to maturity

Time to maturity

Fig 3.7 ● Yield curve in Phase two

Phase three: from expansion to peak

From Phase two of the business cycle it becomes clear that all the indicators of economic expansion, auto sales, consumer credit, retail sales, housing starts are showing improvements. This will initiate broad-based growth as incomes increase in the construction, auto, and other durable goods industries, spilling over and boosting demand for other consumer goods. Boom conditions will intensify as business invests in additional factories and machinery to meet the extra orders.

As the expansion unfolds, capacity utilization increases with the growth in demand and production. Soon factories move from, say, 70 percent to 80 percent of their maximum output. Production facilities strain to meet demand and to retain the loyalty of customers.

Next, high levels of capacity utilization drive labor productivity down and unit labor costs up as efficiency is sacrificed in the name of increased output. Machinery which is always in use cannot be adequately maintained and will tend to break down. Inexperienced workers cannot make the same contribution as old hands. The amount of labor employed increases more rapidly than output, and as output per worker falls, the labor cost per unit of output rises. This generates a surge in production costs.

Rapidly increasing costs are translated into rapidly increasing prices, and a renewed round of inflation begins.

At this stage there will be pressures for the Fed to raise interest rates in an attempt to restrain the ensuing inflation.

This third phase of the business cycle (from expansion to peak) is the inverse of the first. All the forces which led to a reduction in the rate of inflation are now reversed (*see* Figure 3.8, and Figure 3.9 for the yield curve implications).

Gross National Product	↑
Industrial production	↑
Capacity utilization	↑
Labor productivity	↓
Unit labor costs	↑
Producer prices	↑
Interest rate trend	↑

Fig 3.8 ● Phase three (Expansion to peak)

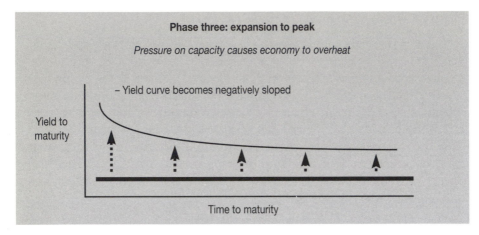

Phase three: expansion to peak

Pressure on capacity causes economy to overheat

– Yield curve becomes negatively sloped

Yield to maturity

Time to maturity

Fig 3.9 ● Yield curve in Phase three

Phase four: from peak to contraction

From Phase three we know that economic expansion generates reduced efficiency and heightened inflation. As production grows, and with it capacity utilization, labor productivity falls. Labor costs increase, driving prices upward. The economy has reached a level of activity which cannot be sustained.

The fourth phase of the business cycle is the inverse of the second. In that phase of the cycle, from recovery to expansion, a declining rate of inflation pushed consumer real income upward, prompting consumers to borrow and spend, thus fueling the economic expansion. Now, in the last phase of the cycle, a rising rate of inflation has the opposite impact on the consumer. Real income falls, and consumer sentiment erodes. Consumers become pessimistic when their salaries don't keep up with inflation, giving them less and less real buying power. They respond by restricting their purchase of postponable items, especially those which require heavy borrowing. The downturn in consumer activity will lead to a general contraction in demand which will continue until the trough of the cycle is reached and the whole cycle starts again (*see* Figures 3.10, and 3.11 for the yield curve implications).

So by observing which phase of the business cycle the economy is passing through we have a strong feeling for the shape of the yield curve and with it the appropriate implications for the financial markets.

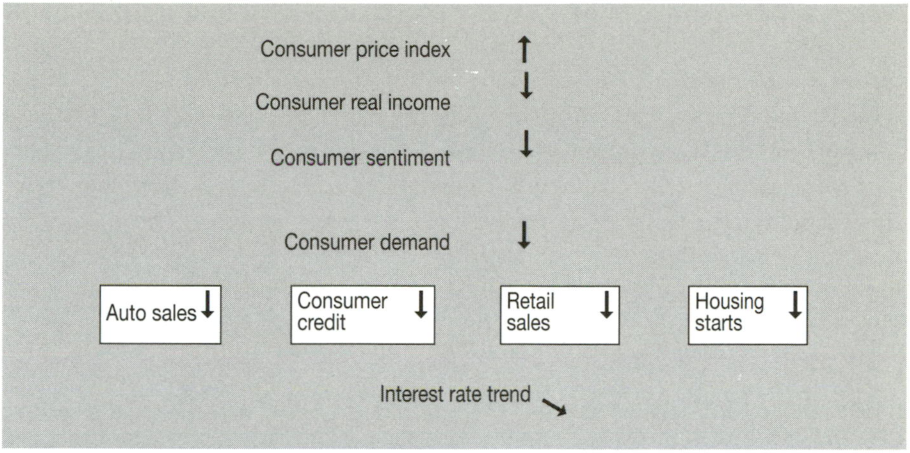

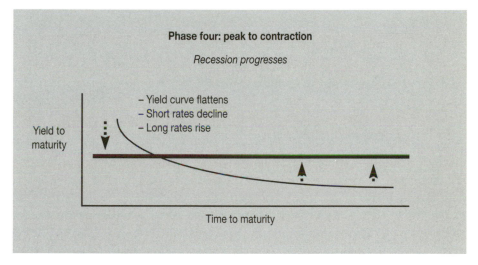

Fig 3.10 ● Phase four (Peak to contraction)

Phase four: peak to contraction

Recession progresses

Yield to maturity

– Yield curve flattens
– Short rates decline
– Long rates rise

Time to maturity

Fig 3.11 ● Yield curve in Phase four

THE ROLE OF INVENTORIES IN RECESSIONS

Historically, most post-war recessions have been characterized by a significant reduction in aggregate inventory investment relative to the reduction from peak to trough of the GNP. In trying to predict the duration of a recession, it is important to monitor the behavior of business inventories. Indeed economic recessions can be triggered by an over-supply of business inventories. The effect of an over-supply of inventories which results in inventory reductions accounted for more than 40 percent of the real GNP decline in each of the nine recessions since 1947. In the recessions of 1948 and 1960, all of the decline in real GNP can be attributed to a drop in inventory investment to negative levels.

Inventory investment, or changes in business inventories, is pro-cyclical and a leading indicator but also extremely volatile. For example, between 1982 and 1990 inventory investment fluctuated sharply, despite the fact that the economy was continuously in expansion.

Inventory behavior cannot be ignored, despite its volatility. Consequently, it must be monitored if the next stage of the business cycle is to be anticipated.

THE BUSINESS CYCLE AND MONETARY POLICY

As already indicated, the outlook for the economy and expectation of households and businesses plays a central role in the magnitude and timing of monetary policy effects on the economy. Households' own experience with the cyclical rise and fall in interest rates may affect their actions. A sustained sharp rise in interest rates, for example, may suggest more uncertain prospects for employment and incomes, resulting in greater household caution toward spending on consumer goods and house purchases. Conversely, a significant fall in interest rates during a period of weak economic activity may encourage greater consumer spending by increasing the value of household assets. Lower mortgage rates, together with greater availability of mortgage credit, also may stimulate the demand for housing.

Businesses plan their inventories and additions to productive capacity (i.e., capital spending) to meet future customer demands and their own sales expectations. Since internal resources – retained earnings and depreciation allowances – do not provide all of their cash requirements, businesses are often obliged to use the credit markets to finance capital spending and inventories.

During a business cycle expansion, the business sector's need for external financing rises rapidly, as firms accumulate inventories to ensure that sales rise rapidly. Firms accumulate inventories to ensure that sales will not be lost because of shortages. At the same time, businesses attempt to finance additions to capacity. Greater business demand for funds tends to bid up interest rates. In making investment decisions, such investors take into account recent experience with inflation and inflation expectations, as well as numerous other factors, including the federal budget deficit, long-term interest rates and the credibility of monetary policy. These same considerations are also important in the transmission of monetary policy to the foreign exchange market.

How monetary policy affects the economy

By causing changes in interest rates, financial markets and the dollar exchange rate, monetary policy actions have important effects on output, employment and prices. These effects work through many different channels, affecting demand. Figure 3.12 shows the main contours of the transmission of monetary policy to the economy. Monetary policy actions influence output, employment and prices through a number of complex channels. These channels involve a variety of forces in financial markets that cause changes in (1) the cost and availability of funds to businesses and households, (2) the value of household assets or net worth, and (3) the foreign exchange value of the dollar with direct consequences for import/export prices. All changes, in due course, affect economic activity and prices in various sectors of the economy.

When the Federal Reserve tightens monetary policy – for example, by draining bank reserves through open market sales of Government securities – the Federal funds rate and other short-term interest rates rise more or less immediately, reflecting the reduced supply of bank reserves in the market. Sustained increases in short-term interest rates lead to lower growth of deposits and money as well as higher long-term interest rates. Higher interest rates raise the cost of funds, and, over time, have adverse consequences for business investment demand, home buying and consumer spending on durable goods, other things remaining the same. This is the conventional money or interest rate channel of monetary policy influence on the economy.

A firming of monetary policy also may reduce the supply of bank loans through higher funding costs for banks or through increases in the perceived riskiness of bank loans. Similarly, non-bank sources of credit to the private sector may become more scarce because of higher lending risks (actual or perceived) associated with tighter monetary conditions. The reduced availability – as distinct from costs – of loans may have negative effects on aggregate demand and output. This is the so-called "credit channel" that may operate alongside the interest rate channel.

Higher interest rates and lower monetary growth also may influence economic activity through the "wealth channel" by lowering actual or expected asset values. For example, rising interest rates generally tend to lower bond and stock prices, reducing household net worth and weakening business balance sheets. As a consequence, business and household spending may suffer.

Finally, a monetary policy tightening affects economic activity by raising the

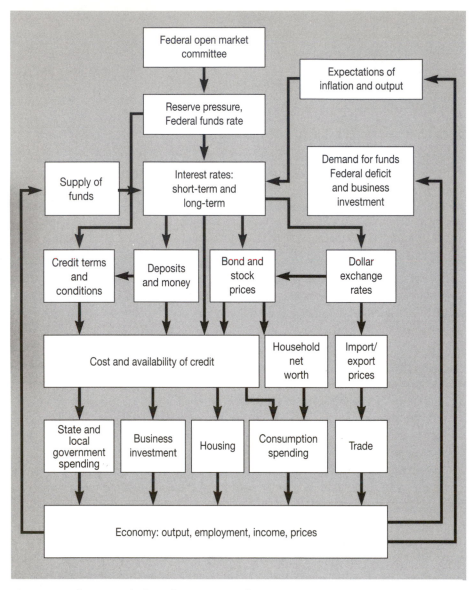

Fig 3.12 ● The transmission of monetary policy

foreign exchange value of the dollar – the exchange rate channel. By making US imports cheaper and by increasing the cost of US exports to foreigners, the appreciation of the dollar reduces the demand for US goods, and, therefore, has adverse consequences for the trade balance and output. On the positive side, lower import prices help in improving the US inflation performance.

Needless to say, all these effects work in the opposite direction when the Federal Reserve eases monetary policy.

FUNDAMENTAL ANALYSIS, THE BUSINESS CYCLE, AND FINANCIAL MARKETS

"Fundamental analysis," as it is known in financial markets, is closely tied to the supply of and demand for money. The money supply, in turn, affects the level of interest rates, bond prices, and the currency markets. Because so many factors – discussed in earlier chapters – influence the supply of and demand for money, the reaction of financial markets is somewhat complex.

In general, however, traders watch three major sources of information:

● the key economic reports issued by various government agencies and private organizations;

● the Federal Reserve Bank; and

● the US Treasury department.

The major financial markets focus on different types of economic indicators. Figure 3.13 provides a survey of some of the more important economic indicators. For a detailed discussion of the sensitivities of financial markets to economic and non-economic indicators refer to *Fed Watching* by Brian Kettell, published by Financial Times Prentice Hall. Fixed-income markets are primarily concerned with reports that address the pace of economic growth and inflation. The foreign exchange markets also look at these figures, as well as at foreign trade imbalances. The stockmarket is affected by economic growth to the extent that this affects general earnings. But stocks are also dependent on specific company and industry fundamentals. In addition, changes in interest rates will affect the stockmarket to the extent that interest rate shifts may cause investors to be more or less attracted to stocks relative to bonds.

Prior to the release of an economic report, many of the news services survey the major dealers and publish forecasts. These surveys are an excellent barometer of the financial markets' expectations and are built into market prices prior to the report's release date.

Report	Description	Degree of impact	Typical release date	Released by	Period covered
Consumer Price Index	The Consumer Price Index measures the average change in prices for a fixed basket of goods and services	High	10th Business Day	Labor Dept. Bureau of Statistics	Prior Month
Durable Goods	One of a series of manufacturing and trade reports. Focuses on new orders	Moderate	18th Business Day	Commerce Dept. Census Bureau	Prior Month
Employment	A survey of households providing very timely information on the rate of unemployment	Very High	First Friday of the Month	Labor Dept. Bureau of Statistics	Prior Month
Gross Domestic Product	Gross Domestic Product measures the value of items produced within the United States	Very High (for initial estimate)	20th Business Day	Commerce Dept. Bureau of Economic Analysis	Prior Quarter
Housing Starts	Measures new residential units started. Most significant for the financial markets during turning points in the business cycle	Moderate	15th Business Day	Commerce Dept. Census Bureau	Prior Month
Industrial Production	Industrial Production measures output in manufacturing, mining and utility industries	Moderate	15th Business Day	Federal Reserve Bank	Prior Month
Merchandise Trade	Details the monthly exports and imports of US goods	Moderate to High	Third Week of the Month	Commerce Dept. Census Bureau	Two Months Prior
NAPM	The (National Association of) Purchasing Managers Index is a composite index of new orders, production, supplier deliveries inventories, and employment	High	First Business Day of the Month	National Association of Purchasing Management	Prior Month
Producer Price Index	The Producer Price Index measures the average domestic change in prices, less discounts received, by wholesale producers of commodities	High	10th Business Day	Labor Dept. Bureau of Statistics	Prior Month
Retail Sales	A measure of consumer spending, reporting sales of both nondurable and durable consumer goods	High	Mid-month	Commerce Dept. Census Bureau	Prior Month
Unemployment Insurance Claims	Reflects actual initial claims for unemployment insurance filed with state unemployment agencies	Moderate	Every Thursday	Labor Dept. Employment and Training Administration	Prior Week ending Saturday

Fig 3.13 ● Major economic reports and their degree of impact on financial markets

Source: Chicago Board of Trade

But the forecasts are not always accurate. Once the number is released, prices quickly adjust to reflect the new information. Figure 3.14 summarizes how the major financial markets typically react to news that varies from initial expectations.

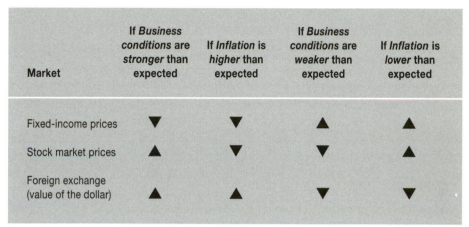

Market	If *Business conditions* are *stronger* than expected	If *Inflation* is *higher* than expected	If *Business conditions* are *weaker* than expected	If *Inflation* is *lower* than expected
Fixed-income prices	▼	▼	▲	▲
Stock market prices	▲	▼	▼	▲
Foreign exchange (value of the dollar)	▲	▲	▼	▼

Source: The information in this table is drawn from *Trading the Fundamentals: The Trader's Complete Guide to Interpreting Economic Indicators and Monetary Policy*, by Michael P. Niemira and Gerald F. Zukowski, Chicago, Probus Publishing Company, Inc., 1994

Fig 3.14 ● The impact of economic news on financial markets

To illustrate the impact of economic news consider the fixed-income markets. Assume that the employment report showed a lower unemployment rate than expected. This would signal stronger business conditions, more consumer income, and increased spending – all signs that the economy is heating up. This news would tend to drive interest rates up. And because prices and yields move inversely in the fixed-income markets, an increase in interest rates would mean a decrease in bond prices.

Over time, the markets tend to favor and follow certain reports over others. For example, if the current concern is centered on inflation, then the CPI and PPI reports will take on more significance. If the value of the dollar and its impact on international trade becomes a major issue, then the merchandise trade report becomes more important.

THE NBER AND BUSINESS CYCLES

In the United States the National Bureau of Economic Research (NBER), a private non-profit organization of economists founded in 1920, pioneered business cycle research. The NBER developed and continues to update "business cycle chronology," a detailed history of business cycles in the United States and other countries. The NBER has also sponsored many studies of business cycles. One landmark study was the 1946 book *Measuring Business Cycles*, by Arthur Burns (who also served as Federal Reserve chairman) and Wesley Mitchell (a principal founder of the NBER). This work was among the first to document and analyze the empirical facts about business cycles. It begins with the following definition:

> Business cycles are a type of fluctuation found in the aggregate economic activity of nations that organize their work mainly in business enterprises. A cycle consists of expansions occurring at about the same time as many economic activities, followed by similarly general recessions, contractions, and revivals which merge into the expansion phase of the business cycle; this sequence of changes is recurrent but not periodic; in duration business cycles vary from more than one year to ten or 12 years.

Explanation of terms

Five points in this definition should be clarified and emphasized.

Aggregate economic activity

Business cycles are defined broadly as fluctuations of "aggregate economic activity" rather than fluctuations in any single specific economic variable such as real GDP. Although real GDP may be the single variable that most closely measures aggregate economic activity Burns and Mitchell also thought it important to look at other indicators of activity, such as employment and financial market variables.

Expansion and contractions

Figure 3.15 – a diagram of a typical business cycle – helps explain what Burns and Mitchell meant by expansions and contractions. The dashed line shows the average, or normal, growth path of aggregate economic activity, and the solid curve shows the rises and falls of actual business activity. The period of time during which aggregate economic activity is falling is a "contraction" or "recession." If the recession is particularly severe, it becomes a "depression." After reaching the low point of the contraction, the "trough" *(T)*, economic activity begins to increase. The period of time during which aggregate economic activity grows is an "expansion" or a "boom." After reaching the high point of the expansion, the "peak" *(P)*, aggregate economic activity begins to decline again. The entire sequence of decline followed by recovery, measured from peak to peak or trough to trough, is a "business cycle."

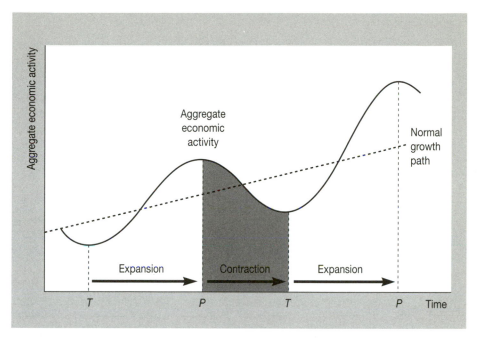

Fig 3.15 ● A typical business cycle

Peaks and troughs in the business cycle are known collectively as "turning points." One goal of business cycle research is to identify when turning points occur. Aggregate economic activity isn't measured directly by any single variable, so there is no simple formula that tells economists when a peak or trough has been reached. In practice, a small group of economists who form the NBER's Business Cycle Dating Committee determine that date. The committee meets only when its members believe that a turning point may have occurred. By examining a variety of economic data, the committee determines whether a peak or trough has been reached and, if so, the month it happened. However, the committee's announcements usually come well after a peak or trough occurs, so their judgments are more useful for historical analysis of business cycles than as a guide to current policymaking.

A specific cycle is a set of turning points observable in a particular series. These turns may or may not correspond to the overall business cycle turning point dates. The selection of a turn must meet the following criteria:

● The cycle duration must be at least 15 months, as measured from either peak to peak or trough to trough.

● If the peak or trough zone is flat, then the latest value is selected as the turn.

● Strike activity or other special factors generally are ignored, if their effect is brief and fully reversible.

Comovement

Business cycles do not occur in just a few sectors or in just a few economic variables. Instead, expansions or contractions occur at about the same time in many economic activities. Thus, although some industries are more sensitive to the business cycle than others, output and employment in most industries tend to fall in recessions and rise in expansions. Many other economic variables, such as prices, productivity, investment, and government purchases, also have regular and predictable patterns of behavior over the course of the business cycle. This tendency is called "comovement."

Recurrent but not periodic

The business cycle is not periodic, in that it does not occur at regular, predictable intervals and does not last for a fixed or predetermined length of time. Although the business cycle is not periodic, it is recurrent; that is, the standard pattern of contraction–trough–expansion–peak recurs again and again in industrial economies.

Persistence

The duration of a complete business cycle can vary greatly, from about a year to more than a decade, and predicting it is extremely difficult. However, once a recession begins, the economy tends to keep contracting for a period of time, perhaps for a year or more. Similarly an expansion, once begun, usually lasts a while. This tendency for declines in economic activity to be followed by more growth, is called "persistence." Because movements in economic activity have some persistence, economic forecasters are always on the lookout for turning points, which are likely to indicate a change in the direction of economic activity.

HOW DO YOU IDENTIFY A RECESSION?

A conventional definition used by the financial media – that a recession has occurred when there are two consecutive quarters of negative real GDP growth – is not widely accepted by economists. The reason that economists tend not to like this definition is that real GDP is only one of many possible indicators of economic activity.

A more complete statement, used by the NBER for spotting a recession would include:

- Real GDP should decline at least one-quarter and industrial production contract for at least four to six months.
- There should be a contraction, for at least four to six months, in one or more of the following series:

(a) industrial production

(b) real disposable personal income

(c) employment and/or

(d) aggregate hours worked.

● The employment diffusion index should decline below 40 percent of all industries expanding their workforce, on a one-month change basis, and remain below that point for at least four to six months. (Diffusion indexes are explained in Appendix 3.1.)

The unemployment rate criteria which is widely discussed seems less useful since it can be affected by demographic influences. For example, during the 1990 recession, the unemployment rate was held down by a "demographic bonus" – a shrinking or very slowly growing labor force.

THE AMERICAN BUSINESS CYCLE: THE HISTORICAL RECORD

An overview of American business cycle history is provided by the NBER's monthly business cycle chronology, as summarized in Table 3.1. It gives the dates of the troughs and peaks of the 31 complete business cycles that the US economy has experienced since 1854. Also shown are the number of months that each contraction and expansion lasted.

Post-World War II US business cycles

As World War II was ending in 1945, economists and policymakers were concerned that the economy would relapse into depression. As an expression of this concern, Congress passed the Employment Act of 1946, which required the government to fight recessions and depressions with any measures at its disposal. But instead of falling into a new depression as feared, the US economy began to grow strongly.

Only a few relatively brief and mild recessions interrupted the economic expansion of the early post-war period. None of the five contractions that occurred between 1945 and 1970 lasted more than a year, whereas 18 of the 22 previous cyclical contractions in the NBER's monthly chronology had lasted a year or more. The largest drop in real GDP between 1945 and 1970 was 3.3 percent during the 1957–58 recession, and throughout this period unemployment never exceeded 8.1 percent of the work force. Historically there has been a strong correlation between economic expansion and war. The 1949–53 expansion corresponded closely to the Korean War, and the latter part of the strong 1961–69 expansion occurred during the military build-up to fight the Vietnam War.

Because no serious recession occurred between 1945 and 1970, some economists suggested that the business cycle had been "tamed," or even that it was "dead." This view, which continues today, was especially popular during the record 106-month expansion of 1961–69, which was widely attributed not only to high rates of military spending during the Vietnam War, but also to the macroeconomic policies of Presidents Kennedy and Johnson. Some argued that policymakers should stop worrying about recessions and focus their attention on inflation, which had been gradually increasing during the 1960s.

Unfortunately, reports of the business cycle's death proved premature. Shortly after the view that the business cycle was dead because the conventional wisdom the Organization of Petroleum Exporting Countries (OPEC) succeeded in quadrupling oil prices in the fall of 1973, the US economy and the economies of many other nations fell into a severe recession. In the 1973–75 recession, American real GDP fell by 4.1 percent and the unemployment rate reached 9 percent – not a depression but a serious downturn, nonetheless. Also disturbing was the fact that inflation, which had fallen during most previous recessions, shot up to unprecedented double-digit levels. Inflation continued to be a problem for the rest of the 1970s, even as the economy recovered from the 1973–75 recession.

More evidence that the business cycle was not dead came with the sharp 1981–82 recession. This contraction lasted 16 months, the same length as the 1973–75 decline, and the unemployment rate reached 11 percent, a post-war high. Inflation did drop dramatically, from about 11 percent to less than 4 percent per year. The recovery from this recession was strong, however, and the ensuing expansion continued until the summer of 1990.

In July 1990 the expansion of almost eight years ended, and the economy entered a recession. This recession was relatively short (the trough came in March 1991, only eight months after the peak) and shallow (the unemployment rate peaked in mid-1992 at 7.7 percent, not particularly high for a recession).

Appendix 3.2 provides a summary of US business cycle surveys. Information is provided on business investment and consumer surveys and these can usefully be used in parallel with the NBER publications.

THE GOLDILOCKS ECONOMY

Figure 3.16 illustrates recent behavior of real gross domestic product since 1972. The shaded areas indicate recessions. It is the length of the non-shaded areas that have suggested to many economists that the business cycle is now dead. This recent enviable combination of steady growth and low inflation is widely referred to as a "Goldilocks economy" after the fairy tale story, *The Three Bears*, in which the character Goldilocks eats the bear's food which is "neither too hot nor too cold."

Table 3.1 ● NBER business cycle turning points and durations of post-1854 business cycles

Trough	Expansion (months from trough to peak)		Peak	Contraction (months from peak to next trough)	
Dec. 1854	30		June 1857	18	
Dec. 1858	22		Oct. 1860	8	
June 1861	46		Apr. 1865	32	
Dec. 1867	18		June 1869	18	
Dec. 1870	34		Oct. 1873	65	
Mar. 1879	36		Mar. 1882	38	
May 1885	22		Mar. 1887	13	
Apr. 1888	27		July 1890	10	
May 1891	20		Jan 1893	17	
June 1894	18		Dec. 1895	18	
June 1897	24		June 1899	18	
Dec. 1900	21		Sep. 1902	23	
Aug. 1904	33		May 1907	13	
June 1908	19		Jan. 1910	24	
Jan. 1912	12		Jan. 1913	23	
Dec. 1914	44	WWI	Aug. 1918	7	
Mar. 1919	10		Jan. 1920	18	
July 1921	22		May 1923	14	
July 1924	27		Oct. 1926	13	
Nov. 1927	21		Aug. 1929	43	(Depression)
Mar. 1933	50		May 1937	13	(Depression)
June 1938	80	WWII	Feb. 1945	8	
Oct. 1945	37		Nov. 1948	11	
Oct. 1949	45	(Korean War)	July 1953	10	
May 1954	39		Aug. 1957	8	
Apr. 1958	24		Apr. 1960	10	
Feb. 1961	106	(Vietnam War)	Dec. 1969	11	
Nov. 1970	36		Nov. 1973	16	
Mar. 1975	58		Jan. 1980	6	
July 1980	12		July 1981	16	
Nov. 1982	92		July 1990	8	
Mar. 1991					

Source: Survey of Current Business, April 1993, page C-25: Business Cycle Expansions and Contractions

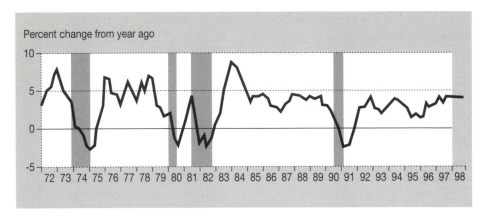

Fig 3.16 ● Real gross domestic product

Source: National Economic Trends

The business cycle expansion period which commenced in March 1991 continues to this day. Suggestions that, yet again, the business cycle has ended are discussed further in Appendix 3.3.

Are long expansions followed by short contractions?

Simple graphical analysis seems to indicate that, in the post-war period, long expansions are followed by short contractions: *see* Figure 3.17.

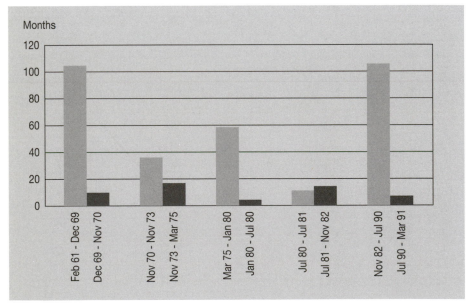

Fig 3.17 ● Lengths of last five expansions and contractions

The long expansion (106 months) of the 1960s was followed by a short contraction of only 11 months. The shorter expansion (36 months) in the early 1970s was followed by a somewhat longer contraction of 16 months. The next expansion in the late 1970s (58 months) was longer, and the following contraction was shorter (six months). Then there was a very short expansion from July 1980 to July 1981 (12 months) followed by a long contraction (16 months). Finally, the great expansion of November 1982 to July 1990 was followed by a brief contraction that ended in March 1991. The expansion from that time continues until today.

THE NON-ACCELERATING INFLATION RATE OF UNEMPLOYMENT (NAIRU)

A new target for the Fed?

The non-accelerating inflation rate of unemployment (NAIRU) is sometimes also referred to as the "natural" rate of unemployment – that rate which can be sustained without a change in the inflation rate. The NAIRU concept features prominently in the Phillips curve. The Phillips curve is the relationship which shows that high rates of unemployment are associated with low rates of change of money wages whilst low rates of unemployment are associated with high rates of change of money wages.

The importance of the Phillips curve was that policy makers (and particularly governments), applying this concept, changed their views about how the economy might be managed. Many became convinced that there was a trade-off between unemployment and inflation. Zero inflation (i.e., price stability) could be achieved but only by keeping unemployment at what, for the time, seemed a relatively high level. On the other hand, lower unemployment could be achieved by accepting higher levels of inflation. But the key to the Phillips curve is that it illustrated that it was impossible to fix both the rate of unemployment and the rate of inflation at desirable levels.

The concept of NAIRU has acquired significance since it seems to be embraced by both Laurence Meyer, a Governor of the Fed and Alan Greenspan, Chairman of the Fed. The application of NAIRU to predicting Fed actions would suggest that if the Fed foresees low unemployment, it will tighten monetary policy and slow the economy. If the current unemployment rate is below the non-accelerating rate, there will be wage and price pressures with inflation rising. Periods when the actual unemployment rate is below the national rate suggest a booming economy and pressure for the Fed to raise interest rates. Periods when the actual unemployment rate is above the natural rate are periods of recessionary pressures when the Fed could be expected to lower interest rates.

The fact that unemployment can remain in an economy which is booming reflects imperfections in labor markets, imperfections that exist regardless of the overall state of the economy. Unemployment may exist as people may have the wrong skills, live in the wrong areas or have little incentive to accept the jobs they are offered. Consequently this unemployment remains irrespective of the cyclical nature of the economy.

Recent estimates of the actual unemployment rate and the natural unemployment rate are given in Figure 3.18. The relationship between unemployment and inflation is given in Figure 3.19. The unemployment gap is calculated from Figure 3.19 by subtracting the natural rate of unemployment from the actual unemployment rate.

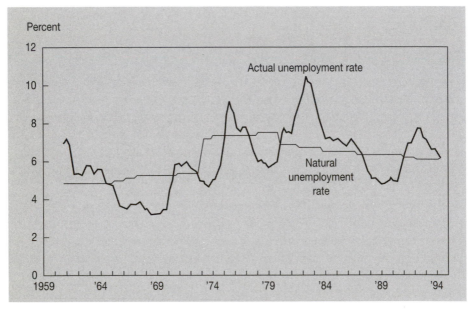

Fig 3.18 ● Actual unemployment rate and the natural unemployment rate

Sources: Actual unemployment rate: US Department of Labor, Natural unemployment rate: Stuart E. Weiner, "New Estimates of the Natural Rate of Unemployment," Federal Reserve Bank of Kansas City, *Economic Review*, 1993: Q4

Historically, the gap between the actual unemployment rate and the natural unemployment rate has been a reliable indicator of future increases in inflation. This can be seen in Figure 3.19. The shaded areas represent periods of sustained rises in inflation, with beginning and ending inflation rates noted along the top edge. The "unemployment gap" is calculated from Figure 3.18 and equals the actual unemployment rate minus the natural unemployment rate. Thus in Figure 3.19, when the gap moves below the zero line, the actual unemployment rate is below the natural rate, and when the gap moves above the zero line, the actual unemployment rate is above the natural rate.

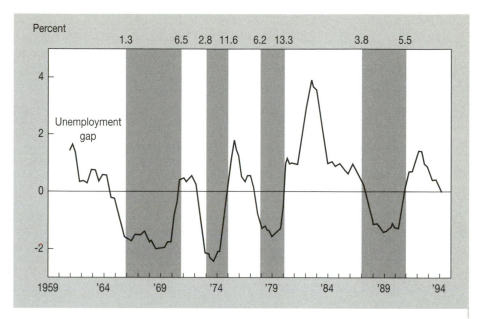

Fig 3.19 ● The unemployment gap and inflation

Sources: Actual unemployment rate and inflation: US Department of Labor, Natural unemployment rate: Stuart E. Weiner, "New Estimates of the Natural Rate of Unemployment." Federal Reserve Bank of Kansas City, *Economic Review*, 1993: Q4

Notes: Shaded areas represent periods of rising inflation as measured by the consumer price index less food and energy; beginning and ending inflation rates are noted along the top edge. The unemployment gap is calculated by subtracting the natural rate of unemployment from the actual unemployment rate.

As shown by the shaded areas in Figure 3.19, the US economy has experienced four periods of sustained increases in inflation between 1959 and 1994. In all four cases, the increases were accompanied by the actual unemployment rate going below the natural unemployment rate. And at no time has there been a false signal; that is, at no time has the actual unemployment rate gone below the natural rate without the economy ultimately experiencing a rise in inflation.

Why might NAIRU be useful to central banks?

One of the problems with monetary policy is that there are time lags between when a policy action is taken and when it takes effect. Therefore in controlling inflation it is dangerous to look only at current rates of inflation. By the time inflation actually begins to rise, inflationary pressures may have been brewing for a year or two and it may take a substantial tightening of policy (possibly leading to a recession) to slow them down.

According to standard thinking of the way the economy works, using the NAIRU concept, if there is an increase in overall spending in the economy it will be followed by inflation. So increases in demand raise real GDP relative to its potential level, which increases the demand for labor to produce the additional goods and services, and therefore lowers the unemployment rate relative to the NAIRU. Excess demand in goods and labor markets leads to higher inflation in goods, prices, and wages with a lag. Because of this, the unemployment rate can help in generating the inflation forecasts that are crucial in formulating monetary policy.

What are the limitations of the use of NAIRU?

There are both empirical and theoretical problems with NAIRU. On the empirical side the estimated NAIRU for the United States has varied in the post-war period. In the 1960s, the NAIRU commonly was estimated at around 5 percent. By the mid-1970s, it had climbed to around 7 percent. And by the mid-1990s, it had fallen back to 6 percent. A number of factors can affect the NAIRU, including changes in labor force demographics, governmental unemployment programs, and regional economic disturbances.

A related empirical criticism is that the NAIRU cannot be estimated with much precision. Based upon comprehensive empirical analysis of Phillips curves the evidence seems to suggest that the NAIRU falls within a range of 4.8 percent to 6.6 percent. Given this kind of uncertainty, the NAIRU can provide misleading signals for monetary policy at various times.

A theoretical objection to the use of the NAIRU for monetary policy is that the short-run trade-off between unemployment and inflation may be unstable over time. This trade-off is sensitive to the way in which expectations about inflation are formed, which in turn will depend upon the nature of the monetary policy regime itself. A further theoretical objection is that the NAIRU makes sense as an indicator of future inflation only when the economy is subjected to a large increase in the demand for goods and services.

However, the economy could also be affected by supply shocks or unexpected changes in the aggregate supply of goods and services. An example of a supply shock would be a sudden increase in productivity. Initially, this kind of shock would raise the quantity of goods and services produced relative to the quantity demanded, and thus put *downward* pressure on prices. At the same time, the increase in real GDP would raise the demand for labor and reduce the unemployment rate. Thus, a falling unemployment rate would be associated with reduced pressure on prices. If a central bank were using the NAIRU to guide policy in this case, it might mistakenly see the lower unemployment rate as a reason to fear higher inflation in the future, and therefore might tighten policy.

Some observers argue that a supply shock in recent years is having an effect on the economy. One explanation for this recent development is a surge in productivity due to the introduction of new computer-related technologies. So a rising real GDP can occur at the same time as falling inflation. Therefore, standard Phillips curve analysis would over-forecast inflation.

Fed Chairman, Alan Greenspan, speaking at his July 1997 Humphrey–Hawkins Testimony, expressed the view that technological change has added to workers insecurity in recent years and made them less willing to push for higher wages and this may be thought of as one version of the effect of new technology. Greater insecurity might reduce the upward pressure on wage rates at any unemployment rate and so lower the threshold rate at which wages (and prices) would begin to move upwards.

THE FUTURE OF THE BUSINESS CYCLE

There is considerable empirical evidence that business cycles have manifested themselves in all market-orientated industrialized economies since detailed statistics have been in existence. Their existence is here to stay, albeit not necessarily in the same shape, form, diffusion, and duration. At least four underlying forces are likely to shape the business cycle of the future and these are described further in Appendix 3.3. They are:

● the maturity of the economy
● the degree of globalization of the economy and related technological developments
● demographic change
● the rapidity at which the post-cold-war environment unfolds.

The ability of an economy to thrive will naturally be bound up with the ability of other economies to thrive. In contemplating growth and stability for any open economy, the problems posed by the diverse stages of maturity reached by other economies will be crucial. The relationship between the structural requirements imposed by the labor force, by advancing technology, by demographic change, of aging and of growth in mature economies has implications for domestic consumption, investment, and government spending with spill-over effects on demand for goods from the rest of the world.

In discussing the future of the business cycle it is instructive to bear in mind the comments made by Alan Greenspan, Chairman of the Federal Reserve in his February 1997 Humphrey–Hawkins Testimony.

> We have had 15 years of economic expansion interrupted by only one recession – and that was six years ago. **There is no evidence, however, that the business cycle has been repealed.** Another recession will doubtless occur some day owing

to circumstances that could not be, or at least were not, perceived by policy makers and financial market participants alike.

History demonstrates that participants in financial markets are susceptible to waves of optimism, which can in turn foster a general process of asset-price inflation that can feed through into markets for goods and services.

Excessive optimism sows the seeds of its own reversal in the form of imbalances that tend to grow over time. When unwarranted expectations ultimately are not realized the unwinding of these financial excesses can act to amplify a downturn in economic activity, much as they amplify the upswing.

REFERENCES

1. Lucas, Robert E., Jr (1977) "Understanding Business Cycles," in Brunner, K. and Meltzer, A. H. (eds) *Carnegie-Rochester Conference Series on Public Policy*, vol. 5, Autumn, p. 10.

2. This section draws heavily on Lehman, M. B. *The Business One Irwin Guide to Using the Wall Street Journal*, 1990.

3. This section also draws on Lehman, M. B.

Diffusion indexes: a note on how to interpret them

Arthur F. Burns, in his book *Measuring Business Cycles* observed that a business cycle expansion does not imply that every underlying economic activity is expanding nor does a business cycle contraction mean that every business cycle firm has declining sales. He further observed that economic activity has two types of cycles: *seen* and *unseen*. One cycle is in the fluctuation of the aggregate measure itself and consequently is seen. But a second cycle – the unseen or *diffusion* cycle – exists in the distribution of components within that aggregate based on the number of expanding or contracting segments. This unseen cycle is important because it helps to monitor and forecast the path of the cycle. In particular, cyclical expansions or contractions diminish in scope before they come to an end and contractions that ultimately become severe are widespread in their early stages.

The concept of diffusion is made operational by defining it as a *time series representing the percentage of components within an aggregate that are expanding*. An index of diffusion is calculated from the percentage of components expanding *(E)*, the percentage of components that are unchanged *(U)* and the percentage of components that are contracting as *(C)*

where $C = E + (\frac{1}{2} \times U)$,

where $E + U + C = 100\%$.

A related concept is the *net percent rising* (NPR), which is defined as:

$$E - C.$$

About 15 regional purchasing manager surveys, including the South Western Michigan Purchasing Management Association referred to below, are taken around the country and many of those surveys report their results using the net percentage rising (NPR) formula, which can range between +100 and –100. Since NPR simply takes the difference between the percentage of the responses reporting "higher" and the percentage reporting "lower" (higher–lower), the bounds are clear. If all the responses are higher, then 100% – 0%, or +100, is the upper bound, while if all the responses are lower, then 0% – 100%, or –100, determines the lower bound.

On the other hand, the National Association of Purchasing Management's survey results are compiled into a diffusion index (DI) that is bounded by 0 percent and 100 percent. The DI is calculated as:

$$100 \times (\text{HIGHER} + (\text{SAME}/2))$$

where HIGHER represents the percentage of the sample reporting an increase, and SAME represents the percentage of the total reporting no change. The relationship between these two summary measures – the NPR and the DI, is straightforward.

HOW DO YOU COMPARE THE TWO METHODS?

Consider the basic information used to calculate both measures, that is, the share of the sample that is higher, lower, and unchanged. For example, assume that the South Western Michigan Purchasing Management Association reported a NPR reading for their new orders series of +20 based on the following responses:

HIGHER	SAME	LOWER
30%	60%	10%

Then the NPR equals the percentage of the sample reporting higher minus the percentage reporting lower, that is:

$$30\% - 10\%,$$

or   20%

and that is expressed as a +20 reading. The DI, however, is:

$$30\% + (60\%/2)$$

or   60%.

The relationship between the two measures is:

$$NPR = 2 \times (DI - 50)$$

where NPR is the net percentage rising (e.g., + 20) and DI is the NAPM-type diffusion index (e.g., 60 percent). Alternatively, the identity can be expressed as:

$$DI = 50 + (NPR/2).$$

The relationship between the aggregate time series and the diffusion index is shown in the chart. There are four stages of the diffusion index and its corresponding phase in the aggregate cycle. Stage 1 occurs when the diffusion index moves up from 50 percent to 100 percent (or simply when the index is above 50 percent and rises), which implies that the aggregate series is increasing at an increasing rate. In Stage 2, the diffusion index is declining from its upper bound of 100 percent to 50 percent (or simply the index moves from a higher to a lower number above 50 percent); this implies that the aggregate series is increasing at a decreasing rate. At Stage 3, the diffusion index is below 50 percent and declining, which implies that aggregate series is decreasing at an increasing rate. Finally, Stage 4 takes place when the diffusion index is moving up from its lower bound of 0 percent to 50 percent; this implies that the aggregate series is declining at a decreasing rate.

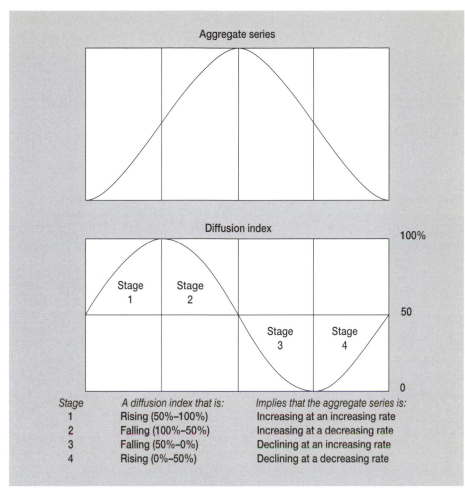

The relationship between the aggregate series and the diffusion index

Source: Economic Review, Federal Reserve Bank of Cleveland, January 1971, p. 6

US business cycle surveys (selected business, investment, and consumer surveys)

Performed by	Since	Frequency	Sectors	Sample size	Form of publication
Business surveys					
National Association of Purchasing Management	1931	Monthly	Purchasing managers	300	"Report on Business"
Dun & Bradstreet New York	1947	Quarterly	Manufacturing, wholesale, retail non-financial services	3,000	"Dun & Bradstreet Looks at Business"
	1987	Quarterly	Business executives in 14 countries	9,000	"Dun & Bradstreet Looks at Business"
	1990	Monthly	Manufacturers	1,000	Press Releases
Federal Reserve Bank Philadelphia, PA	1967	Monthly	Regional manufacturers		"Business Outlook Survey"
Manpower Temporary Services, Inc. Milwaukee, WI	1977	Quarterly	Public and private industries in all regions	15,000	Hiring intentions survey; in-press release
National Federation of Independent Business (NFIB) Washington, DC	1973	Quarterly	Small business in manufacturing, wholesale, retail trade, services, construction, and transportation	2,000	Quarterly press release
The Conference Board New York	1976	Quarterly	All industries	1,600	"Report on Business Expectations"
Mitsubishi Bank, Ltd New York	1988	Monthly	Air cargo companies, seaports, and trucking firms	65	Foreign trade survey press release
Investment surveys					
US Department of Commerce Washington, DC	1947	Quarterly	All industries	13,000	"Survey of Current Business"

Performed by	Since	Frequency	Sample size	Form of publication
Consumer surveys				
ABC News/Money Magazine New York	1985	Weekly	1,000	Consumer Comfort Index report to clients
Sindlinger & Co. Wallingford, PA	1957	Weekly	2,000	Reports to clients
Conference Board New York	1968	Monthly	5,000	Reports to clients; press releases
University of Michigan Survey Research Institute Ann Arbor, MI	1946	Monthly	500	Reports to clients

The business cycle: what are its prospects?*

THE BUSINESS CYCLE IS ALIVE AND KICKING

Are business cycles a thing of the past? Rumours of their demise persist in the United States, although business cycles still seem to be alive in Europe and kicking in Japan and Asia. But does the US experience point the rest of us toward a brave new world free of serious business fluctuations? Unfortunately, the US experience reveals more a string of luck than a new economic template. The absence of economic shocks – trade disruptions, financial panics, trend growth declines – in the United States appears more the source of the recent stability than any structural change brought on by a growing service sector, stronger international competition, or improved inventory and production technology.

A more stability oriented monetary policy, helped perhaps by falling fiscal deficits, has also contributed to the recent US stability, but similar policies elsewhere have not led to equal success. Thus, post-industrial economies are still sensitive to unexpected economic and political shocks that touch off business cycles. Most businessmen, workers, and investors around the world should not expect a less troubled future than they have experienced over the past half century.

The end to business cycles ...

Are business cycles dying? This question can only be seriously considered from an American perspective. Asian "tiger" economies are now entering their steepest recessions ever. Japan remains mired in its longest stagnations in half a century. Most of Europe is only now beginning to recover from business downturns that have raised unemployment to levels not seen since the Great Depression. If the US has really found a better economic system, now is a good time to unveil it.

The US economy certainly has performed better than most over the past decade, and better than during most of its own history. Americans have experienced seven years of uninterrupted economic expansion, following a then-record peace-time expansion in the Reagan-Bush years and punctuated only by a short 1990–91 recession. Unemployment has fallen to a 25 year low with inflation still showing no clear signs of rekindling. Many commentators have taken this as grounds to pronounce the business cycle dead, and even some academics have jumped on the new era bandwagon. A feature in the influential political journal Foreign Affairs (Weber, 1997) received widespread attention last year. While most economists remain sceptical, so much talk of a new economic era has taken US financial markets to euphoria. The long-awaited stock market correction seems, so far,

*This appendix is reprinted, with permission, from *UBS International Finance*, Issue 32, March 1998. Its original title was "The Business Cycle is Alive and Kicking."

to have been more of an upward pause. More recently, international capital fleeing the emerging Asian markets have taken refuge in US government bonds and driven their yields to a 25 year low.

... would be good news for everyone

If the proposition that business cycles are a thing of the past were indeed true, the implications would be considerable:

● With greater business stability we could expect more stable employment and less volatility in prices and interest rates.

● Greater economic stability would reduce risks in the credit system, and interest rate stability would generally ease the planning and risk control process for financial and non-financial enterprises alike.

● Less volatile interest rates would tend to raise the relative value of risk-capital (equities) relative to bonds. This would promote real investment and economic growth.

US economy becoming more stable, again   **Chart 1**

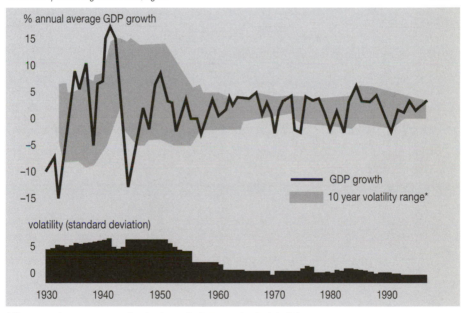

*10 year moving average growth rate plus and minus one standard deviation.

Sources: US Department of Commerce, and Martin (1997)

Whatever our first reaction to the proposition that the business cycle is dead, the benefits of greater cyclical stability certainly warrant giving the matter careful consideration.

Is the US leading a brave new world?

To explain a new economic era, American commentators have focused on several structural changes that may have reduced the cyclical variability in economic activity.

In particular:

- Service oriented economies may be less prone to cyclical stress
- Computerised inventory control has dampened manufacturing inventory cycles
- Globalisation may be diminishing cycles by enforcing greater flexibility of prices and wages and requiring smaller adjustments in output
- Policymakers may have learned to manage growth without creating recessions
- Capital markets may have become more efficient in directing funds away from over-extended firms and industries and into those most able to generate profitable investment.

We consider these arguments in both the US and international context below. But first, it is useful to review a few basic facts about business cycles.

Business cycles: some facts

A longer term view helps assess the arguments for a recent decline in business cycles (see Chart 2).

Milder cycles after World War II   Chart 2

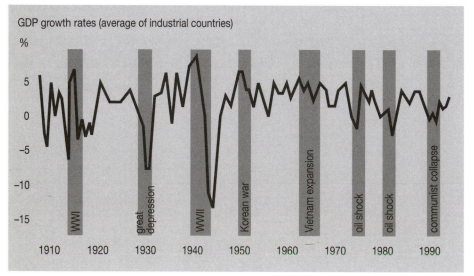

Source: Martin (1997)

Whether one looks at the industrial world as a whole or at the United States, Europe and Japan individually, business cycles have become much less pronounced in the post-war period.

Extreme shocks like the two World Wars and the Great Depression caused big swings in economic growth. But business cycles in the US and major European countries were at least as severe in the 18th and 19th century when frequent financial panics amplified other sources of economic fluctuation.

Only US now shows falling volatility   Chart 3

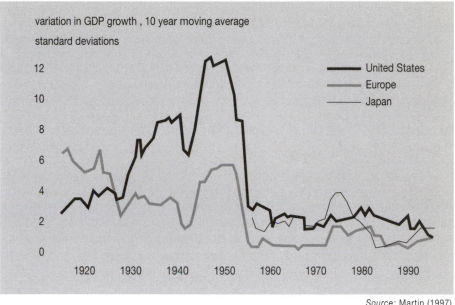

variation in GDP growth , 10 year moving average

standard deviations

Source: Martin (1997)

Since the 1950s, the Vietnam War boom and the oil-shock busts produced considerable economic swings, but these were still much less pronounced than the pre-war cycles.

Little improvement since the 1960s

While there has been a significant improvement in the post-war period, there has been lit-tle decline in the volatility of business cycles since the mid 1950s. Whether one looks at the industrial world as a whole or major regions (Chart 3), the variability of economic growth has not changed very much since the mid-1950s.

Economic stability declined sharply after the Korean war boom-bust in the early 1950s in nearly all industrial countries. By the late 1960s business cycles had become so mild that many began to consider them a dead issue – defeated by modern Keynesian macro-economic management. At the time, Paul Samuelson, paraphrasing Mark Twain, noted that "it is premature to speak of the death of the business cycle" (Samuelson, 1967). Indeed, the oil price shocks of the early and late 1970s brought the business cycle back with a vengeance. Only in the United States has GDP growth become more stable in the 1990s than it was in the 1960s. For Europe, the 1990s have not been a particularly stable period as the fall of communism and German reunification have produced strong shocks, while efforts to regain price and fiscal stability have continued to drag on economic growth. Japan has got the worse of both in the 1990s, increased instability and sharply lower trend growth rates.

While the European economy as a whole appears to have been much more stable than the United States or Japan over most of the recorded period, this stability was largely the result of individual country cycles being slightly out of sync. Recessions in one country have fre-quently been offset by recoveries in others, so that the combined European economy looks more stable than do its constituent national parts. Since the 1970s, at least, individual Euro-pean countries have not been less cyclical than the United States or Canada (Chart 4).

Among the individual economies in Europe, only Switzerland and Italy now show signifi-cantly lower cyclical variability than they enjoyed in the 1960s. Getting stuck at the bottom of a business cycle, as has Switzerland, may be stable but does not help unemployed workers, bankrupt businessmen, or government budgets. Germany now shows about the same stability as in the 1960s, but Germany's income has fluctuated more as a result of its political reunion in the 1990s than from the earlier oil shocks. France and the UK show greater instability in the current decade than in the 1960s, although the UK is regaining ground lost during the oil swings. Even Canada shows more cyclical instability in the 1990s than during the 1960s.

Why is the US more stable?

While the US is now enjoying particularly mild business fluctuations, some of the factors behind the diminished US cycle could point to a similar "brave new world" in Europe as the recent shocks wear off, and in Japan as the financial and services sector are modernised.

Few gains for individual countries   **Chart 4**

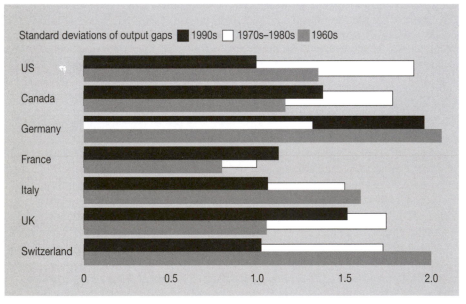

Source: UBS Economic Research

Five arguments are commonly made for the death of the US business cycle:

● The growing service sector is inherently more stable than declining manufacturing industries

- Computers have significantly improved inventory control, making the economy less responsive to shocks
- Globalised production forces firms and workers to adjust prices and wages more rapidly in order to remain internationally competitive
- Less ambitious fiscal and monetary policies produce fewer policy shocks
- The US economy has simply been subject to fewer external shocks than in the past.

How valid are these arguments?

Shocks have been key

The most obvious and widely accepted reason for the reduced volatility of US business cycles since the 1970s is that the severity of supply shocks, in particular those creating oil price variability, has declined sharply. The link between real oil price shocks and the volatility of the US business cycle is well documented (Tatom, 1981). The severe price shocks in 1973 and 1979 both contributed to the recessions that followed, as the sudden surge in the cost of production translated into a jump in most prices and reduced aggregate demand. Similarly, the rapid decline in the real cost of oil in the early 1980s contributed to the recovery. The further drop in 1986 boosted GDP growth in the late 1980s. The shock at the beginning of the Kuwait crisis in 1991 was one of the factors which led to a downturn in the early 1990s (see Chart 5).

Oil price shocks caused major cycles   **Chart 5**

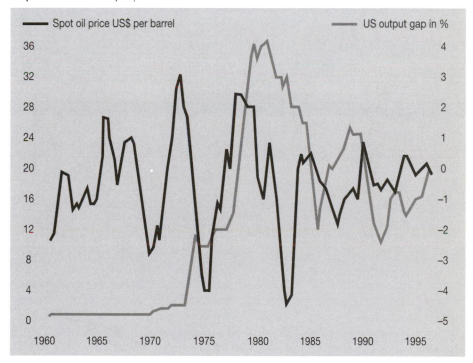

Source: UBS Economic Research

While oil prices have been relatively well behaved since 1991, future oil shocks cannot be ruled out. Yet, global energy markets have become more competitive with a broader supply base, new alternative sources of energy and maturing technologies to reduce consumption. Thus, future oil price shocks are likely to be less pronounced, and less likely to deteriorate into generalised business depressions than in the past.

However, other supply shocks can also be severe. Major natural disasters can have significant fallout. The Kobe earthquake, Indonesian forest fires and El Nino are all reminders. Major political shifts, like the fall of communism or the rise of militant religious movements, can have powerful effects as well. War has not been eliminated just because we have not suffered a major one in half a century. Financial panics reminiscent of those in the past century also wait in the wings, as the Asian crisis has shown. Speculative "bubbles" ranging from real estate to derivatives have occurred in most industrial countries not too long ago. All in all, the absence of shocks is a very thin reed upon which to build the case for a new economic era.

Structural shifts less important

The structural arguments for the death of the business cycle have received wide attention because they represent factors that other countries, in principle, can copy. Unfortunately, these structural changes do not account for much of the reduction in US business cycle volatility.

Steady manufacturing shares limit the scope for servce stability   Chart 6

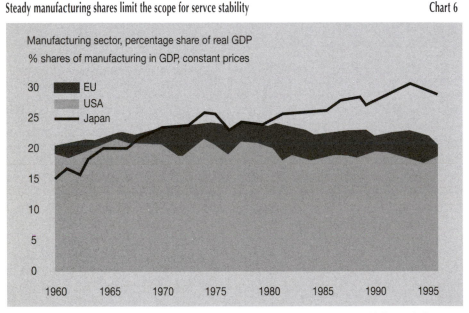

Source: UBS Economic Research

Growing service sector

Service sector employment has been growing and proved less volatile than work in the industrial sector. But since the mid-1980s service sector employment itself has become more volatile. This likely reflects the increased private provision of government services and the outsourcing of jobs previously done within industrial firms to independent service providers and consultants. Moreover, the total share of services in the output of the economy as a whole has not risen much because service productivity growth has been slower than that in industry. Thus, while the growth of services may have made employment less variable over the business cycle, it has not significantly reduced the variability of total output (see Chart 6).

Better inventory management

With most of the reduced cyclical swings coming from the goods sector, it is natural to look to better inventory management as a major factor. In fact, just-in-time production has greatly reduced the level of inventories, diminishing their impact on the economy. However, inventory changes are often counter-cyclical. Rising inventories support output when final demand is falling. Declining inventories substitute for new production when final demand exceeds current production. Inventory movements tend to offset changes in final demand.

While inventory variability has declined in the 1990s, particularly as petroleum inventory swings have become more muted, it is in the non-inventory components of GDP that the major volatility declines have taken place (see Chart 7). Inventory changes are an important indicator of business cycle conditions, but do not themselves contribute greatly to the volatility of overall output.

Globalisation of production

It has been claimed that the globalisation of markets is stabilising cycles, mainly because tougher competition increases the flexibility of wages and prices. Nevertheless, the share of "new" competitors, principally from emerging economies, in GDP of advanced countries is too small to have a major effect on overall cyclical behaviour.

Deregulation and the decline of labour union power have significantly increased competition within the US economy. More effective competition in key sectors like transportation, health care, and basic manufacturing has likely increased the flexibility of wages and prices more than has competition from globalised production.

In sum, these often-cited structural changes to the US economy do not seem to be the key to lower business cycle swings. Moreover, while the US may well lead the world in information technology, openness to trade, and service sector size, many other industrial countries have started to catch up in these respects and have still not seen lower business cycle volatility.

Fiscal policies little changed

Better government policies are also a candidate for explaining the improvement. Policies to promote competition and market efficiency should make economies better able to absorb shocks by encouraging wage and price adjustments rather than changes in output, income and employment. The effects of fiscal and monetary policies are more difficult to disentangle.

Fiscal policies have two components. Automatic stabilisers like unemployment compensation and progressive tax rates automatically offset fluctuations in private sector demand. With taxes becoming less progressive and unemployment compensation lagging behind incomes, US automatic stabilisers have probably lost somewhat in effectiveness. Active fiscal policies – discretionary changes in taxes and spending – can also compensate for business cycles. Paradoxically, due to their generally temporary nature and long lags in their effect, discretionary policy changes are often themselves a destabilising factor. Moreover, with governments everywhere trying to trim deficits and debt levels, many observers have concluded that fiscal policies have become less, not more active. In any event, we find no evidence that discretionary fiscal policy has become more or less counter-cyclical in the United States, or in Europe (Martin, 1997).

Inventories not a major source of business cycles   **Chart 7**

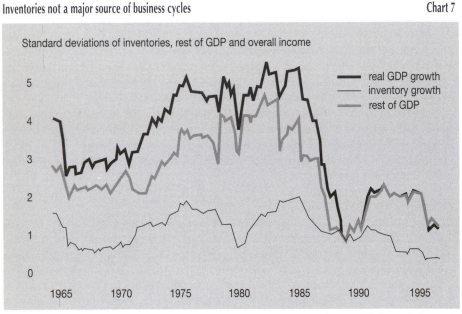

Source: UBS Economic Research

On the other hand, attempts to cut government budgets and debt should eventually add modestly to stability everywhere as this will contribute to a more stable monetary environment.

More stable monetary policy helps

There is general agreement that part of the explanation for the improved US cyclical performance is in the shift of monetary policy emphasis away from fine-tuning the economy to establishing price stability. Nevertheless, the quantitative importance of this factor is difficult to determine.

Monetary policy errors were clearly a major source of shocks in the late 1960s. Stop-and-go policies, sometimes inadvertent, sometimes tuned to political election calendars, had contributed to business fluctuations in the 1960s and 1970s. Moreover, the generally easy monetary policies pursued in the 1960s and 1970s aggravated the commodity price swings which themselves became important sources of cyclical instability. Finally, the inflation in the 1970s made it very difficult for financial and other markets to gauge changes in relative prices and adjust to other cyclical disturbances. Inflation made big price misalignments and abrupt corrections like the oil shocks more likely.

The shift in US monetary policy to focus on price stability rather than fine-tuning the economy was dramatically announced by Paul Volcker in 1979. While the strict monetary targeting first applied has since been abandoned for a more eclectic approach, the focus on price stability has been retained. This shift in policy emphasis showed up in lower and less volatile inflation expectations. Changes in nominal interest rates were therefore increasingly perceived as variations in the real cost of capital, enhancing the effectiveness of financial markets in stabilising investment demand. In addition, in a more stable monetary environment, pricing and allocation errors by firms and households are likely to be reduced, improving economic stability.

This new emphasis on price stability has not only been at work in the United States. Other countries that were prone to high inflation, including Canada, Australia and New Zealand, have changed the rules of monetary policymaking and succeeded in dramatically lowering inflation, without however seeing significantly milder business fluctuations yet. In Europe, Germany's long-standing commitment to price stability has not prevented the shocks from reunification to echo across the Continent. Less activism in monetary policy cannot alone sustain the argument that the business cycle is truly dead.

Prospects for Europe

We find that the improvement in the US principally reflects an absence of shocks and improved monetary policy. Europe, in contrast, has suffered peculiar shocks in the 1990s, although monetary policies have been strongly oriented toward price stability for some time. Once the recent shocks have dissipated, Europe should enjoy greater cyclical stability as well.

Nevertheless, a new uncertainty has arisen in Europe: the introduction of a single currency, the euro, and a new central bank. Many pessimists argue that Europe is not ready for monetary union. They reason that the loss of exchange rate flexibility will be costly because labour still cannot move easily among European nations and fiscal transfers among member nations are quite limited. This would increase cyclical instability. However, Europe's labour market inflexibility cannot be offset by independent monetary policies and flexible exchange rates in any event. European labour is inflexible even within countries, and among sectors in the same region of these countries. Unemployment is high and rising and workers are dropping out of the labour force nearly everywhere in Europe (see UBS International Finance October 1997). This unemployment cannot simply be exported to neighbours in similar circumstances. It must be resolved within each country.

Box 1

Better monetary policy adds real stability

- Tighter focus on price stability rather than output and employment reduces stop-and-go policies.
- With lower, less variable inflation expectations interest rate fluctuations are more effective in stabilising credit and investment flows.
- Lower, less variable inflation makes goods, service, and labour markets more efficient.

The lack of large government transfers among participating countries will not make fiscal policies impotent. It is not the size of the transfer among regions that determines the stabilisation effect of fiscal policy, but by how much these transfers change. Monetary union need not reduce the flexibility of tax and revenue programs in any country, although trend deficits, tax burdens and the size of debt may impose constraints on some national governments. But it is not the size of the deficit or surplus that determines the fiscal effect, but changes in this deficit or surplus. Once they have attained a sustainable fiscal position, nations can be as ambitious as they wish in countering temporary business fluctuations.

Monetary union alone will not likely boost member economies enough to resolve their long-standing labour rigidities and fiscal excesses. But the single currency will also not make these problems more intractable. The major gain from European Monetary Union will be a low inflation monetary policy for all of Europe. The major cost will arise if this stability is not achieved.

Financial risks to stability

In the 1800s and early 1900s, financial market failures generally magnified and often caused cyclical instability. Financial booms and busts, runs on banks and the resulting business failures frequently degenerated into general depressions. In most industrial countries, financial fragility as a cause of business cycles has been eliminated over most of this century due to the introduction of deposit insurance, better accounting and supervisionary

---

Box 2

Why does Business Cycle?

Shocks start business cycles ...

Supply shocks
- technological innovations
- sudden changes in the supply of natural resources (e.g. oil)
- wars, strikes or other political disruptions

Demand shocks
- changes in government tax and spending policy
- changes in consumer taste, saving rates, business sentiment

Financial shocks
- unexpected monetary policy shifts
- financial and banking crises

... economies respond with recurring patterns
- Some markets respond very quickly – financial markets, commodity markets
- Others take more time to adjust – manufacturing inventories
- A few take a long time – constructing new factories, retraining labour

standards, tighter regulations on capital adequacy and exposure limits, and more profes-sional central banks. Nevertheless, many argue that deregulation and the expansion of domestic and international financial markets threaten to bring back the earlier instability.

Risks are certainly greater in times of change and new institutions, markets, and partici-pants always generate increased uncertainty. But we must keep in mind that central banks today are directing monetary policy according to the needs of the economy rather than let-ting shifts in the world supply of gold determine how expansive or contractive credit becomes. Regulators certainly play catch-up with the markets, and they have generally been conservative in reacting to change. But problems in particular sectors of industrial countries, like in savings and loans in the US or construction in Switzerland, have not spread into general financial collapse.

Moreover, regulation is a two-edged sword. Over-regulation can cause even bigger busts by encouraging over-expansion, reducing due diligence and raising a moral hazard. Mistaken monetary policy and regulatory errors have themselves been sources of cyclical behaviour in some countries. Easy money in Switzerland and Japan in the late 1980s, for example. contributed to real estate and asset price booms that then turned into busts. In Japan, the failure to impose adequate capital and accounting standards further aggra-vated the problems by delaying adjustment as the bubble collapsed.

Global finance a new challenge

Does the globalisation of finance pose a special risk? International financial interdepen-dence has reached record proportions and raises many questions. New entrants into these markets have certainly found them difficult, and even old participants are continually learn-ing from new mistakes. But this has not been a seriously destabilising factor for most industrial economies.

Problems in Latin America, and more recently Asia, have resulted mainly from misman-agement of the local economy and domestic financial systems. Their effects have largely been felt locally. Each crisis has revealed new aspects of the problem – external debt bur-dens for Latin America in the 1980s, the lack of an effective legal system in Eastern Europe, foreign exchange and monetary policy mismanagement in Mexico in the 1990s, and fragile domestic financial systems in Asia most recently.

Box 3

Global finance: stabilising or destabilising?

- International capital market integration has moved to an unprecedented level.
- Record exposures, particularly to untested "emerging" markets, imply new risks.
- International flows may finance unsustainable policies and amplify cycles.
- Growing experience and international cooperation should keep the risks in check – but we must learn and adjust.

Markets did not recognise these problems before they arose and quickly looked for similarly placed economies elsewhere, leading to widely discussed contagion effects. There are clearly lessons to learn and even to re-learn here. Will politicians and regulators turn against capital flows? This would mean giving up opportunities for economic growth. A better approach is for everyone to learn from experience and to cooperate internationally.

Conclusions and implications

What does this review of business cycles mean for financial institutions and all those who rely on them to save and invest?

The business cycle is not dead

This means that asset prices and credit risks will continue to swing, sometimes widely. This poses risks not only for banks, but for all segments of the economy.

Monetary policy is key for stability

There has been a global trend to lower inflation, but full confirmation that cycles will be less severe as a result is certainly missing.

If monetary policy were to improve permanently, we could look forward to lower and less volatile interest rates and even better equity valuations.

We cannot predict shocks

The notion that the business cycle is dead has surfaced at least twice before in the United States – just before the great depression, and again before the 1970s oil and commodity shocks. This does not mean another serious shock is just around the corner, but it does suggest that Paul Samuelson's 1967 advice is worth repeating: "The naive belief that a new era of stability has begun is certainly a dangerous path to follow".

REFERENCES

Analysis underlying this summary review is available in:

Cabiallavetta, Mathis (1997). "Are Business Cycles a Thing of the Past?", Working Paper for the Institut International d'Etudes Bancaires October 1997 Conference. Zurich: UBS.

Related references:

Kindleberger, Charles (1978). *Manias, Panics and Crashes: A History of Financial Crises*. New York: Basic Books.

Maddison, Angus (1995). *Monitoring the World Economy*, 1820–1992. Paris: OECD.

Martin, William (1997). *Cycles and Securities*. UBS Global Research: London, April.

Rodrick, Dani (1997). *Has Globalisation Gone Too Far?*. Institute for International Economics, Washington, D.C., March.

Samuelson, Paul (1967). *Economics: An Introductory Analysis*. New York: McGraw Hill.

Schumpeter, Joseph (1939). *Business Cycles: A Theoretical, Historical and Statistical Analysis of the Capitalist Process.* New York: McGraw Hill.

Tatom, John A. (1981). "Are the Macroeconomic Effects of Oil Price Changes Symmetric?" in: Karl Brunner and Allan H. Meltzer, eds., *Stabilization Policies and Labor Markets*, Carnegie-Rochester Conference Series in Public Policy 28:325–68.

UBS International Finance (1997). "Putting Europe to Work." Issue 31, October.

Weber, Steven (1997). "The End of the Business Cycle?" *Foreign Affairs* July/August.

Zarnowitz, Victor (1992). *Business cycles: Theory, History, Indicators and Forecasting*. University of Chicago Press.

CHAPTER 4

The Federal Reserve at work: the implementation of monetary policy

INTRODUCTION

United States monetary policy is the pre-eminent responsibility of the Federal Reserve. Monetary policy refers to the actions the Federal Reserve takes to influence national and international monetary and financial conditions with a view to helping achieve the nation's basic economic objectives of price stability, high employment, and reasonable balance in its trade and payments relations with other nations.

This conception of monetary policy implies certain relationships. First, the Federal Reserve must be able to influence monetary and financial conditions. Second, monetary and financial conditions must have some impact on at least some of the objectives – or, to employ the jargon of economists, the "goal variables" – of economic policy, such as stability in the price level.

It is generally recognized that the Federal Reserve, like other central banks, can influence domestic monetary and financial conditions. It is essential to understand, however, that the Federal Reserve's influence over most financial variables is indirect. The Federal Reserve has direct administrative control over only one interest rate, the discount rate, and it has no direct control over cash, bank deposits and other liquid assets that comprise the various measures of the money supply. What the Federal Reserve can influence directly is the volume and growth of reserves held by private commercial banks and other depository institutions, i.e., balances held by depository institutions at one of the 12 Federal Reserve Banks. The role of Federal Reserve Banks is discussed in Chapter 3.

The use of the word "influence" rather than "control" here is deliberate. The technicalities of reserve controls are discussed in later chapters. At this stage it is sufficient to appreciate that the Federal Reserve cannot control total reserves in the short run because total reserves include reserves borrowed from the discount window, and depository institutions play a significant role in determining the level of borrowing in the short run. The Federal Reserve can, however, control non-borrowed reserves, the other type of reserves, with considerable precision in the short run.

Through its influence on bank reserves, the Federal Reserve can indirectly affect interest rates and the growth of money and credit. For example, if the public's demand for money and credit is substantial, due, perhaps, to strong growth in the general economy, a restrictive approach to the provision of reserves by the Federal Reserve tends to put immediate upward pressure on the

Federal Reserve funds rate, which is the short-term interest rate charged for the use of reserves when they are sold (lent) and bought (borrowed) in the so-called Federal Reserve funds market. The rise in the Federal funds rate, in turn, causes other interest rates to rise, which acts to reduce both the supply and demand for money and credit and hence their growth. Conversely, if the Federal Reserve supplies reserves generously in relation to the demand for money and credit, interest rates will come under downward pressure, and the growth of money and credit will tend to increase.

The second basis for the conduct of monetary policy is the presumption that relationships exist between the monetary and financial variables that the Federal Reserve can influence, on the one hand, and the goal variables of economic policy on the other. The nature of these relationships and their empirical characteristics have been the subject of extensive research and analysis by monetary economists for many years.

Most economists agree that a stable and predictable positive relationship exists over the long run between the rate of growth of the money supply and the rate of inflation. Specifically, a sustained rise in the growth rate of the money supply is followed eventually by a rise in the trend rate of inflation. Some economists also believe that short-run relationships exist between changes in the growth rates of monetary variables, and real economic variables such as the rates of growth of production and employment. Views regarding the nature of these short-run relationships and their usefulness as a basis for monetary policy changed substantially in the 1980s and 1990s. In particular, the research of the rational expectations school of economists has produced a growing consensus that the only changes in the growth rate of the money supply that affect real economic variables are those that are not anticipated by the public. Since the public's anticipations are difficult to observe and quantify accurately on a current basis, this view implies that these short-run relationships cannot be predicted reliably, and for that reason the Federal Reserve cannot exploit them to fine tune the economy.

HOW DO BANKS CREATE MONEY? – THE PRINCIPLE OF MULTIPLE DEPOSIT CREATION

An appreciation of the principles of how the Federal Reserve can control the banking system starts with an explanation of how banks create money. The mechanism whereby banks do this is known as the bank credit multiplier, described below. The relationships described here are considerably simplified. They should not be interpreted as being as mechanical as they seem – however, they do provide the essential building blocks to an understanding of how the banking system operates which can then be suitably modified in later chapters.

Today, in the US, money used in transactions is mainly of three kinds – currency (paper money and coins in the pockets of the public); demand deposits (non-interest-bearing checking accounts in banks); and other checkable deposits, such as negotiable order of withdrawal (NOW) accounts, at all depository institutions, including commercial and savings banks, savings and loan associations, and credit unions.

Who creates money?

Changes in the quantity of money may originate with actions of the Federal Reserve System (the central bank), depository institutions (principally commercial banks), or the public. The major control, however, rests with the central bank.

The actual process of money creation takes place primarily in banks. Checkable liabilities of banks are money. These liabilities are customers' accounts. They increase when customers deposit currency and checks and when the proceeds of loans made by the banks are credited to borrowers' accounts.

In the absence of legal reserve requirements, banks can build up deposits by increasing loans and investments so long as they keep enough currency on hand to redeem whatever amounts the holders of deposits want to convert into currency. This unique attribute of the banking business was discovered many centuries ago.

It started with goldsmiths. As early bankers, they initially provided safekeeping services, making a profit from vault storage fees for gold and coins deposited with them. People would redeem their "deposit receipts" whenever they needed gold or coins to purchase something, and physically take the gold or coins to the seller who, in turn, would deposit them for safekeeping, often with the same banker. Everyone soon found that it was a lot easier simply to use the deposit receipts directly as a means of payment. These receipts, which became known as notes, were acceptable as money since whoever held them could go to the banker and exchange them for metallic money.

Bankers then discovered that they could make loans merely by giving their promises to pay, or bank notes, to borrowers. In this way, banks began to create money. More notes could be issued than the gold and coin on hand because only a portion of the notes outstanding would be presented for payment at any one time. Enough metallic money had to be kept on hand, of course, to redeem whatever volume of notes was presented for payment.

Transaction deposits are the modern counterpart of bank notes. It was a small step from printing notes to making book entries crediting deposits of borrowers, which the borrowers in turn could "spend" by writing checks, thereby "printing" their own money.

What limits the amount of money banks can create?

If deposit money can be created so easily, what is to prevent banks from making too much – more than sufficient to keep the nation's productive resources fully employed without price inflation? Like its predecessor, the modern bank must keep available, to make payment on demand, a considerable amount of currency and funds on deposit with the central bank. The bank must be prepared to convert deposit money into currency for those depositors who request currency. It must make remittance on checks written by depositors and presented for payment by other banks (settle adverse clearings). Finally, it must maintain legally required reserves, in the form of vault cash and/or balances at its Federal Reserve Bank, equal to a prescribed percentage of its deposits. There are 12 Federal Reserve Banks in the US.

These operating needs influence the minimum amount of reserves an individual bank will hold voluntarily. However, as long as this minimum amount is less than what is legally required, operating needs are of relatively minor importance as a restraint on aggregate deposit expansion in the banking system. Such expansion cannot continue beyond the point where the amount of reserves that all banks have is just sufficient to satisfy legal requirements under a "fractional reserve" system. For example, if reserves of 20 percent were required, deposits could expand only until they were five times as large as reserves. Reserves of $10 million could support deposits of $50 million. The lower the percentage requirement, the greater the deposit expansion that can be supported by each additional reserve dollar. Thus, the legal reserve ratio together with the dollar amount of bank reserves are the factors that set the upper limit to money creation.

What are bank reserves?

Currency held in bank vaults may be counted as legal reserves as well as deposits (reserve balances) at the Federal Reserve Banks. Both are equally acceptable in satisfaction of reserve requirements. A bank can always obtain reserve balances by sending currency to its Reserve Bank and can obtain currency by drawing on its reserve balance. Because either can be used to support a much larger volume of deposit liabilities of banks, currency in circulation and reserve balances together are often referred to as "high-powered money" or the "monetary base."

Where do bank reserves come from?

Increases or decreases in bank reserves can result from a number of factors, again discussed in later chapters. From the standpoint of money creation, however, the essential point is that the reserves of banks are, for the most part, liabilities of the Federal Reserve Banks, and net changes in them are largely determined by actions of the Federal Reserve System. Thus, the Federal Reserve, through its ability to vary both the total volume of reserves and the required ratio of reserves to deposit liabilities, influences banks' decisions with respect to their assets and deposits. One of the major responsibilities of the Federal Reserve System is to provide the total amount of reserves consistent with the monetary needs of the economy at reasonably stable prices.

BANK DEPOSITS – HOW THEY EXPAND OR CONTRACT

Let us assume that an expansion in the money stock is desired by the Federal Reserve to achieve its policy objectives. One way the central bank can initiate such an expansion is through purchases of securities in the open market. Payment for the securities adds to bank reserves. Such purchases (and sales) are called "open market operations."

How do open market purchases add to bank reserves and deposits? Suppose the Federal Reserve System, through its trading desk at the Federal Reserve Bank of New York, buys $10,000 of Treasury bills from a dealer in US government securities. The Federal Reserve Bank pays for the securities with an "electronic" check drawn on itself. Via its "Fedwire" transfer network, the Federal Reserve notifies the dealer's designated bank (Bank A) that payment for the securities should be credited to (deposited in) the dealer's account at Bank A. At the same time, Bank A's reserve account at the Federal Reserve is credited for the amount of the securities purchased. The Federal Reserve System has added $10,000 of securities to its assets, which it has paid for, in effect, by *creating* a liability on itself in the form of bank reserve balances. These reserves on Bank A's books are matched by $10,000 of the dealer's deposits that did not exist before.

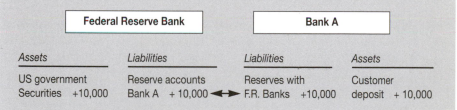

When the Federal Reserve Bank purchases government securities, bank reserves increase. This happens because the seller of the securities receives payment through a credit to a designated deposit account at the Bank (Bank A) which the Federal Reserve effects by crediting the reserve account of Bank A.

Federal Reserve Bank		Bank A	
Assets	Liabilities	Liabilities	Assets
US government Securities +10,000	Reserve accounts Bank A + 10,000 ◄►	Reserves with F.R. Banks +10,000	Customer deposit + 10,000

The customer deposit at Bank A likely will be transferred, in part, to other banks and quickly loses its identity amid the huge interbank flow of deposits.

How the multiple expansion process works

If the process ended here, there would be no "multiple" expansion, i.e., deposits and bank reserves would have changed by the same amount. However, banks are required to maintain reserves equal to only a fraction of their deposits. Reserves in excess of this amount may be used to increase earning assets – loans and investments. Unused or excess reserves earn no interest. Under current regulations, the reserve requirement against most transaction accounts is 10 percent. Assuming, for simplicity, a uniform 10 percent reserve requirement against all transaction deposits, and further assuming that all banks attempt to remain fully invested, we can now trace the process of expansion in deposits which can take place on the basis of the *additional* reserves provided by the Federal Reserve System's purchase of US government securities.

The expansion process may or may not begin with Bank A, depending on what the dealer does with the money received from the sale of securities. If the dealer immediately writes checks for $10,000 and all of them are deposited in other banks, Bank A loses both deposits and reserves and shows no net change as a result of the System's open market purchase. However, other banks have received them. Most likely, a part of the initial deposit will remain with Bank A, and a part will be shifted to other banks as the dealer's checks clear.

It does not really matter where this money is at any given time. The important fact is that *these deposits do not disappear*. They are in some deposit accounts at all times. All banks together have $10,000 of deposits and reserves that they did not have before. However, they are not required to keep $10,000 of deposits. All they need to retain, under a 10 percent reserve requirement, is $1,000. The remaining $9,000 is "excess reserves." This amount can be loaned or invested.

As a result, all banks taken together now have 10,000 "excess" reserves on which deposit expansion can take place.	Total reserves gained from new deposits	
	less: required against new deposits (at 10 percent)	1,000
	equals: excess reserves	9,000

If business is active, the banks with excess reserves probably will have opportunities to loan the $9,000. Of course, they do not really pay out cash from the money they receive as deposits, when they make loans. If they did this, no additional money would be created. What they do when they make loans is to credit the borrowers' transaction accounts. Loans (assets) and deposits (liabilities) both rise by $9,000. Reserves are unchanged by the loan transactions. But the deposit credits constitute new additions to the total deposits of the banking system.

Expansion – Stage 1

Expansion takes place only if the banks that hold these excess reserves (Stage 1 banks) increase their loans or investments. Loans are made by crediting the borrower's deposit account, i.e. by creating additional deposit money.

Stage 1 banks		
Assets		*Liabilities*
Loans	+ 9,000	Borrower deposits + 9,000

This is the beginning of the deposit expansion process. In the first stage of the process, total loans and deposits of the banks rise by an amount equal to the excess reserves existing before any loans were made (90 percent of the initial deposit increase). At the end of Stage 1, deposits have risen a total of $19,000 (the initial $10,000 provided by the Federal Reserve's action plus the $9,000 in deposits created by Stage 1 banks).

As a result of the process so far, total assets and total liabilities of all banks together have risen 19,000

All banks			
Assets		*Liabilities*	
Reserves with		Deposits:	
FR Banks	+10,000	Initial	+10,000
Loans	+ 9,000	Stage 1	+ 9,000
Total	+19,000	Total	+19,000

However, only $900 (10 percent of $9,000) of excess reserves have been absorbed by the additional deposit growth at Stage 1 banks.

Excess reserves have been reduced by the amount required against the deposits created by the loans made in Stage 1.

Total reserves gained from initial deposits		10,000
less: required against initial deposits	1,000	
less: required against Stage 1 deposits	900	1,900
equals: excess reserves		8,100

The lending banks, however, do not expect to retain the deposits they create through their loan operations. Borrowers write checks that probably will be deposited in other banks. As these checks move through the collection process, the Federal Reserve Banks debit the reserve accounts of the paying banks (Stage 1 banks) and credit those of the receiving banks.

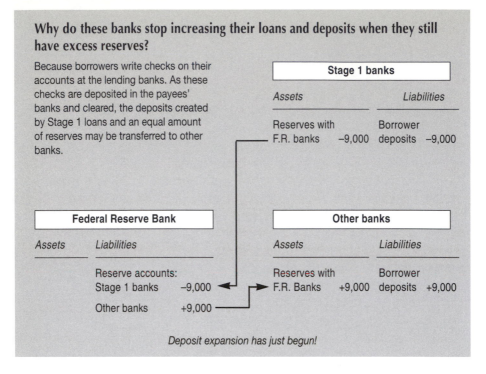

Why do these banks stop increasing their loans and deposits when they still have excess reserves?

Because borrowers write checks on their accounts at the lending banks. As these checks are deposited in the payees' banks and cleared, the deposits created by Stage 1 loans and an equal amount of reserves may be transferred to other banks.

Stage 1 banks

Assets		Liabilities	
Reserves with F.R. banks	−9,000	Borrower deposits	−9,000

Federal Reserve Bank

Assets	Liabilities	
	Reserve accounts:	
	Stage 1 banks	−9,000
	Other banks	+9,000

Other banks

Assets		Liabilities	
Reserves with F.R. Banks	+9,000	Borrower deposits	+9,000

Deposit expansion has just begun!

Whether Stage 1 banks actually do lose the deposits to *other* banks or whether any or all of the borrowers' checks are redeposited in these *same* banks makes no difference in the expansion process. If the lending banks *expect* to lose these deposits – and an equal amount of reserves – as the borrowers' checks are paid, they will not lend more than their excess reserves. Like the original $10,000 deposit, the loan-created deposits may be transferred to other banks, but they remain somewhere in the banking system. Whichever banks receive them also acquire equal amounts of reserves, of which all but 10 percent will be "excess."

Assuming that the banks holding the $9,000 of deposits created in Stage 1 in turn make loans equal to their excess reserves, then loans and deposits will rise by a further $8,100 in the second stage of expansion. This process can continue until deposits have risen to the point where all the reserves provided by the initial purchase of government securities by the Federal Reserve System are just sufficient to satisfy reserve requirements against the newly created deposits.

Expansion continues as the banks that have excess reserves increase their loans by that amount, crediting borrowers' deposit accounts in the process. This creates still more money.

Stage 2 banks			
Assets		*Liabilities*	
Loans	+8,100	Borrower deposits	+8,100

Now the banking system's assets and liabilities have risen by 27,100.

All banks			
Assets		*Liabilities*	
Reserves with F.R. Banks	+10,000	Deposits Initial	+10,000
		Stage 1	+ 9,000
Loans:		Stage 2	+ 8,100
Stage 1	+ 9,000		
Stage 2	+ 8,100		
Total	+27,100	Total	+27,100

But there are still 7,290 of excess reserves in the banking system.

Total reserves gained from initial deposits		10,000
less: required against initial deposits	1,000	
less: required against Stage 1 deposits	900	
less: required against Stage 2 deposits	810	2,710
equals: excess reserves		7,290

to
Stage 3
banks

As borrowers make payments, these reserves will be further dispersed, and the process can continue through many more stages, in progressively smaller increments, until the entire 10,000 of reserves have been absorbed by deposit growth. As is apparent from the summary below, more than two-thirds of the deposit expansion potential is reached after the first ten stages.

Thus through stage after stage of expansion, "money" can grow to a total of ten times the new reserves supplied to the banking system ...

	Assets				Liabilities
	Reserves			Loans and	
	Total	[Required]	[Excess]	Investments	Deposits
Initial reserves provided	10,000	1,000	9,000	–	10,000
Expansion - Stage 1	10,000	1,900	8,100	9,000	19,000
Stage 2	10,000	2,710	7,290	17,100	27,100
Stage 3	10,000	3,439	6,561	24,390	34,390
Stage 4	10,000	4,095	5,905	30,951	40,951
Stage 5	10,000	4,686	5,314	36,856	46,856
Stage 6	10,000	5,217	4,783	42,710	52,170
Stage 7	10,000	5,695	4,305	46,953	56,953
Stage 8	10,000	6,126	3,874	51,258	61,258
Stage 9	10,000	6,513	3,487	55,132	65,132
Stage 10	10,000	6,862	3,138	58,619	68,619
.	.	.	.	.	.
.	.	.	.	.	.
.	.	.	.	.	.
Stage 20	10,000	8,906	1,094	79,058	89,058
.	.	.	.	.	.
.	.	.	.	.	.
.	.	.	.	.	.
Final Stage	10,000	10,000	0	90,000	100,000

... as the new deposits created by loans at each stage are added to those created at all earlier stages and those supplied by the initial reserve-creating action.

Cumulative expansion in deposits on basis of 10,000 of new reserves and reserve requirements of 10 percent

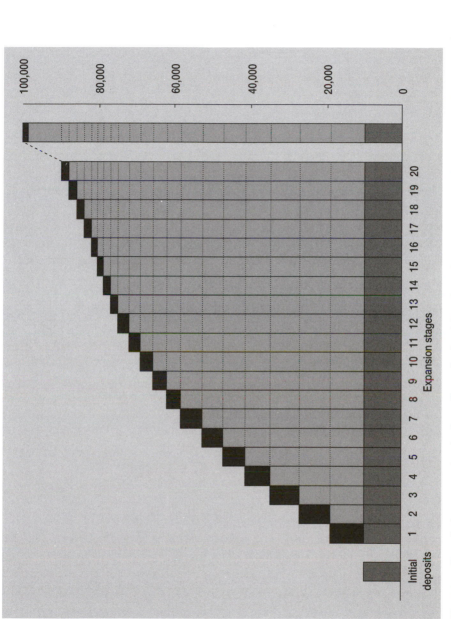

Fig 4.1 ● Cumulative expansion in deposits on basis of $10,000 of new reserves and reserve requirements of 10 percent

The individual bank, of course, is not concerned as to the stages of expansion in which it may be participating. Inflows and outflows of deposits occur continuously. Any deposit received is new money, regardless of its ultimate source. But if bank policy is to make loans and investments equal to whatever reserves are in excess of legal requirements, the expansion process will be carried on.

How much can deposits expand in the banking system?

The total amount of expansion that can take place is illustrated above. Carried through to theoretical limits, the initial $10,000 of reserves distributed within the banking system gives rise to an expansion of $90,000 in bank credit (loans and investments) and supports a total of $100,000 in new deposits under a 10 percent reserve requirement. The deposit expansion factor for a given amount of new reserves is thus the reciprocal of the required reserve percentage (1 divided by 0.10 = 10). Loan expansion will be less by the amount of the initial injection. The multiple expansion is possible because the banks as a group are like one large bank in which checks drawn against borrowers' deposits result in credits to accounts of other depositors, with no net change in total reserves.

Expansion through bank investments

Deposit expansion can proceed from investments as well as loans. Suppose that the demand for loans at some Stage 1 banks is slack. These banks would then probably purchase securities. If the sellers of the securities were customers, the banks would make payment by crediting the customers' transaction accounts; deposit liabilities would rise just as if loans had been made. More likely, these banks would purchase the securities through dealers, paying for them with checks on themselves or on their reserve accounts. These checks would be deposited in the sellers' banks. In either case, the net effects on the banking system are identical with those resulting from loan operations.

How open market sales reduce bank reserves and deposits

Now suppose some reduction in the amount of money is desired. Normally, this would reflect temporary or seasonal reductions in activity to be financed since, on a year-to-year basis, a growing economy needs at least some monetary expansion. Just as purchases of government securities by the Federal Reserve System can provide the basis for deposit expansion by adding to bank reserves, sales of securities by the Federal Reserve System reduce the money stock by absorbing bank reserves. The process is essentially the reverse of the expansion steps just described.

Suppose the Federal Reserve System sells $10,000 of Treasury bonds to a US government securities dealer and receives in payment an "electronic" check drawn on Bank A. As this payment is made, Bank A's reserve account at a Federal Reserve Bank is reduced by $10,000. As a result, the Federal Reserve System's holdings of securities and the reserve accounts of banks are both reduced by $10,000. The $10,000 reduction in Bank A's deposit liabilities constitutes a decline in money stock.

Deposit contraction

When the Federal Reserve Bank sells government securities, bank reserves decline. This happens because the buyer of the securities makes payment through a debit to a designated deposit account at a bank (Bank A), with the transfer of funds being effected by a debit to Bank A's reserve account at the Federal Reserve Bank.

Federal Reserve Bank			
Assets	Liabilities		
US government securities −10,000	Reserve accounts Bank A −10,000		

Bank A			
Assets	Liabilities		
Reserves with F.R. Banks −10,000	Customer deposit −10,000		

Contraction is also a cumulative process

While Bank A may have regained part of the initial reduction in deposits from other banks as a result of interbank deposit flows, all banks taken together have $10,000 less in both deposits and reserves than they had before the Federal Reserve's sales of securities. The amount of reserves freed by the decline in deposits, however, is only $1,000 (10 percent of $10,000). Unless the banks that lose the reserves and deposits had excess reserves, they are left with a reserve deficiency of $9,000.

Although they may borrow from the Federal Reserve Banks to cover this deficiency temporarily, sooner or later the banks will have to obtain the necessary reserves in some other way or reduce their needs for reserves.

The loss of reserves means that all banks taken together now have a reserve deficiency.	Total reserves lost from deposit withdrawal	10,000
	less: reserves freed by deposit decline (at 10 percent)	1,000
	equals: deficiency in reserves against remaining deposits	9,000

One way for a bank to obtain the reserves it needs is by selling securities. But, as the buyers of the securities pay for them with funds in their deposit accounts in the same or other banks, the net result is a $9,000 decline in securities and deposits at all banks.

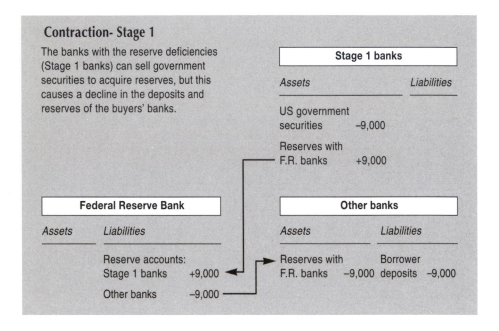

At the end of Stage 1 of the contraction process, deposits have been reduced by a total of $19,000 (the initial $10,000 resulting from the Federal Reserve's action plus the $9,000 in deposits extinguished by securities sales of Stage 1 banks).

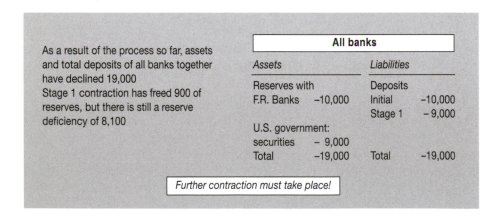

However, there is now a reserve deficiency of $8,100 at banks whose depositors drew down their accounts to purchase the securities from Stage 1 banks. As the new group of reserve-deficient banks, in turn, makes up this deficiency by selling securities or reducing loans, further deposit contraction takes place.

Thus, contraction proceeds through reductions in deposits and loans or investments in one stage after another until total deposits have been reduced to the point where the smaller volume of reserves is adequate to support them. The contraction multiple is the same as that which applies in the case of expansion. Under a 10 percent reserve requirement, a $10,000 reduction in reserves would ultimately entail reductions of $100,000 in deposits and $90,000 in loans and investments.

As in the case of deposit expansion, contraction of bank deposits may take place as a result of either sales of securities or reductions of loans. While some adjustment of both kinds would undoubtedly be made, the initial impact probably would be reflected in sales of government securities. Most types of outstanding loans cannot be called for payment prior to their due dates. But the bank may cease to make new loans or refuse to renew outstanding ones to replace those currently maturing. Thus, deposits built up by borrowers for the purpose of loan retirement would be extinguished as loans were repaid.

There is one important difference between the expansion and contraction processes. When the Federal Reserve System adds to bank reserves, expansion of credit and deposits *may* take place up to the limits permitted by the minimum reserve ratio that banks are required to maintain. But when the System acts to reduce the amount of bank reserves, contraction of credit and deposits *must* take place (except to the extent that existing excess reserve balances and/or surplus vault cash are utilized) to the point where the required ratio of reserves to deposits is restored. But the significance of this difference should not be overemphasised. Because excess reserve balances do not earn interest, there is a strong incentive to convert them into earning assets (loans and investments).

The exact size of the reserve multiplier does, in practice vary. Some of the reasons for this are illustrated in Appendix 4.1.

THE INSTRUMENTS OF MONETARY POLICY

Having discussed the basic idea of credit creation we must now turn to examine all the instruments available to the Federal Reserve to control monetary policy.

It is not enough for the Federal Reserve to have a longer-term strategy in conducting monetary policy. Like other institutions, it lives in the short term, and it must respond to an endless series of economic and financial disturbances – some of which can be anticipated, but most of which cannot – in implementing policy.

For this reason, the Federal Reserve uses a set of tactical procedures to assist in implementing the longer-term strategy and in attaining its strategic objectives.

The Federal Reserve uses three principal instruments in conducting monetary policy on a day-to-day basis. These are:

- open market operations
- the discount rate
- reserve requirements.

Open market operations

Open market operations are the most important instruments used by the Federal Reserve for controlling monetary growth. We discussed the basic principles earlier in this chapter. When using this policy instrument the Federal Reserve simply purchases or sells securities in the open money and bond markets. The purpose of these purchases and sales is to affect the aggregate reserve position of depository institutions; that is, the level and growth of the non-interest-bearing reserve deposits these institutions hold, in the aggregate, at Federal Reserve Banks. These operations also affect the Federal funds rate, which is the interest rate charged for the use of reserve funds in the open market.

The basic mechanics of these operations are quite simple and were illustrated earlier in the description of the bank credit multipliers. If the Federal Reserve wishes to increase the level of reserves, it purchases securities in the open market. It ultimately pays for the purchase by crediting the reserve account of some depository institution for the amount purchased, which increases the level of aggregate reserves by that amount. Conversely, if the Federal Reserve wants to reduce the level of reserves it sells securities in the market. (Or, more importantly in practice, if it wishes to reduce the rate of growth of reserves, it buys securities at a less rapid pace.) Payment for the sales is eventually effected by reducing some depository institution's reserve account for the amount of the sale, which reduces the aggregate level of reserves. This description of the mechanics of open market operations focuses on individual transactions in isolation. In reality, of course, such individual transactions are part of a continuous stream of transactions involving the public and other institutions in addition to the Federal Reserve. Therefore, it is not generally useful in practice to think of Federal Reserve open market operations in terms of the isolated effect of particular purchases and sales. Instead, the focus is on the broader effects of operations on the growth of reserves over time: purchases tend to increase growth; sales reduce it.

The Federal Reserve's open market operations are controlled and supervised by the Federal Reserve Open Market Committee (FOMC). They are executed in the market, under the Committee's direction, by the Federal Reserve Bank of

New York acting as the Committee's agent. A department at the New York Bank, known popularly as the "trading desk," or simply the "desk," actually carries out the operations. A manager for domestic operations, who is a senior officer of the New York Bank, supervises the trading desk. The manager has direct day-to-day control of open market operations, reports directly to the Committee and receives instructions from the Committee.

Although in principle, the Federal Reserve could conduct open market operations using any public or private securities, it is restricted by law to the use of US government (i.e., US Treasury) securities, obligations issued or guaranteed by agencies of the US, and a few short-term securities. In practice, the vast majority of operations are carried out using Treasury securities, and they would undoubtedly be concentrated in Treasuries even in the absence of legal restrictions. To be effective in an economy and financial system as large as that of the US, it is essential that the Federal Reserve be able to conduct large purchases and sales flexibly without unduly disrupting the market. The market for US government securities is extremely broad and active, and is therefore ideal for open market operations.

The Federal Reserve's open market operations are an important factor affecting the aggregate volume of reserves available to depository institutions, but by no means the only factor. Independent actions on the part of the general public and the US Treasury also have important effects on reserves. When the public's demand for currency increases, for example, as it typically does before important holidays, depository institutions obtain the currency from the Federal Reserve. They pay for it through reductions in their reserve balances at the Federal Reserve, which reduce aggregate reserves, and could lead to a fall in the money supply. Conversely, a reduction in the public's desire for currency increases reserves, and could lead to an increase in the money supply.

As discussed earlier, open market operations represent the New York Federal Reserve buying and selling US Treasury securities. The buying of securities by the Federal Reserve causes the seller to deposit the proceeds of the sale in a bank account, thereby increasing bank reserves. And because the bank needs to hold only a fraction of the deposit in reserve, the balance can be lent to borrowers. This action creates new checking account balances, which, in turn, increases the money supply. When the Federal Reserve sells securities, the buyer pays with funds withdrawn from the bank. The withdrawal decreases bank reserves and therefore, the money supply. Higher reserves make it easier for banks to lend. This lending stimulates the economy. Lower reserves make it more difficult for banks to lend, which restrains the economy. However, banks cannot change their reserves through their own actions (*see* Figure 4.2).

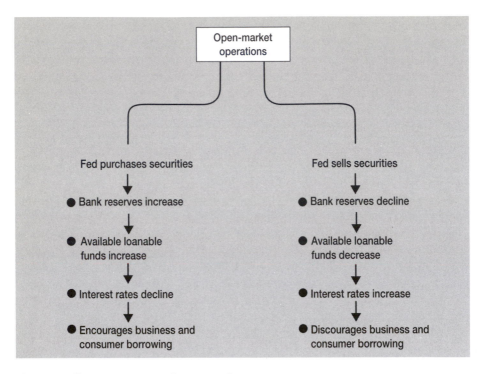

Fig 4.2 ● Effects on open market operations

Source: Chapter 3, *Essentials of Finance*, George W. Gallinger and Jerry B. Poe, Prentice Hall 1995.

The discount rate

All depository institutions with deposits against which they are obliged to maintain reserves may borrow reserves from the Federal Reserve. This is known as
discount window borrowing. There are, however, several restrictions regarding
their access.

The discount rate itself is the interest rate charged on these loans. A depository institution can borrow from the window in one of two ways:

- by "discounting," i.e., selling loans or other assets carrying its endorsement
  to the Federal Reserve;

- through an advance, which is a loan from the Federal Reserve to the institution, which must be secured by acceptable collateral.

At present, nearly all borrowing at the window is via advances because of their
greater convenience. In the early days of the system, however, discounting was
the more common procedure, and this historical legacy is the origin of the terms
discount window borrowing and *discount rate*. Most borrowing at the window is
at the basic discount rate. Higher rates are charged for certain categories of
extended credit.

Essentially, the Federal Reserve uses the discount rate to reinforce its efforts to manage reserves through open market operations. Although many depository institutions are reluctant to borrow from the window, and all institutions are subject to various rules and administrative constraints when they do borrow, a discount rate that is low in relation to other short-term rates tends to encourage borrowing, and, conversely, a high discount rate in relation to other rates tends to discourage borrowing. Therefore, if the Federal Reserve, for example, were trying to restrain the growth of reserves, and this restraint put upward pressure on the Federal Reserve funds rate and other market rates, the maintenance of an unchanged discount rate might tend to raise the aggregate level of borrowing at the window at least temporarily, which would work against the thrust of open market operations. In this situation, the Federal Reserve might raise the discount rate to reinforce its open market operations. In addition to its direct impact on borrowing, the announcement of the discount rate increase would be a strong signal of the direction of Federal Reserve policy both to the financial markets and the general public, because such changes are highly visible and receive considerable attention from the news media. Similarly, if the Federal Reserve were trying to stimulate reserve growth through open market operations, it might reduce the discount rate at some point.

The short-term impact of discount rate changes on market interest rates depends to some extent on the particular short-term operating procedures the Federal Reserve is using in implementing policy, and the Federal Reserve has to take these relationships into account in deciding on discount rate actions in particular circumstances.

The discount rate is the interest rate at which member banks borrow from the Federal Reserve. The Federal Reserve considers use of the discount window a last resort for members that are in urgent need of additional reserves. As Figure 4.3 illustrates, the Federal Reserve views an increase in the discount rate as a discouragement to bank lending with the ultimate objective of discouraging business and consumer borrowing. A decrease in the discount rate has the intended opposite effect by encouraging borrowing through lower interest rates.

In reality the discount rate appears to have little policy significance because the Federal Reserve has generally kept this rate below the market rate for money. As a result the discount rate, in practice, is not a penalty rate.

Reserve requirements

Under current law, all depository institutions operating in the US (including not only domestic commercial banks but also savings banks, savings and loan associations, credit unions, Edge Act and agreement corporations, and US branches and agencies of foreign banks) must hold required reserves against their:

- net transaction accounts
- non-personal time deposits
- Eurocurrency liabilities.

These required reserves must be held in the form either of vault cash or deposits at a Federal Reserve Bank. The Board of Governors of the Federal Reserve establishes these requirements in terms of percentages of particular categories of liabilities against which they must hold reserves. These are known as *reservable liabilities*.

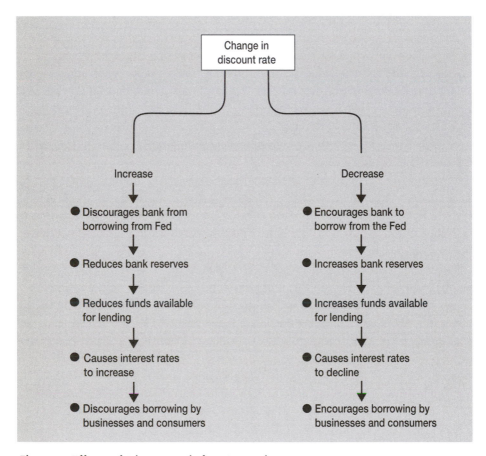

Fig 4.3 ● Effects of Discount Window Borrowing

Figure 4.4 illustrates the intended effect of increases and decreases in bank reserves. When reserve requirements increase banks must hold more funds in reserve against their deposits. The effect is that banks have less funds available to lend. The intent of higher reserves is to reduce the money supply, increase interest rates, and reduce inflationary pressure in the economy through lower economic activity. The Federal Reserve hopes that a decrease in reserves has opposite effects.

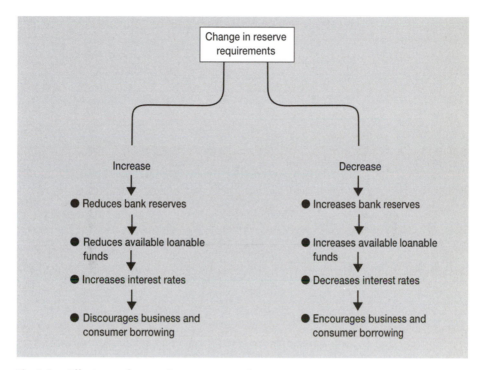

Fig 4.4 ● Effects on changes in reserve requirements

With regard to monetary policy and monetary control, reserve requirements affect the quantitative relationship between the aggregate reserves held by depository institutions and the various monetary aggregates the Federal Reserve seeks to influence, all of which include some reservable liabilities. More precisely, reserve requirements put limits on the volume of reservable deposits and other liabilities that can be supported by any given volume of aggregate reserves. Therefore, the Federal Reserve, if it chose to do so, could manipulate reserve requirements to reinforce its other policy actions. For example, if it had adopted a generally restrictive posture, it might raise reserve requirements, and vice versa.

In practice, the Federal Reserve rarely uses reserve requirements in this way. Frequent changes in the requirements would obviously be a substantial administrative burden on both the Federal Reserve itself and the institutions subject to the requirements. Furthermore, even relatively small changes in reserve requirements can have a sizable impact on the availability and cost of reserves and are therefore not appropriate for effecting the generally incremental changes in reserve conditions that the Federal Reserve is usually trying to achieve on a day-to-day basis. For this reason, the System tends to focus on reserve requirements as a central element of the institutional apparatus linking reserves quantitatively to the monetary aggregates rather than as an instrument to be manipulated.

The reserve multiplier – why it varies

The deposit expansion and contraction associated with a given change in bank reserves, as illustrated earlier, assumed a fixed reserve-to-deposit multiplier. That multiplier was determined by a uniform percentage reserve requirement specified for transaction accounts. Such an assumption is an oversimplification of the actual relationship between changes in reserves and changes in money, especially in the short run. For a number of reasons, as discussed in this Appendix, the quantity of reserves associated with a given quantity of transaction deposits constantly changes.

One slippage affecting the reserve multiplier is variations in the amount of excess reserves. In the "real world," reserves are not always fully utilized. There are always some excess reserves in the banking system, reflecting frictions and lags as funds flow among thousands of individual banks.

Excess reserves present a problem for monetary policy implementation only because the amount changes. To the extent that new reserves supplied are offset by rising excess reserves, actual money growth falls short of the theoretical maximum. Conversely, a reduction in excess reserves by the banking system has the same effect on monetary expansion as the injection of an equal amount of new reserves.

Slippages also arise from reserve requirements being imposed on liabilities not included in money as well as differing reserve ratios being applied to transaction deposits according to the size of the bank. From 1980–1990, reserve requirements were imposed on certain non-transaction liabilities of all depository institutions, and before then on all deposits of member banks. The reserve multiplier was affected by flows of funds between institutions subject to differing reserve requirements. The extension of reserve requirements to all depository institutions in 1980 and the elimination of reserve requirements against non-personal time deposits and Eurocurrency liabilities in late 1990 reduced, but did not eliminate, this source of instability in the reserve multiplier. The deposit expansion potential of a given volume of reserves is still affected by shifts of transaction deposits between large institutions and those exempt from reserve requirements.

In addition, the reserve multiplier is affected by conversions of deposits into currency or vice versa. This factor was important in the 1980s as the public's desired currency holdings relative to transaction deposits in money shifted considerably. Also affecting the multiplier are shifts between transaction deposits included in money and other transaction accounts that also are reservable but not included in money, such as demand deposits due to depository institutions, the US government, and foreign banks and official institutions. In aggregate, these non-money transaction deposits are relatively small in comparison to total transaction accounts, but can vary significantly from week to week.

A net injection of reserves has widely different effects depending on how it is absorbed. Only a dollar-for-dollar increase in the money supply would result if the new reserves were paid out in currency to the public. With a uniform 10 percent reserve requirement, a $1 increase in reserves would support $10 of additional transaction accounts. An even larger amount would be supported under the graduated system where smaller institutions are subjected to reserve requirements below 10 percent. One dollar of new reserves would also support an additional $10 of certain reservable transaction accounts that are not counted as money (see Figure 4.1.1). Normally, an increase in reserves would be absorbed by some combination of the currency and transaction deposit changes.

All of these factors are to some extent predictable and are taken into account in decisions as to the amount of reserves that need to be supplied to achieve the desired rate of monetary expansion. They help explain why short-run fluctuations in bank reserves often are disproportionate to, and sometimes in the opposite direction from, changes in the deposit component of money.

Money creation and reserve management

Another reason for short-term variation in the amount of reserves supplied is that credit expansion – and thus deposit creation – is variable, reflecting uneven timing of credit demands. Although bank loan policies normally take account of the general availability of funds, the size and timing of loans and investments made under those policies depend largely on customers' credit needs.

In the real world, a bank's lending is not normally constrained by the amount of excess reserves it has at any given moment. Rather, loans are made, or not made, depending on the bank's credit policies and its expectations about its ability to obtain the funds necessary to pay its customers' checks and maintain required reserves in a timely fashion. In fact, because Federal Reserve regulations in effect from 1968–1984 specified that average required reserves for a given week should be based on average deposit levels two weeks earlier ("lagged" reserve accounting), deposit creation actually preceded the provision of supporting reserves. In early 1984, a more "contemporaneous" reserve accounting system was implemented in order to improve monetary control.

In February 1984, banks shifted to maintaining average reserves over a two-week reserve maintenance period ending Wednesday against average transaction deposits held over the two-week computation period ending only two days earlier. Under this rule, actual transaction deposit expansion was expected to more closely approximate the process explained at the beginning of Chapter 4. However, some slippages still exist because of short-term uncertainties about the level of both reserves and transaction deposits near the close of reserve maintenance periods. Moreover, not all banks must maintain reserves according to the contemporaneous accounting system. Smaller institutions are either exempt completely or only have to maintain reserves quarterly against average deposits in one week of the prior quarterly period.

On balance, however, variability in the reserve multiplier has been reduced by the extension of reserve requirements to all institutions in 1980, by the adoption of contemporaneous reserve accounting in 1984, and by the removal of reserve requirements against non-transaction deposits and liabilities in late 1990. As a result, short-term changes in total reserves and transaction deposits in money are more closely related now than they were before.

Ironically, these modifications contributing to a less variable relationship between

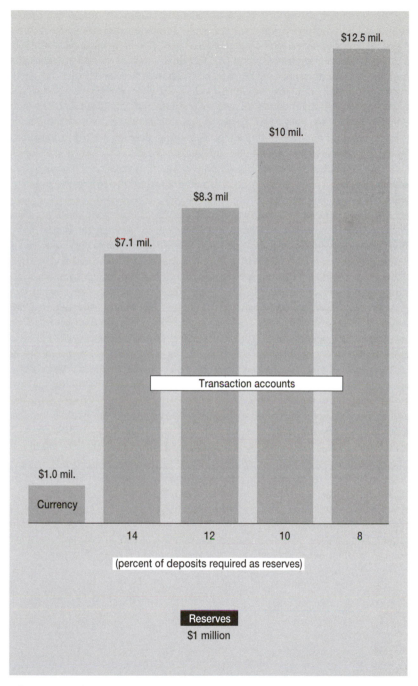

Fig 4.1.1 ● The growth potential of a $1 million reserve injection

changes in reserves and changes in transaction deposits occurred as the relationship between transaction money (M1) and the economy deteriorated. Because the M1 measure of money has become less useful as a guide for policy, somewhat greater attention has shifted to the broader measures M2 and M3. However, reserve multiplier relationships for the broader monetary measures are far more variable than that for M1.

Although every bank must operate within the system where the total amount of reserves is controlled by the Federal Reserve, its response to policy action is indirect. The individual bank does not know precisely what its reserve position will be at the time the proceeds of today's loans are paid out. Nor does it know when new reserves are being supplied to the banking system. Reserves are distributed among thousands of banks, and the individual banker cannot distinguish between inflows originating from additions to reserves through Federal Reserve action and shifts of funds from other banks that occur in the normal course of business.

To equate short-term reserve needs with available funds, therefore, many banks turn to the money market – borrowing funds to cover deficits or lending temporary surpluses. When the demand for reserves is strong relative to the supply, funds obtained from money market sources to cover deficits tend to become more expensive and harder to obtain, which, in turn, may induce banks to adopt more restrictive loan policies and thus slow the rate of deposit growth.

Federal Reserve open market operations exert control over the creation of deposits mainly through their impact on the availability and cost of funds in the money market. When the total amount of reserves supplied to the banking system through open market operations falls short of the amount required, some banks are forced to borrow at the Federal Reserve discount window. Because such borrowing is restricted to short periods, the need to repay it tends to induce restraint on further deposit expansion by the borrowing bank. Conversely, when there are excess reserves in the banking system, individual banks find it easy and relatively inexpensive to acquire reserves, and expansion in loans, investments, and deposits is encouraged.

CHAPTER **5**

How does economic activity affect financial markets?

WHAT IS MACROECONOMICS ALL ABOUT?

In order to best appreciate the impact of economic activity on the financial markets, it is essential to first appreciate what are the major constituent items which drive the economy. This is based on what economists refer to as the *standard macroeconomic model*.

Macroeconomics concentrates on the behavior of entire economies. Rather than looking at the price and output decisions of a single company, macroeconomists study overall economic activity, the unemployment rate, the price level and other broad categories. These are referred to as *economic aggregates*.

An "economic aggregate" is nothing but an abstraction that people find convenient in describing some salient feature of economic life. Among the most important of these abstract notions is the concept of national product, which represents the total production of a nation's economy. The process by which real objects like automobiles, tickets to sports events and laptop computers get combined into an abstraction called national product is one of the foundations of macroeconomics.

EXAMPLE 1

Imagine a nation called Titanica whose economy is far simpler than the more developed economies of the West. Business firms in Titanica produce nothing but food to sell to consumers. Rather than deal separately with all the markets for sandwiches, ice cream and fried chicken and so on, macro-economists group them all into a single abstract "market for output." Thus when macroeconomists in Titanica announce that output in Titanica rose 10 percent this year, are they referring to more potatoes, hamburgers or onions? The answer is that they do not care; overall output has risen by 10 percent.

During economic fluctuations, markets tend to move in unison. When demand in the economy rises, there is more demand for fruit, vegetables and complete meals. This reverses when the economy slows down.

There are several ways to measure the economy's total output, the most popular being the gross national product (GNP). The GNP is the most comprehensive measure of the output of all the factories, offices and shops in the economy. Specifically it is the sum of the money values of all final goods and services produced within the year. This is often referred to as *nominal GNP*. Real GNP is nominal GNP adjusted for inflation. Gross domestic product (GDP) is the market value of final goods and services newly produced within a nation's borders during a fixed period of time.

Aggregate demand within the economy, another application of the aggregation principle, refers to the total amount that all consumers, business firms, government agencies, and foreigners wish to spend on all domestically produced goods and services. The level of aggregate demand depends on a variety of factors, like consumer incomes, the price level, government economic policies and events in foreign countries.

The big picture

The nature of aggregate demand can best be understood if it is split into its major components. These are:

- consumer expenditure (C)
- investment spending (I)
- government spending (G)
- level of exports (X) minus level of imports (IM).

This gives us the familiar macroeconomic relationship that:

Aggregate demand (GNP) is the sum of C + I + G + (X – IM)

Definitions

Consumer expenditure (C) is the total amount spent by consumers on newly produced goods and services (excluding purchases of new homes, which are considered investment goods).

Investment expenditure (I) is the sum of the expenditure of business firms on new plant and equipment, plus the expenditures of households on new homes. Financial "investments" such as bonds or equities are not included.

Government spending refers to all the goods (such as airplanes and pencils) and services (such as school teaching and police protection) purchased by all levels of government. It does not include government transfer payments, such as social security and unemployment benefits.

Net exports (X – IM) is the difference between exports and imports. It indicates the difference between what a country sells abroad and what it buys from abroad.

National income is the sum of the incomes of all the individuals in the economy earned in the form of wages, interest, rents, and profits. It excludes transfer payments, such as unemployment benefits, and is calculated before any deductions are taken for income taxes.

Disposable income (DI) is the sum of the incomes of all the individuals in the

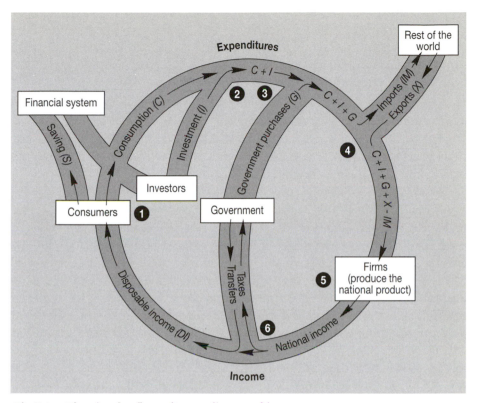

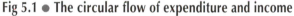

Fig 5.1 ● The circular flow of expenditure and income

Source: Baumol & Blinder: Economics

economy after taxes have been deducted and all transfer payments have been added.

Having introduced the concepts of national product, aggregate demand and national income, Figure 5.1 illustrates how they interact in the market economy.

Figure 5.1 is called a circular flow diagram. It depicts a large circular tube in which a fluid is circulating in a clockwise direction. There are several breaks in the tube where either some of the fluid leaks out or additional fluid is injected in.

At point 1 on the circle there are consumers. Disposable income (DI) is flowing into them, and two things are flowing out: consumption (C), which stays in the circular flow, and savings (S) which "leaks out." This just means that consumers normally spend less than they earn and save the balance. This "leakage" to savings, of course, does not disappear, but flows into the financial system.

The upper loop of the circular flow represents expenditure, and as we move clockwise to point 2, we encounter the first "injection" into the flow: investment spending (I). The diagram shows this as coming from "investors" – a group that includes both business firms and consumers who buy new homes. As the circular flow moves beyond point 2, it is bigger than it was before. Total spending has increased from C to C + I.

At point 3, there is yet another injection. The government adds its demand for goods and services (G) to those of consumers and investors (C + I). Now aggregate demand is up to C + I + G.

The final leakage and injections comes at point 4. Here we see export spending coming into the circular flow from abroad and import spending leaking out. The net effect of these two forces, net exports, may increase or decrease the circular flow. In either case, by the time we pass point 4 we have accumulated the full amount of aggregate demand, C + I + G + (X − IM).

The circular flow diagram shows this aggregate demand for goods and services arriving at the business firms, which are located at point 5 at the south-east portion of the diagram. Responding to this demand, firms produce the national product.

As the circular flow emerges from the firms it has been renamed as national income. National product is the sum of the money values of all the final goods and services provided by the economy during a specified period of time, usually one year. National income and national product must be equal. Why is this the case? When a firm produces and sells $100 worth of output, it pays most of the proceeds to its workers, to people who have lent it money, and to the landlord who owns the property on which it is located. All of these payments are income to some individuals. But what about the rest? Suppose, for example, that the wages, interest, and rent that the firm pays add up to $90, while its output is $100. What happens to the remaining $10? The answer is that the owners of the firm receive it as profits. But these owners are also citizens of the country, so their incomes count in national income too. Thus, when we add up all the wages, interest, rents, and profits in the economy to obtain the national income, we must arrive at the value of national output.

The lower loop of the circular flow diagram traces the flow of income by showing national income leaving the firms and heading for consumers. But there is a detour along the way. At point 6, the government does two things. First, it siphons off a portion of the national income in the form of taxes. Second, it adds back government transfer payments, like unemployment compensation and social security benefits, which are sums of money that certain individuals receive as outright grants from the government rather than as payments for services rendered to employers.

When taxes are subtracted from GNP, and transfer payments are added, we obtain disposable income.

$$DI = GNP − Taxes + Transfer Payments$$

Disposable income flows unimpeded to consumers at point 1, and the cycle repeats.

FINANCIAL MARKETS AND THE ECONOMY

Now that we have an appreciation of how the economy works it is essential to examine how the financial markets interrelate with the real economy. In trying to assess the significance of an economic indicator to the financial markets, it is imperative to understand that each particular indicator provides a piece of information about some aspect of nominal GNP. Analysts are concerned about nominal GNP because there is a relationship between nominal GNP and monetary growth. This relationship comes about because as nominal GNP accelerates there is increased demand for transactions balances, i.e., as incomes grow we need more cash to spend. Not surprisingly, therefore, the growth of the money supply and nominal GNP are related.

What is important here is that there is an identifiable relationship between the growth rates of nominal GNP and the various monetary aggregates. Because of this long-standing historical relationship, the Federal Reserve has adopted specific growth rate targets for several of the monetary aggregates. Therefore, if something causes nominal GNP to grow more quickly, then it will translate almost assuredly into more rapid growth of the money supply. If money supply growth picks up, the Federal Reserve is likely to respond by tightening its grip on monetary policy. It does this by raising interest rates.

As interest rates rise the price of fixed income securities declines. This was discussed in detail in Chapter 2, but as an example, take a situation in which somebody holds a Treasury bond that yields 10 percent. If the economy expands rapidly and the Federal Reserve is eventually forced to tighten so that interest rates rise to 12 percent, the 10 percent bond becomes less attractive and its price declines. People would rather own the higher-yielding 12 percent security. Thus, any factor that causes nominal GNP to rise increases the likelihood that the Federal Reserve will tighten by raising interest rates which, in turn, causes security prices to decline.

It is also important to recognize that nominal GNP consists of two parts – real (or inflation-adjusted) GNP, and the inflation rate which is measured by the GNP deflator (defined further in Chapter 6). The growth rate of nominal GNP equals the sum of the growth rates of real GNP and of the inflation rate. Thus, 8 percent nominal GNP growth might consist of 4 percent real GNP growth and 4 percent inflation, or 2 percent real GNP growth and 6 percent inflation. From the market's point of view any factor that results in *either* more rapid GNP growth *or* a higher rate of inflation will cause *nominal* GNP to grow more rapidly which, as noted earlier, causes monetary growth to accelerate, increases the likelihood of a Federal Reserve tightening move, and implies higher interest rates and lower securities prices. Conversely, lower GNP growth and lower inflation imply slower GNP growth which could cause the Federal Reserve to ease monetary policy. A Federal Reserve easing move would bring about lower interest rates and higher securities prices. The fact of the matter is that the fixed income markets thrive when the economy collapses and moves into a recession, and they suffer when the economy is doing well and expanding rapidly. Therefore, when interpreting an economic indicator it is critical to determine the effect that particular indicator will have on either GNP growth or the inflation rate. By adding the two together we can get a feel as to the direction of monetary policy and consequently the direction that financial asset prices will move.

It is useful to carry the breakdown of real GNP one step further in order to focus on specific sectors of the economy which can at times move in several different directions. As we discussed earlier real GNP consists of the sum of consumption expenditures (C), investment spending (I), government expenditures (G) and net exports (or exports–imports) (X – IM). This equation is frequently referred to as GNP = C + I + G + (X – IM). If one is looking at an economic indicator that refers to the real economy, it is extremely helpful to be able to identify the particular component of GNP that it affects. For example, when retail sales are released one should immediately recognize that retail sales provide information about consumer spending which in turn has implications for the consumption component of GNP. Then, having determined the effect on GNP, one can say something about the likelihood of a change in Federal Reserve policy.

Appendix 5.1 describes in detail the way an experienced analyst would use the plethora of data on the US economy to gain a feel for the prospects for the economy, and in turn, the financial markets. We will return to these economic indicators in later chapters.

Having stressed the importance of determining how an economic indicator affects nominal GNP, it is also important to remember, as discussed in Chapter 1, that it is not so much the *absolute* change in an indicator that is important, but how it compares to market expectations. Indeed the critical judgment to be made when analyzing market behavior is on what the market is expecting and why. In financial market language, this is called knowing what has been "discounted" by the market.

For example, if it is widely believed that the Federal Reserve is likely to cut the discount rate over the next several weeks, then bond prices will reflect that belief. When the discount rate is actually cut, bond prices may not move very much, because the expectation that was discounted into the market was actually realized. On the other hand, if for some reason the Federal Reserve chooses not to cut the discount rate, when the financial markets expected it was going to, then bond prices may react quite negatively, because the expectation of a discount rate cut proved to be incorrect.

What this example shows is the important function that expectations play in the timing of a price movement. Major events that are widely anticipated may have absolutely no effect on prices at the time they occur. Other, equally major, events can have profound impacts on prices if they were not anticipated. The first lesson, then, of market dynamics and expectations is that one must know what future events have already been discounted by the market.

We must now break down the components of GNP and analyze which regularly published data will best indicate the likely future trend of the US economy and their likely impact on financial markets.

Economic data is analyzed using the following classification system, in order that a consistent analytical approach can be applied:

- title of the indicator
- definition
- who publishes it and when
- how to interpret it
- its impact on financial markets.

Figure 5.2 provides a useful taxonomy of the interrelationship between the different components of nominal GNP and those economic indicators which most closely influence it. The remaining chapters are based around Figure 5.2 so it is useful if you familiarize yourself with it.

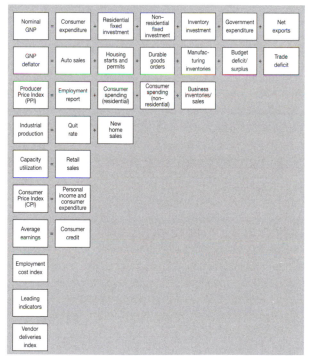

Fig 5.2 ● Economic indicators and financial markets

A primer on short-term linkages between key economic data series

In the United States, economy watchers are blessed (or cursed, depending on one's viewpoint) with a plethora of data. To the casual or new observer of the economy, the information content of the many indicators may be unclear. Moreover, the way experienced analysts use the data to evaluate the economy may seem counterintuitive. To the newcomer the question often is, Why do those interested in future economic developments look at these numbers? Or how does one use these data series? There may be as many answers as there are analysts.

Why do analysts look at economic data? The simple answer is that investors and planners must look forward, and economic data help them forecast. If there is new information on the economy, on demand, on profit potential, or on prices, among other factors, then the underlying value of financial and real investments may shift, changing values, project projections, and plans.

The release of economic data can have an impact on the value of financial instruments and investment projects because it may change analysts' views of the strength or weakness of the economy. These views in turn may affect their forecasts for company or project earnings, general or specific prices, and interest rates. Because major decisions may depend on economic reports, market participants need to squeeze as much information as possible out of data so as to make intelligent decisions about financial holdings and investments.

There are a number of time horizons relevant to how market watchers evaluate economic data and use them for forecasting. The evaluation of various longer-run fundamentals often begins with examining short-run relationships among economic variables. This article focuses on these relationships – many of which involve lagged effects taking place over a few months or at least within a year and a half. Clarifying the source data linkages and the statistical linkages will help explain how and why financial markets track and react to economic data the way they do. Source data are series from one statistical agency used by another statistical agency to derive a new series (discussed below).

This article is a brief guide to some of the well known short-term relationships between economic data series upon which many analysts focus. It explains how analysts use data in concurrent month forecasts and what some key relationships are, outlines the monthly calendar of economic releases, and, finally, reports on typical lags between various dependent and explanatory variables.

This appendix was originally published in The Federal Reserve Bank of Atlanta *Economic Review*, Second Quarter 1998. The author is R. Mark Rogers.

CONCURRENT MONTH LINKAGE – SOURCE DATA AND STATISTICAL LINKS

There are at least two basic approaches to linking two or more economic series over a short time horizon. Analysts try to use prior-released data to project later-released data for the same period. This practice is called "forecasting" concurrent data. Linkages between the earlier and later data sets may be based on common source data or on some statistical relationship.

Source data

Source data are series used by a statistical agency (usually a government bureau such as the Commerce Department's Bureau of Economic Analysis [BEA]) to derive other economic statistical series. For example, the BEA uses average hourly earnings data from the Labor Department to help produce the wages-and-salaries component in personal income data; the BEA also uses residential construction outlays to help estimate the residential investment component of gross domestic product (GDP).

Analysts should be aware that analyzing source data to forecast concurrent data for the derived data series is less than straightforward because the statistical agencies typically make numerous adjustments to the source data at levels of detail not always accessible to the public. Adjustments may have been made for differences in definition, geographic coverage, or timing and obvious or subtle differences in economic concepts. Additionally, a subsequent data series may be based on more than one set of source data. Some examples follow.

The industrial production index has three principal components: manufacturing production, utilities production, and mining. For the initial release of the index, the Federal Reserve Board of Governors bases the manufacturing production component primarily on production worker hours in the manufacturing sector, available from the establishment survey in the employment report produced by the Bureau of Labor Statistics (BLS). The Federal Reserve Board uses this measure as its primary input for the initial estimate because so little hard data for actual production are available for the month about to be released. (For example, data on kilowatt hours of electricity used in production are not available until later in the month. For later revisions to the initial estimates of industrial production, the Federal Reserve Board incorporates these other types of data.) The production worker hours data become publicly available on the first Friday of each month following the reference month; the industrial production report for the same reference month is released around the fifteenth of the following month. Thus, on average, the production worker hours data are available about ten days prior to the production index release. Analysts use this data to judge the strength of the manufacturing sector in terms of estimated output. As a percentage of value added in 1994, production worker hours data underlay 29.1 percent of the initial estimate directly and 53.1 percent indirectly (for heavily judgmentally based series). These percentages, respectively, were 29.1 percent and 2.5 percent for the fourth month estimates.[1]

1. These figures are unpublished estimates by Federal Reserve staff, October 1997.

Because production workers hours data are key inputs for initial estimates of industrial production, market analysts often attempt to forecast an upcoming release with a regression model based on production worker hours data, shown in Table 1.[2] This regression estimates manufacturing output as a function of production worker hours plus a constant over the 1980–97 period. Both output and hours are in monthly percentage change form. The percentage change in manufacturing output is estimated to be 0.631 times the percentage change in production worker hours plus a constant of 0.268. This simple model has reasonably good explanatory power with an adjusted R^2 of 0.5015 and with t-statistics for both explanatory variables statistically significant. (R^2 is the coefficient of determination, a statistical measure of the "explained" variation in the data as a percentage of the total variation in the data. Values for R^2 range from 0 to 1.00 so that, for a simple regression model with only one explanatory variable, all the data lie on the regression line when R^2 equals 1.00 – that is, there are no unexplained variations in the data. Adjusted R^2 is a measure that takes into account how many explanatory variables are used in the regression model.) Based on its moderately high adjusted R^2, the regression confirms that a percentage change in manufacturing production worker hours is useful for forecasting manufacturing output for the current month.

Table 1● A simple model for forecasting IP with production worker hours

Regression using OLS
Dependent variable: FRB industrial output, manufacturing, percent change
Explanatory variable: production worker hours, percent change
1980M1–97M10

Variable	Coefficient	Standard error	t-statistic	Significance
Constant	0.267801	0.380935E-01	7.03011	0.000
Production worker hours, percent change	0.631322	0.430306E-01	14.6715	0.000

Equation summary

Number of observations	=	214	R^2 (adjusted)	=	0.5015
Sum of squared residuals	=	65.6672	Standard error of regression	=	0.556553
R^2	=	0.5038	Durbin-Watson	=	2.36697

2. This particular regression model is discussed in more detail in Rogers (1992). Importantly, one should note that the Federal Reserve Board estimates production with procedures for individual components. About 82 percent of the series is based on production worker hours, directly and indirectly, for the initial estimate. Even for these series, the Federal Reserve Board makes estimates using production factor coefficients (PFCs) based on more than just production hour data (see Board of Governors 1986, 33–128).

PFCs are used to estimate individual industrial production series, which are estimated over historical periods, taking into account trend and cyclical relationships between production and the hours input and adjusting the hours data to be representative of the month as a whole. This procedure is more complex than is represented by a simple production hours regression model, but market analysts have found this type of model to have some usefulness.

Statistical relationships

A second way that analysts may make forecasts – short-term or long-term – is by linking different data series that have relatively dependable statistical relationships. Two data series may have a common near-term link either to each other or to separate variables even though statistical agencies do not use one series to produce the other. An example of such a concurrent-month – or same-reference-month – statistical relationship is using producer price index (PPI) data, released earlier in the month, to project the consumer price index (CPI), even though the BLS derives these indexes independently.

Another example involving short-term linkages of data for concurrent forecasting is using the purchasing managers index to predict the later-released industrial production index.[3] Even though the former index is not used to produce the latter, there is a statistical relationship between the direction and magnitude of movement in the purchasing managers' index and the industrial production index on a concurrent month basis. The National Association for Purchasing Management (NAPM) releases a survey of manufacturers in its association on the first business day of each month following the reference month. This release is timed so that manufacturing sector data are available on average about two or three days before the employment situation data on production worker hours. This early release date for manufacturing sector data makes this release a very important one for profit-driven analysts, who are motivated to determine whether it contains any significant information that will help them assess the strength of the economy before the employment report is released.

The purchasing managers' survey release contains a composite index, the components of the composite index, and a number of indexes not included in the composite. The composite index is based on subcomponents for production, new orders, employment, inventories, and vendor performance. To predict the release of industrial production later in the month – but prior to the release of the employment situation – analysts typically regress the percentage change in industrial production against the NAPM composite diffusion index. This diffusion index measures not levels of activity but percentages of respondents indicating an increase, decrease, or no change in activity. NAPM's diffusion index is the percentage of respondents indicating an increase in activity plus half the percentage indicating no change. Hence, the level of these diffusion indexes is associated with percentage changes in corresponding government data series based on actual dollar values or output level. For this article's statistical comparison, the Federal Reserve Board's manufacturing output index in monthly percent changes is regressed against the NAPM's production diffusion index level. This regression model, shown in Table 2, estimates that the percentage change in manufacturing output is equal to 0.055 times the NAPM production index plus a constant of –2.758. The explanatory power of this model, with an adjusted R^2 of 0.2991, is lower than the production worker hours model (Table 1), but analysts use this type of model because the NAPM data are released prior to the production worker hours data and the NAPM data's explanatory power is significant.

Statistical relationships can be expanded beyond the current month when one variable "explains" a second series over an extended time horizon (even if only for a few months). One series in a base time period typically has some known economic impact on another series in a subsequent time period. For example, changes in housing permits over time lead to changes in housing construction outlays.

---

3. For more detailed discussion of these types of models, see Rogers (1988, 1992, 1994, and 1998), Harris (1991), and Harris and Vega (1996).

Table 2 ● A simple model for forecasting IP with the NAPM production index

Regression using OLS
Dependent variable: FRB industrial output, manufacturing, percent change
Explanatory variable: NAPM production diffusion index level
1980M1–97M10

Variable	Coefficient	Standard error	t-statistic	Significance
Constant	−2.75805	0.315984	−8.72845	0.000
NAPM Production Index	0.554479E-01	0.578480E-02	9.58510	0.000

Equation summary

Number of observations	=	214	R^2 (adjusted)	=	0.2991
Sum of squared residuals	=	92.3292	Standard error of regression	=	0.659936
R^2	=	0.3023	Durbin-Watson	=	2.21014

In summary, short-term analysis of data can involve concurrent forecasting using either source data or well known statistical relationships among explanatory variables. The use of independent variables can be expanded beyond current period analysis to longer-term forecasting.

MONTHLY RELEASES AND CONCURRENT LINKAGES

Analysts' abilities to predict economic strengths as much in advance as possible depend on the fact that there is a regular cycle to economic news releases. Federal government statistical agencies typically give dates for economic news releases for a given year during the latter part of the previous year. The relative order of each release during the calendar month has changed little over the years. For example, the U.S. Department of Labor generally releases the employment situation report on the first Friday of each month. Industrial production is usually released by the Federal Reserve Board of Governors around midmonth, and GDP estimates typically are released during the last week of each month. Other government – and private-sector – release dates are also generally known well in advance and have followed much the same sequence relative to each other for years. For example, the PPI always precedes the CPI, usually by about three days. Table 3 gives a typical schedule of key economic releases over a monthly release cycle.

What series are used to project subsequently released concurrent month data? And what are the basic relationships between the released and the projected series? Table 4 lists the primary linkages for concurrent month forecasting according to when key data series are first made public. Series in the left-hand column are released to the public prior to those in the right-hand column. Table 5 shows the primary source data specifically for GDP components. Financial markets track economic series in the sequence that they are released publicly. The key reports shown in Tables 4 and 5 and linkages from those reports to later-released data are discussed below.

The purchasing managers' report

Several individual series from the monthly report by the National Association of Purchasing Managers are used to predict other, later-released economic data. Although the most notable instance is the use of the purchasing managers' production index to predict the industrial production index produced by the Federal Reserve discussed earlier, there are others. Some analysts use the NAPM composite index rather than the production index as the explanatory variable. Other series are used to a lesser degree because the statistical relationship is less reliable. The NAPM employment index is used to predict BLS data for nonfarm payroll employment – or, more specifically, for the manufacturing employment component of the establishment employment report. The NAPM prices paid index is often correlated with the BLS producer price index. The NAPM new orders index has a small predictive capability for the Census Bureau's new factory orders. Finally, the Conference Board uses the NAPM vendor performance index as source data directly for that component in the Conference Board's index of leading indicators.

Table 3 ● Monthly release schedule for October 1997

Release date	Indicator	Reference period
October		
1	Construction expenditures	August
1	Purchasing managers' index, NAPM	September
1	Conference Board's composite indicators	August
2	Manufacturers shipments, inventories, and orders	August
2	Initial unemployment claims	September 25
3	Employment situation	September
6	Auto sales, AAMA	September
8	Wholesale trade	August
9	Initial unemployment claims	October 4
10	Producer price index	September
14	Atlanta Fed manufacturing survey	September
14	Richmond Fed manufacturing survey	September
15	Advance monthly retail sales	September
16	Consumer price index	September
16	Initial unemployment claims	October 11
16	Philadelphia Fed manufacturing survey	October
16	Business inventories and sales	August
17	Housing starts and permits	September
17	Industrial production and capacity utilization rate	September
21	U.S. international trade in goods and services	August
23	Initial unemployment claims	October 18
28	Employment cost index	Third Quarter
29	Advance report on durable goods	September
30	New one-family house sales	September
30	Initial unemployment claims	October 25
31	GDP	Third Quarter
November		
3	Personal income, outlays, and saving	September
3	Purchasing managers' index, NAPM	October

The employment situation report

The employment situation report, released the first Friday of each month after the reference month, contains four major sets of data series used for concurrent month forecasting. The report's primary importance stems from the fact that it is the first major release each month with comprehensive coverage of all major sectors of the economy; the report provides key data on the strength of the manufacturing and consumer sectors. As already discussed, the manufacturing production worker hours index is used by the Federal Reserve Board to estimate the first release figure for manufacturing output. Second, the BEA uses nonfarm payroll data on employees, the average work week, and average hourly earnings to estimate the private-sector portion of wage and salary disbursements in the personal income report. Next, the manufacturing average workweek is one of the components of the Conference Board's composite index of leading indicators. Finally, the series for nonfarm payroll employment is part of the Conference Board composite index of current indicators.

American Automobile Manufacturers Association (AAMA)

The AAMA, formerly known as the Motor Vehicle Manufacturers Association, produces data on unit sales for autos and light trucks. The BEA uses these data to estimate portions of GDP components - notably durables personal consumption expenditures, producers durable equipment, and government consumption expenditures and gross investment. These components reflect purchases or leases of light motor vehicles.

Chain store sales – LJR Redbook

Several private firms produce reports on weekly or monthly chain store sales. The most widely known is the weekly series produced by the New York investment firm of Lynch, Jones, and Ryan, published in their Redbook report. (This report was previously called the Johnson Redbook, named after the individual who started the report.) The LJR chain-store data are compiled from public reports from major chain stores in the United States. The weekly data, which are released on Tuesday afternoons, are not source data for any government statistics on retail sales. But analysts take an interest in the LJR Redbook data because they are available prior to the Commerce Department's retail sales report, are somewhat indicative of the strength of consumer spending, and have moderate predictive power for the narrowly defined department store series within the retail sales report.

Table 4 ● Indicators for "forecasting" within the monthly cycle

Precursor/explanatory series and producing agency	Series being "forecast" and producing agency
Purchasing managers' report, NAPM (a) composite or production index (b) employment index (c) prices paid index (d) inventory index	(a) industrial production, FRB (b) manufacturing employment, BLS (c) producer price index, BLS (d) manufacturers inventories, Census
Employment report, BLS (a) aggregate production hours in manufacturing[a] (b) average hourly earnings, payroll employment, average workweek[a] (c) average manufacturing workweek[a] (d) nonfarm payroll employment[a]	(a) industrial production, FRB (b) wage and salary disbursements in personal income report, BEA (c) component of index of leading indicators, Conference Board (d) component of index of current indicators, Conference Board
Unit new auto sales, MMA (a) auto and light truck sales[a]	(a) durables PCEs in personal income report, BEA
LJR Redbook (a) chain store sales	(a) department store sales in retail sales report, Census
Retail sales, Census (a) retail sales[a]	(a) durables and nondurables PCEs in personal income report, BEA
Producer Price Indexes, BLS (a) consumer product components	(a) goods components in CPI, BLS
Manufacturers' shipments, inventories, and orders, Census (a) nondefense capital goods shipments[a] (b) manufacturers inventories[a]	(a) producers' durable equipment in GDP, BEA (b) change in inventories, manufacturers, in GDP, BEA
Monthly business inventories, census (a) business inventories[a]	(a) inventory change in GDP, BEA
Monthly international trade, Census and BEA (a) goods and services exports and imports[a]	(a) net exports in GDP, BEA
Construction outlays, Census (a) residential outlays[a] (b) nonresidential outlays[a] (c) public outlays[a]	(a) residential investment in GDP, BEA (b) nonresidential structures in GDP, BEA (c) structures component in government purchases in GDP, BEA

Note: FRB indicates Federal Reserve Board of Governors; BLS indicates Bureau of Labor Statistics; BEA indicates Bureau of Economic Analysis.

[a] Source data for forecast series

Table 5 ● Principal source data for GDP: availability for the advance GDP release

GDP component and monthly series	Months available
Personal consumption expenditures	
Retail sales	3
Unit auto and truck sales	3
Nonresidential fixed investment	
Unit auto and truck sales	3
Value of construction put in place	2
Manufacturers' shipments of machinery and equipment	2
Exports and imports of machinery and equipment	2
Residential investment	
Value of construction put in place	2
Housing starts	3
Change in business inventories	
Manufacturing and trade inventories	2
Unit auto inventories	3
Net exports of goods and services	
Merchandise exports and imports	2
Government consumption expenditures and gross investment	
Federal outlays	2
Value of construction put in place by state and local government	2
GDP prices	
CPI	3
PPI	3
Nonpetroleum merchandise export and import price indexes	3
Values and quantities of petroleum imports	2

The retail sales report

Commerce's report on retail sales is released around midmonth following the reference month. The Census data on retail sales are used by the BEA to produce estimates for portions of personal consumption expenditures, which are part of GDP. The retail sales data are also used in the "disposition of income" portion of the Personal Income report, which is released the next business day after GDP estimates. Markets look at the retail sales data because they are a major indicator of consumer strength and they precede the personal consumption numbers by about two weeks. However, retail sales do not cover services and as such are only source data for durables and nondurables portions of personal consumption expenditures (PCEs). (In 1997 durables and nondurables PCEs were 12.0 percent and 29.0 percent, respectively, of total nominal PCEs. Thc BEA uses AAMA data for motor vehicle consumption because those numbers are more reliable than the Census survey-based data for retail sales. The AAMA data essentially cover all sales as tallied by the auto manufacturers themselves.)

Producer price index

The producer price index is released midmonth following the reference month. It precedes the CPI report by about three days, and analysts use the PPI numbers to project the CPI release figures. PPI data are not source data for CPI data; the data sets are derived from two independent surveys. The predictive power of PPI data for CPI numbers is only moderately strong, as suggested by standard regression statistics (see Rogers 1988). There are some notable definitional differences between the PPI for finished goods and the all-urban CPI. For example, the PPI does not cover services but does cover capital equipment; about half of the CPI component weight is services, but the CPI does not cover capital equipment. Also, even for components that are very similar for the PPI and CPI, such as food and energy, the rate at which prices at the producer level pass through to the consumer level varies by component.

Manufacturers' inventories, orders, and sales

This report, produced by the Census Bureau, contains source data for two components of GDP. The manufacturers' inventories data from the monthly Census report form the backbone of the manufacturers' component of inventory investment within GDP. However, the relationship is not as tight as might be expected because the BEA must make substantial adjustments in the Census data to convert them to the proper form for National Income and Product Accounts (NIPA).[4]

The monthly manufacturers' report also provides source data for a second GDP component: producers durable equipment. Analysts focus on data for nondefense capital goods equipment shipments within the orders report as a barometer of future spending on producers durable equipment. But the relationship of nominal shipments of nondefense capital goods shipments with nominal producers durable equipment investment is not as tight as might be expected. The relationship is not one-for-one for two primary reasons: not all capital equipment produced in the United States is sold to domestic users, and U.S. businesses obtain capital equipment not only from domestic producers but also from those overseas. Therefore, in the manufacturers' inventories, orders, and sales report, exports of capital equipment are subtracted from domestic equipment investment – that is, producers durable equipment and imports of capital equipment are added, but the latter are not part of (domestic) shipments of nondefense capital goods as measured in the Census report.

---

4. The National Income and Product Accounts, produced by the BEA, are broad "double-entry" accounts that track economic activity in the United States. With double-entry accounts, for every expenditure series there is a corresponding income account; the NIPA accounts attempt to follow economists' definition that spending generates an equal amount of income. For GDP estimates based on expenditures (such as personal consumption and investment, among others), there are GDP estimates based on personal income, corporate profits, and other income components.

Monthly business inventories

The business inventories report is a later-published, broad report on overall business inventories. It includes the earlier-released manufacturers' inventories plus data for merchant wholesale inventories and retail inventories. These data are source data for nonfarm inventory investment within the GDP accounts. As with the manufacturers' data, there are a number of adjustments made by the BEA in converting the wholesale and retail series to their NIPA equivalents.

Monthly international trade

Monthly international trade data, jointly produced by the Census Bureau and the BEA, are source data for goods and services exports and imports in the GDP accounts as well as in the balance of payments accounts. There are a notable number of coverage and timing differences between the monthly series and the balance of payments series and, in turn, the GDP series. One coverage difference is that the customs data that go into Census data are based on the geographic authority of U.S. Customs, which includes U.S. territories. Data that include U.S. territories are appropriate for balance of payments data but are not appropriate for GDP accounts within NIPA since GDP is defined by national borders exclusive of territories.

Monthly construction outlays

Monthly construction outlays data, or construction spending data, produced by the Census Bureau, are key source data for various structures components within GDP. Monthly construction spending data serve as a measure of production in the construction sector. Data on private residential outlays are source data for GDP's residential investment component; nonresidential outlays, for nonresidential investment; and public construction outlays, for structures components within government consumption expenditures and gross investment. The statistical relationship between these series is moderately strong, based on regression analysis, because the monthly outlay series source data are not the only source data used for GDP structures components. Additional source data includes for example, a quarterly survey used to estimate spending on additions and alterations, which are part of the GDP residential investment series, and a subcomponent for brokerage commissions.

Key source data for GDP

Analysts project GDP ahead of its official release because it is viewed as a summary measure of overall economic performance. Tracking various releases for source data is important for developing an estimate for current-quarter GDP as the release months of the quarter progress. Most of the key series of GDP source data are listed in Table 5, which pulls together many of the series listed by separate reports. A more complete listing is available from the U.S. Commerce Department (1996).

One key difference between estimating GDP from earlier-released source data and using source data to estimate other monthly series is that one or more months of data are missing for some component series when the first release for GDP is made to the public. Quarterly GDP is revised each month for two months after the initial release. The first release is referred to as "advance"; the second, as "preliminary"; and third, as "revised." Table 5 shows how many months of data are available for each source data series when GDP is initially released for a given quarter. The BEA also uses additional unpublished data that may not be available to the public. In addition, some source data may not be available at all for the early estimates of current quarter GDP and become available only by the time of the annual revisions during the subsequent year. In these cases the services components are projected for the current quarter since they are derived from private sector annual surveys.

When the BEA releases the advance estimate for GDP, it also publishes its assumptions for missing months of data for monthly source data that are public. This table, titled "Summary of Major Data Assumptions for Advance Estimates," is published in the *Survey of Current Business* with the advance GDP report. Comparing subsequent releases of missing monthly data with the BEAs assumptions provides some clue toward the direction of later revisions to current-quarter GDP. However, because monthly source data are only one part of the estimation procedure, differences between BEA assumptions and subsequent releases provide only part of the explanation for subsequent revisions to GDP estimates.

BEHAVIORAL LINKS BETWEEN DATA SERIES

Analysts use economic data to forecast other economic series by observing various behavioral links. That is, one type of economic activity appears to have an impact on another type of economic activity, and often with a lag. For example, a rise in factory orders is believed to lead to an increase in industrial production. Although a detailed explanation of econometric models for various sectors in the economy is beyond the scope of this article, a brief discussion of some basic behavioral linkages between economic data series and what type of lagged impact one variable has on the other will round out this primer on data series.

The consumer – income and expenditures

An income-expenditure flow analysis of the consumer sector is relatively straightforward. Income is the "driver" behind consumer spending, although other factors play a role. Additional fundamentals include changes in employment and wealth, changes in interest rates, and changes in prices. Nonetheless, a key to understanding the consumer income-expenditure flow is to examine what determines – in simple terms – consumer income. Aggregate consumer income, in a definitional sense, is based on the product of the number of workers, the average number of hours worked, and the average wage. The data series that correspond to these concepts are nonfarm payroll employment, the nonfarm average workweek, and average hourly earnings. All of these series are part of the employment situation report produced by the BLS and form the backbone of the BEA's estimates of the wage and salary disbursement portion of personal income. Analysts track these series in part so that they can gauge the strength of consumers' ability to spend.

As the flow diagram in Chart 1 shows, an increase in either employment, the average workweek, or average hourly earnings leads to an increase in personal income, and, in turn, an increase in personal consumption. Of course, this flow assumes that all other factors are held constant as the factors in the behavioral flow change. Clearly, other factors come into play in determining consumer spending, but in this simplified model these outside factors have no impact on explaining changes in consumer spending. Similarly, as the article discusses other behavioral flows between economic data series, for variables not discussed, the assumption of ceteris paribus is made.

Manufacturing and the inventory cycle

Income and expenditures flows play a more complex role in the manufacturing sector in what is traditionally called an inventory cycle. Essentially, changes in consumer spending affect actual and desired inventory levels; when desired inventory levels differ from actual levels, manufacturers, wholesalers, and retailers make necessary adjustments to bring the two together. These actions, in turn, affect consumer income and spending. Essentially, the consumer plays a key role in the inventory cycle.

The flow diagram in Chart 2 illustrates this cycle. At the beginning of the cycle, if retail sales to consumers are unexpectedly strong, retail inventories will decline below desired levels. Retailers will then place new orders with domestic producers or order additional imports. Domestic producers respond by increasing shipments, which in turn cause manufacturers' inventories to drop below desired levels. This drop in turn boosts manufacturing output. Initially, manufacturers merely increase the average workweek, but when demand is sufficiently strong they hire additional workers. Average hourly earnings may rise in order to attract the additional workers. As personal income rises, the cycle is renewed because this income gain can fuel additional consumer spending.

Table 6 lists the data series that analysts track to follow this cycle. The left-hand column shows the generalized economic concepts in the behavioral flow for manufacturing while the right-hand column indicates the specific data series that correspond to the economic concept.

Analysts are interested in determining the average length of time it takes for a change in one variable to affect a second variable. But a complicating factor in estimating some of these average lag lengths is that the direction of causality is not always consistent, especially for sales series and inventory data. During a business cycle, businesses may do a better job of anticipating sales at some times than at others; inventory changes may anticipate sales changes and vice versa. This reciprocity reduces the likelihood that measures of average lag length are statistically meaningful for these data series. For other data series, the causal relationships may be more consistent so that average lag lengths can be estimated. For example, housing starts essentially always precede housing outlays, and changes in durables factory orders precede changes in durables production.

For manufacturing sector analysis, it is useful, for a couple of reasons, to segment the discussion between durable goods and nondurable goods. First, durable goods, especially heavy capital equipment, tend to have longer production cycles than nondurables, and durables output is more cyclically sensitive. Changes in durables and nondurables share of output over the business cycle would affect the reliability of estimates of various lag coefficients (such as orders to production) if estimated using data that were not disaggregated between durables and nondurables. Second, differences in methodologies for nondurables orders affect lag estimates.

Chart 1 Behavioral flow for consumer spending

↑ Employment × average hours worked × average wage rate → ↑ Income → ↑ Spending

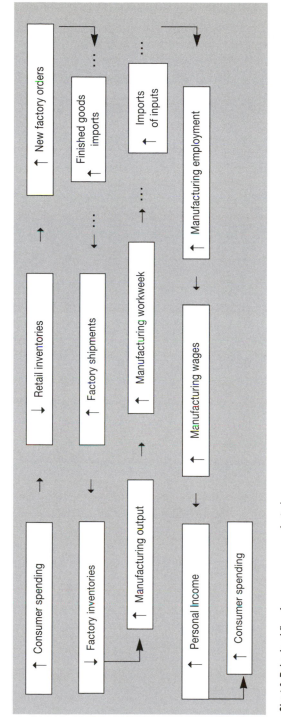

Chart 2 Behavioral flow for consumer manufacturing

Table 6 ● Behavioral flow for manufacturing: economic concepts and corresponding data series

Economic concept	Data series
Consumer spending	Retail sales, Census Personal consumption expenditures, BEA Unit new motor vehicle sales, AAMA and BEA Chain store sales, LJR
Retail inventories	Retail inventories, Census
New factory orders	Manufacturers new orders, Census
Factory shipments	Manufacturers shipments, Census
Factory inventories	Manufacturers inventories, Census
Imports	Imports of goods and services, BEA and Census
Manufacturing output	Industrial production index, Federal Reserve Board Manufacturing surveys: NAPM, Chicago Purchasing Managers, Atlanta Fed, Kansas City Fed, Philadelphia Fed, and Richmond Fed
Manufacturing workweek	Average workweek, manufacturing, BLS
Manufacturing employment	Nonfarm payroll employment, manufacturing, BLS
Manufacturing wage	Average hourly earnings, manufacturing, BLS
Personal income	Personal income, BEA

Table 7 shows the average (mean) lags, estimated by the Almon distributed lag technique, between various manufacturing sector indicators for durables. The mean lag between changes in new factory orders for durables (real) and industrial production for durables manufactured goods in all durables industries is 2.3 months;[5] the lag from production to shipment is relatively short – only 1.654 months. Lags would vary if they were estimated on an industry-by-industry basis. For example, the orders-to-production mean lag would be much longer for the aircraft industry than for the lumber industry. Estimates of lag length also vary depending on the model and lag structure chosen (see Greene 1993, 519–25).

5. Because output for durables and nondurables is in real (inflation-adjusted) terms, it is appropriate that the orders and shipments data be converted from current dollars to real dollars. Durables and nondurables orders and shipments data were deflated using BLS data for producer price indexes for durables manufactured goods and nondurables manufactured goods, respectively.

Durables industries include lumber and products, furniture, and fixtures; clay, glass, and stone products, primary metals, fabricated metal products, industrial and commercial machinery, and computer equipment, electrical machinery, transportation equipment, instruments, and miscellaneous manufactures. Nondurables industries include foods, tobacco products, apparel products, paper and paper products, printing and publishing, chemical and products, petroleum products, rubber and miscellaneous plastics products, and leather and leather products.

For nondurables, data methodology for orders has an interesting impact on lag estimates. The Census Bureau's monthly estimates for new orders are defined as current-month shipments plus current-month unfilled orders minus prior-month unfilled orders (see Rogers 1994, 145). This formula works reasonably well for industries with unfilled orders. However, most nondurables industries report no unfilled orders – for December 1997 only 25.5 percent of the dollar value of new orders for nondurables was for industries that report unfilled orders. For industries with no unfilled orders, Census uses shipments data for new orders – that is, new orders are assumed to equal the available shipments numbers and to represent post-production activity. Official data indicate that most nondurables production takes place during the same month as the shipments/new orders. Table 8, which reports on the regression output of nominal shipments regressed against contemporaneous nominal new orders and a constant, shows the high correlation (an adjusted R^2 of 0.9378) between nondurables new orders and nondurables shipments.

Construction sector linkages

Just as there are inventory cycle effects in manufacturing, there are similar linkages in the construction sector (see Table 9). An unexpected increase in housing sales leads to a drop in houses for sale as well as in the months' supply of houses for sale. Houses for sale and months' supply are the housing sector's equivalent of manufacturers' inventories data and of the inventories-to-sales ratio. If housing stocks decline below desired levels, then builders take out housing permits, initiate housing starts, and work toward completing houses by making construction outlays (spending), as Chart 3 demonstrates. As in manufacturing, this cycle can differ when production is based on expectations of changes in the business cycle. For example, housing stocks may be built up in anticipation of housing sales rather than housing being replenished after a rise in sales. There clearly are times that the direction of causality among some of the inventory-sales-permits-starts linkages reverses, reducing the statistical reliability of these relationships.

Table 7 ● Manufacturing indicators: lags between key series

	Estimation technique: Almon distributed lag			
	Observation period: 1970M1-97M9			
Series and predecessor series	Mean lag (months)	Standard error of mean lag	Adjusted R^2 of equation	Lag specification (order, lag length, endpoint constraint)
Industrial production, durables/ durables orders, real	2.342	Undefined	0.401	2, 12, None
Durables shipments, real/ industrial production, durables	1.654	Undefined	0.309	3, 9, None

Table 8 ● High correlation between same-month nondurables new orders and shipments

Regression: Dependent variable is
nondurables, shipments, nominal, percent change
1970M1-97M9

Variable	Coefficient	Standard error	t-statistic	Significance
Constant	0.320391E-01	0.192568E-01	1.66378	0.097
New orders, nominal percent change	0.940697	0.132951E-01	70.7552	

Equation summary

Number of observations	=	333	R^2 (adjusted)	=	0.9378
Sum of squared residuals	=	34.8928	Standard error of regression	=	0.324679
R^2	=	0.9380	Durbin-Watson	=	2.92446

Table 10 shows that the average lag (using the Almon distributed lag estimation technique) between changes in housing permits and housing starts is very short – only 1.026 months. The average lag from changes in starts to changes in construction outlays is 4.032 months.

Price sector linkages

To some degree there are linkages in prices in various sectors of the economy through cost pass-through. The cost for crude materials may be passed through to costs for intermediate goods, for producer prices for finished goods, and on to the consumer (see Chart 4).

The relationship between the PPI for finished goods and the CPI should be measured using the CPI for goods only (that is, excluding services, since the PPI for finished goods has no services other than electricity from public utilities). In addition, the length of pass-through from the PPI for finished goods to the CPI is rather short, with most of the impact taking place within the current and following months. Finally, the relationship between any two price series above is not particularly strong because there is a great deal of volatility in the data, more so for producer prices for crude materials than for finished goods. Crude materials prices and diffusion indexes provide many false signals of building price pressures at the consumer level. However, rising crude and intermediate prices are generally precursors of an increase in consumer price inflation.

Table 11 shows a very short lag time from changes in producer prices for finished goods and consumer prices – only 1.573 months. Movement in prices for finished goods and intermediate goods is essentially coincident, with an estimated lag of 0.100 month. The apparent pass-through of changes in crude materials prices to intermediate products is somewhat longer, with an estimated mean lag of 5.056 months.

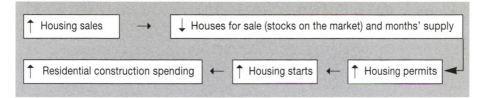

Chart 3 Behavioral flow for construction

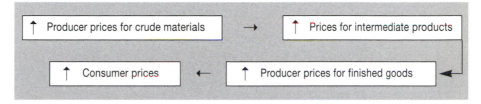

Chart 4 Behavioral flow for prices

Note: The individual units in the chart are the names of indexes produced by the BLS. However, producer prices for crude materials refers not only to the index published by the BLS but also to series by the Commodity Research Bureau (CRB) and the *Journal of Commerce* and the prices paid diffusion index from the NAPM.

SUMMARY

This article is a primer on some of the key short term economic relationships among data series upon which economic analysts focus. Certainly, market participants closely watch the calendar of economic releases and, as each release is made, enter the new information into their calculations – with either formal models or with judgment – regarding the strength of the economy. The article, though it touches only on selected data relationships, should clarify how analysts carry information from one economic release into their view of the strength of other economic indicators.

Table 9 ● Behavioral flow for construction: economic concepts and corresponding data series

Economic concept	Data series
Housing sales	New single-family housing sales, Census Existing single-family housing sales National Association of Realtors (NAR)
Houses for sale, ratio stocks/sales	Months supply, new single-family houses, Census Months supply, existing single-family houses, NAR
Housing permits	Housing permits, Census
Housing starts	Housing starts, Census
Residential construction spending	Residential construction outlays, Census

Table 10 ● Construction indicators: lags between key series

Estimation technique: Almon distributed lag
Observation period: 1970M1-97M9

Series and predecessor series	Mean lag (months)	Standard error of mean lag	Adjusted R^2 of equation	Lag specification (order, lag length, endpoint constraint)
Housing starts/ housing permits	1.026	Undefined (Lag signs switch)	0.389	3, 6, None
Residential construction outlays, 1992, $ housing starts	4.032	0.450	0.537	2, 15, None

Table 11 ● Inflation indicators: lags between key series

Estimation technique: Almon distributed lag
Observation period: 1970M1-97M9

Series and predecessor series	Mean lag (months)	Standard error of mean lag	Adjusted R^2 of equation	Lag specification (order, lag length, endpoint constraint)
CPI, total/ PPI, finished goods	1.573	0.144	0.621	3, 6, None
PPI, finished goods/ PPI, intermediate products	0.100	0.105	0.561	2, 4, None
PPI, intermediate products/ PPI, crude materials	5.056	0.460	0.347	4, 12, None

REFERENCES

Board of Governors of the Federal Reserve System. 1986. *Industrial Production: With a Description of the Methodology*. Washington, D.C.

Greene, William H. 1993. *Econometric Analysis*. 2nd edn. Englewood Cliffs, N.J.: Prentice Hall.

Harris, Ethan S. 1991. "Tracking the Economy with the Purchasing Managers' Index." Federal Reserve Bank of New York *Quarterly Review* 16 (Autumn): 61–69.

Harris, Ethan S. and Clara Vega. 1996. What Do Chain Store Sales Tell Us about Consumer Spending?" Federal Reserve Bank of New York, *Economic Policy Review* 2 (October): 15–5.

Rogers, R. Mark. 1988. "Improving Monthly Models for Economic Indicators: The Example of an Improved CPI Model." Federal Reserve Bank of Atlanta, *Economic Review* 73 (September/October): 34–50.

— —. 1992. "Forecasting Industrial Production: Purchasing Managers' versus Production-Worker Hours Data." Federal Reserve Bank of Atlanta, *Economic Review* 77 (January/February): 25–36.

— —. 1994. *Handbook of Key Economic Indicators*. Burr Ridge, Ill.: Irwin Professional Publishing.

— —. 1998. *Handbook of Key Economic Indicators*. 2nd edn. Burr Ridge, Ill.: McGraw-Hill Professional Publishing.

U.S. Department of Commerce. 1996. "Updated Summary Methodologies." *Survey of Current Business* (August): 81–103.

CHAPTER **6**

A survey of market-sensitive economic indicators

- Introduction
- Gross National Product and Gross Domestic Product
- GDP Deflator
- Producer Price Index (PPI)
- Index of Industrial Production
- Capacity utilization rate
- Commodity prices – general
- Commodity prices – crude oil
- Commodity prices – food
- Commodity price indicators – a checklist
- Consumer Price Index (CPI)
- Average hourly earnings
- Employment Cost Index (ECI)
- Index of Leading Indicators (LEI)
- Vendor deliveries index
- Appendix 6.1: Computation of price indexes
- Appendix 6.2: Macroeconomic announcements

INTRODUCTION

As discussed in Chapter 5, it is essential in appreciating the reaction of financial markets to economic news to be able to break down the components of nominal GNP. The key indicators affecting nominal GNP are shown in Figure 6.1. Appendix 6.2 gives the announcement time, title, and reporting entities for 18 monthly economic indicators and one weekly economic indicator. Appendix 6.2 is the staple diet for traders. This table is their bible for analyzing what is and what is not "expected" news and is at the heart of their whole trading strategy.

GROSS NATIONAL PRODUCT AND GROSS DOMESTIC PRODUCT

Definition

Gross domestic product (GDP) measures the total value of US output. It is the total of all economic activity in the US, regardless of whether the owners of the means of production reside in the US. It is "gross" because the depreciation of capital goods is not deducted.

GDP is measured both in *current prices*, which represent actual market prices, and *constant prices*, which measure changes in volume. Constant price, or real, GDP is current-price GDP adjusted for inflation.

The financial markets focus on the seasonally adjusted annualized percentage change in real-expenditure based GDP in the current quarter compared to the previous quarter.

The difference between GDP and gross national product (GNP) is that GNP includes net factor income, or net earnings, from abroad. This is made up of the return on US investment abroad (profits, investment income, workers' remittances) minus the return on foreign investment in the US. GNP is national, because it belongs to US residents, but not domestic, since it is not derived solely from production in the US.

Who publishes it and when?

Three reports on quarterly GDP are published by the Department of Commerce. Advance, preliminary and final GDP growth rates are released during the first, second and third months of the following quarter. So in April the advance report

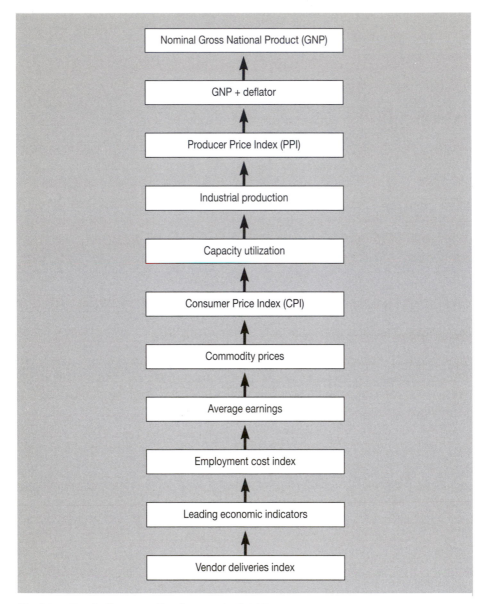

Fig 6.1 ● Key indicators affecting nominal GNP

for Q_1 would be published, in May the preliminary report for Q_1 would be published and in June the final report for Q_1 would be published.

How should you interpret it?

Look at the annualized growth in seasonally adjusted, real expenditure-based GDP for the latest quarter compared to the previous quarters. Breaking the figure down to final sales and inventories can provide an indication of the future behavior of the economy.

What is its impact on financial markets?

Financial market behavior to this economic indicator is often restrained since it is usually expected news, with many of its key components having already been published. When there is reaction in the financial markets it will always be to an unexpected advance report rather than to the preliminary or final GDP growth rates (*see* Box 6.1).

Box 6.1: Market reaction to an unexpected change in GNP

Degree of market sensitivity:
High   ✓
Medium
Low

GNP	↑	↓
Bond market	↓	↑
Equity market	↑	↓
US dollar	↑	↓

GDP DEFLATOR

Definition

The GDP deflators are comprehensive measures of inflation since they encompass changes in prices in all sectors of the economy – consumer products, capital goods, the foreign sector, and the government. In general it is calculated as

$$\text{GNP price deflator} \ = \ \frac{\text{Nominal GNP}}{\text{Real GNP}} \ \times \ 100$$

There are actually three GDP deflators: the implicit deflator, the fixed weight deflator, and the chain-price index. Until the late 1980s, the implicit deflator was the primary focus of attention. Since 1989, the Commerce Department has promoted the fixed weight deflator instead. The implicit deflator measures changes in prices as well as changes in the composition of output. Some goods are less expensive than other goods, so depending on the combination of goods and services produced in any given quarter, *regardless of the price changes*, the implicit price deflator can rise or fall. This makes the implicit price deflator a *variable* basket of goods. It is rare to see an outright decline in the implicit GDP deflator, but its rate of increase varies significantly from one quarter to the next.

The fixed weight deflator works on the same principle as the consumer and producer price indexes since it measures prices for a composition of GDP chosen in a certain time-period. Currently, 1987 weights are used. Consequently, the fixed weight deflator only reflects changes in prices.

The chain-price index combines the variable and fixed weight baskets. For any given quarter, it shows the basket of goods of the previous quarter. Over time, however, the basket of goods is changing. Admittedly, this has questionable relevance to the inflation picture and gets little attention, if any.

Who publishes it and when?

The Bureau of Economic Analysis releases the GDP deflators together with the gross domestic product and national income about four weeks after the end of the quarter. The figures are seasonally adjusted and annualized.

How do you interpret it?

The fixed weight GDP deflator is more meaningful, and therefore more market sensitive, than the implicit price deflator. The implicit price deflator reflects changes in the composition of GDP as well as changes in prices. Both the implicit and fixed weight GDP deflators can be skewed from time to time. For example, government pay rises typically occur in the first quarter, boosting the deflator overall. Seasonal adjustment factors cannot be utilized to account for the annual pay rise because the magnitude of increase is not stable from year to year.

(*See* Appendix 6.1 for details of how price indexes can be measured.)

What is its impact on financial markets?

Financial market participants closely follow the GDP deflators. In the past few years, more attention has focused on the fixed weight deflator than on the implicit price deflator. An increase in the deflator is unfavorable news to all markets. Stock prices will decline, bond prices will fall (yields will rise), and the value of the dollar will increase on the back of expected interest rate increases. A moderation in the inflation measure will lead to the opposite effect. Stock prices and bond prices will rise and the value of the dollar will fall on expectations of falling interest rates (*see* Box 6.2).

Box 6.2: Market reaction to an unexpected change in GDP deflator

Degree of market sensitivity:
High   ✓
Medium
Low

GDP deflator	▲	▼
Bond market	▼	▲
Equity market	▼	▲
US dollar	▲	▼

PRODUCER PRICE INDEX (PPI)

Definition

The PPI measures the prices that manufacturers and farmers charge to the shops.

The US producer price indices (PPIs) are calculated in three different ways: type of commodity produced; net output of particular industries; and stage of the processing cycle. Of these, the latter is by far the most market sensitive.

Under the "stage of processing" methodology, there are three indices:

● *crude materials* for further processing, covering items like oil and livestock which cannot be sold to consumers before being used in manufacturing;

● *intermediate materials, supplies and components* including items that have been manufactured but require work before they are salable;

● *finished goods* which can be used by consumers.

By separating the stages of production in this way, it is possible to gauge inflation as it works its way through the production process. A fourth index combines the three subdivisions into the "all commodities index." Financial market attention is focused on the percentage change in the monthly finished goods PPI. However, because food prices tend to be seasonal, and energy prices are frequently volatile, analysts prefer to watch the "core" rate of producer price inflation which strips out food and energy prices.

Who publishes them and when?

The PPIs are published in a Department of Labor press release towards the middle of the month following that to which they refer.

How do you interpret them?

Concentrate on the seasonally adjusted finished goods PPI and look at how this has behaved on a month-to-month, quarter-on-quarter, six-monthly and year-on-year basis. This should give a good guide to whether the trend is changing.

To establish whether the change is merely due to volatile items, repeat the above for "core" PPI, i.e., headline figure minus food and energy.

However, core PPI includes the sometimes volatile auto component. This makes up about 5 percent of the finished goods index and may be subject to huge volatility as the result of auto incentive programs and discounts. Care should be taken to ensure that what appears to be an underlying change in trend is not just due to this "noisy" component. Particularly vulnerable months are September and October. September is when prices usually fall by as much as 3 percent ahead of the new model year.

Analyze the category headings for any suspicious rises. These are frequently reversed the next month and should be excluded from the above analysis unless there are strong reasons for thinking the upward trend will be sustained.

What is their impact on financial markets?

Financial market participants anxiously await the producer price index figures. The fixed-income market will obviously prefer to see low inflation over high inflation. Thus, the larger the monthly rise in the PPI, the more negative the impact on the bond and the money markets. High inflation leads to high interest rates. Low inflation points to declining interest rates.

The equity will also view accelerating inflation negatively. Stock prices may decline. The value of the dollar will probably rise when producer price increases are large and accelerating, if they expect the Federal Reserve to respond by raising interest rates.

As mentioned above, financial market participants will often look at the PPI for finished goods excluding food and energy prices. Large changes in food and energy components are less likely to cause market reactions than changes in the core rate (*see* Box 6.3).

Box 6.3: Market reaction to an unexpected change in Producer Price Index (PPI)

Degree of market sensitivity:
High   ✓
Medium
Low

Producer Price Index	↑	↓
Bond market	↓	↑
Equity market	↓	↑
US dollar	↑	↓

INDEX OF INDUSTRIAL PRODUCTION

Definition

The industrial production figures are a set of index numbers which measure the monthly physical output of US factories, mines and gas and electric utilities. The index is broken down by type of industry (manufacturing, mining or utilities) and by type of market (consumer, equipment, intermediate or materials). The financial markets tend to focus on the seasonally adjusted monthly change in the aggregate figure.

Who publishes it and when?

The Federal Reserve publishes the preliminary estimate of the previous month's industrial production in a press release around the 15th of each month. The first revision of the index comes with the next month's preliminary data about 45 days after the reference month and there are second, third and fourth estimates in the following months. After the fourth estimate the index is regarded as final.

How do you interpret it?

The US Index of Industrial Production is a derivative statistic, based in a large part on the Bureau of Labor Statistics (BLS) employment report which comes out 2–3 weeks earlier, and consequently normally is expected news.

Industrial production is pro-cyclical, i.e., it rises during economic expansions and falls during contraction. It is included as one of the four coincident indicators. It is typically used as a proxy for GDP even though it only covers 20 percent of total production in the country. Typically the index rises more during economic downturns than the aggregate real GDP series.

Some analysts think that because the seasonally adjusted monthly index follows a relatively smooth path and is subject to few revisions, it can be taken as representative of the trend. But it is probably safest to compare the past three months with the previous three to eliminate monthly volatility. Beware the seasonally adjusted series when the weather is abnormal.

An eye should be kept on volatile motor vehicles output. This fluctuates a great deal and can pull the aggregate figure with it. But it should be borne in mind that motor vehicles are an extremely important component of industrial output and should only be excluded if there are strong reasons for supposing that its deviation is only temporary.

What is its impact on financial markets?

A rise in industrial production signals economic growth, whereas a decline in production indicates contraction. Thus fixed income participants view a rise in industrial production as a warning of inflationary pressures. This would mean that there were pressures for interest rates to rise which is bad news for fixed income markets. Similarly, a drop in industrial production provides a warning signal that economic contraction is on the way with an expectation that interest rates will fall, which is good news for fixed-income markets.

Participants in the stock and foreign exchange markets favor gains in industrial production together with the capacity utilization rate, discussed below, since they portend economic strength. Equity market professionals will look toward the benefits of increases in corporate earnings whereas foreign exchange professionals will look toward the benefits of higher interest rates. High interest rates in the US relative to other countries increase the demand for US securities and therefore US dollars (*see* Box 6.4).

Box 6.4: Market reaction to an unexpected change in industrial production

Degree of market sensitivity:
High
Medium
Low   ✓

Industrial production	▲	▼
Bond market	▼	▲
Equity market	▲	▼
US dollar	▲	▼

CAPACITY UTILIZATION RATE

Definition

Capacity utilization measures the extent to which the capital stock of the nation is being employed in the production of goods. Technically defined, the utilization rate for an industry is equal to:

$$\frac{\text{Output Index}}{\text{Capacity Index}}$$

The Output is measured by the Index of Industrial Production. The Capacity Index attempts to capture "sustainable practical capacity" as indicated by work schedules and the availability of inputs to operate machinery and equipment in place.

Who publishes it and when?

The Federal Reserve Board publishes it at the same time as the Index of Industrial Production, about two weeks after the end of the month.

How do you interpret it?

Once capacity reaches a certain point, it is expected that excess demand pressures will result in inflation. The actual point at which these pressures have occurred has risen over time, largely due to technological progress. At certain times the market has used this indicator as a good leading indicator of inflation although its value has become limited recently as it has risen without inflationary pressures also rising.

One problem with this index is that it covers many industries which do not uniformly suffer inflationary pressures at the same level. The paper industry for example normally operates at around 95 percent whereas non-electrical machinery normally operates at 78 percent.

The capital utilization rate rises during expansions and falls during recessions.

What is its impact on financial markets?

A rise in capacity utilization has the same effect on financial markets as a rise in industrial production as the two indicators are inextricably linked. It is not necessary to view them as two separate indicators. They always move in the same direction, and they will always tell a similar story. However, they serve a different purpose.

Industrial production will signal economic growth. The capacity utilization rate reflects the extent of resources utilization and the point at which inflationary pressures set in. For example, a 1 percent rise in industrial production should not cause fears of inflationary pressures when the operating rate is 78 percent. However, it could indicate inflation will accelerate when the utilization rate is around 85 percent (*see* Box 6.5).

Box 6.5: Market reaction to an unexpected change in capacity utilization

Degree of market sensitivity:
High
Medium
Low   ✓

Capacity utilization	↑	↓
Bond market	↓	↑
Equity market	↑	↓
US dollar	↑	↓

COMMODITY PRICES – GENERAL

Inflationary pressures can often come from increases in commodity prices. A list of the key commodity prices which financial markets focus on is given in Table 6.1.

Table 6.1 ● Key commodity prices

Commodity Prices	Unit
Agricultural raw material	yoy %
Cotton (Liverpool index)	cts/lb
Wool (Aus-NZ; UK)	cts/kg
Rubber (New York)	cts/lb
Food	yoy %
Cocoa (LCE)	USD/t
Coffee (CSCE)	cts/lb
Sugar (CSCE)	cts/lb
Wheat (CBT)	USD/bu
Base metals	yoy %
Aluminum (LME)	USD/t
Copper (LME)	USD/t
Nickel (LME)	USD/t
Crude oil	yoy %
Brent	USD/bbl
WTI	USD/bbl
Gold	USD/ounce

Oil and food prices are closely scrutinized key commodities. Oil as a source of energy or a natural resource in the production of goods, is a key component of economic activity used in manufacturing, and it is an important product used by consumers as well. Food is an indispensable item in every person's budget.

COMMODITY PRICES – CRUDE OIL

Definition

Crude oil is traded at the New York Mercantile Exchange (NYMEX). Both spot and futures prices of crude oil are determined in the market. The spot price reflects the current value of the commodity, whereas the futures price reflects the price at some point in the future such as three or six months hence.

Who publishes it and when?

The price is quoted continuously and is available on screen-based information systems.

How do you interpret it?

This is not straightforward. Financial market participants in the fixed income, equity and foreign exchange markets often look at the future price of crude oil as an indicator of inflation. Oil is an important commodity in the US economy. However oil prices change hourly and it is not always clear as to what the inflationary implications are. Oil prices are particularly prone to movements based on rumor, which may or may not prove to be fact.

What is its impact on financial markets?

Financial markets are well aware that the oil price rises of the 1970s did cause major US recessions. Largely speaking the announcement that oil prices are rising in a sustainable manner will cause a negative reaction in the bond and stock markets, but it could well strengthen the prospects for the dollar. All price falls will provoke the opposite reaction.

COMMODITY PRICES – FOOD

Definition

Food prices are also monitored closely by financial market participants. The most monitored indicator of food prices is the *Index of Prices Received by Farmers*, more commonly known as the "Ag Price Index."

The Index of Prices Received by Farmers comprises crops (44.2 percent) and livestock and products (55.8 percent). The main crop items reported are corn, hay, soybeans and wheat with the principal livestock and products items being eggs, milk, steers, and barrows and gilts. The price changes are based on average prices for all grades and qualities at the point of sale (such as the local market) about the middle of the month. All the prices are then revised in the following month when averages are calculated for the entire month for some of the commodities.

Who publishes it and when?

The Department of Agriculture releases the Index of Prices Received by Farmers at the end of the month for the current month, but it only reflects price changes through the middle of that month. The index is not adjusted for seasonal variation.

How do you interpret it?

The "Ag Price Index" needs to be compared to other inflation indicators. Although it is related to food price changes in the Producer Price Index and the Consumer Price Index, it can vary significantly over time. First, the Ag Price Index is not adjusted for seasonal variations. The food components in both the Consumer Price Index and the Producer Price Index are seasonally adjusted. Second, the Ag Price Index measures prices at the first point of sale and is based on average price for all grades. The Producer Price Indexes and the Consumer Price Index typically adjust for quality and grades. Because this series is not seasonally adjusted, you should look at year-to-year changes rather than month-to-month changes.

Generally speaking, the index should decline or post small increases during periods of harvest, and tends towards larger increases during off seasons.

What is its impact on financial markets?

The Ag Price Index is reported late in the afternoon and gets little attention from financial market participants. However, an unexpectedly large rise in the index can spur a drop in bond prices if market psychology is already negative. Conversely, an unexpectedly large drop in the index may lead to a rise in bond prices if market psychology is positive. The foreign exchange and stock markets tend to ignore this index altogether (*see* Box 6.6).

Box 6.6: Market reaction to an unexpected change in commodity prices

Degree of market sensitivity:
High
Medium ✓
Low

Commodity prices	↑	↓
Bond market	↓	↑
Equity market	↑	↓
US dollar	↑	↓

COMMODITY PRICE INDICATORS – A CHECKLIST

The most popular commodity price indicators for financial markets have been the Commodity Research Bureau (CRB) futures index, the Journal of Commerce (JOC) index, the crude PPI, the change in the Sensitive Materials Prices Index (SMPs), the National Association of Purchasing Managers Prices Index and the PHIL Index, all discussed below.

The CRB index

The Commodity Research Bureau's future index (CRB), compiled since 1957, measures prices of non-financial contracts traded on public futures exchanges.

The CRB contains nearby and deferred (up to but not including one year away) futures prices for 21 separate commodities contracts.

CRB component groups

Imports	:	Cocoa, coffee, sugar
Precious metals	:	Gold, platinum, silver
Industrials	:	Cotton, copper, crude oil, lumber, silver
Livestock and meats	:	Cattle, hogs, pork bellies
Grains	:	Corn, oats, soybean meal, wheat
Energy	:	Crude oil, heating oil, unleaded gasoline

Since 13 of the 21 commodities are foodstuffs and the remaining eight are atypical industries, the CRB is not the best indicator of general inflation.

Journal of Commerce industrial index (JOC)

The Journal of Commerce tracks an index of prices of 18 industrial materials and supplies used in the first stage of manufacturing, energy production, or building construction.

The components have been chosen on the basis that they have been sensitive to price pressures that show up 6–9 months later in the PPI or Consumer Price Index (CPI).

The JOC is more sensitive to actual economic developments than the CRB.

Each commodity in the JOC index is weighted by its importance to overall economic output and how well it predicts inflation.

The base year is 1980. The JOC index is subdivided into three major categories: Textiles, metals, and miscellaneous.

JOC index composition

Textiles	:	Cotton (5.9 percent), Burlap (5.5 percent), Polyester (2.7 percent), Print cloth (3.3 percent)
Metals	:	Scrap steel (6.3 percent), Copper scrap (6.7 percent), Aluminum (6.1 percent), Zinc (5.1 percent), Tin (5 percent)
Miscellaneous	:	Hides (5.5 percent), Rubber (6.3 percent), Tallow (5.2 percent), Plywood (7.9 percent), Boxes (5 percent), Red Oak (6.3 percent), Benzene (4.7 percent), Crude oil (7.1 percent)

Change in sensitive materials prices (SMPs)

This index is calculated on spot prices of 12 crude and intermediate materials and 13 raw industrial materials. It is calculated as a moving average and is compiled by the US Department of Commerce, US Department of Labor and Commodity Research Bureau Institute.

Table 6.2 ● Composition of commodity price indexes

	CRB	JOC	SMP
Prices	futures	spot	spot
Components	21	18	25
Weights	equal	individual	equal
Weights by category:			
metals	19%	38%	38%
energy	14%	12%	0%
livestock	14%	0%	0%
Grains, food and fibre	43%	17%	29%
Other	10%[a]	36%[b]	33%[c]

[a] Orange juice and lumber
[b] Rubber, red oak, hides, tallow, boxes and plywood
[c] Rubber, hides, resin, tallow, wastepaper, sand and timber

The crude PPI

The crude PPI is divided about evenly into three parts – food, energy and other. It is weighted according to the actual value of commodity shipments. This was discussed earlier in this chapter.

The NAPM Prices Index

The NAPM Prices Index measures the percentage of manufacturing firms reporting higher material prices, plus half the percentage of those firms reporting no change in prices. It therefore has a value of roughly 50 percent when aggregate prices are unchanged. The NAPM is discussed further in Chapter 8.

The PHIL Index

The PHIL Index, calculated slightly differently from the NAPM Prices Index, is the percentage of firms in the Philadelphia region reporting higher prices, minus the percentage reporting lower prices. Hence, it should have a value of roughly zero when aggregate prices are unchanged.

CONSUMER PRICE INDEX (CPI)

Definition

The consumer price index (CPI) is a measure of the prices of a fixed basket of consumer goods and as such a measure of inflation. There are two versions, the CPI-U and the CPI-W. The CPI-U is more widely used because it measures inflation as it affects all urban households (including the unemployed and the retired). The CPI-W covers only urban wage earners and clerical workers in blue-collar occupations. However, this index is used by many unions in wage negotiations.

Who publishes it and when?

The CPI is published monthly in a press release from the Bureau of Labor Statistics, a division of the US Department of Labor. Publication of the data is usually in the second week of the following month. The CPI is seasonally adjusted.

How do you interpret it?

Financial markets generally disregard the CPI-W, which covers only urban wage earners and clerical workers in blue collar occupations.

The seasonally adjusted CPI-U is the main starting point for analysis.

However, there are times when seasonal factors diverge from the trends embodied in the official seasonal adjustment. The most notable case of this is drought. When this happens, it is probably best to use unadjusted data. One other seasonal factor to watch is the impact of the new season's introduction of new (and more highly priced) clothing.

The month-on-month CPI change is regarded as being too "noisy," or volatile, to give any clues on a change in the trend of inflation. The year-on-year comparison is the most widely used, but this suffers from the "base-effect." Changes in the yearly rate can have as much to do with what happened 12 months ago as with what happened last month. The three-monthly change is a better indicator.

Reluctantly, many economists exclude parts of the index for analytical purposes: "reluctantly," because those excluded prices affect inflation. Food and energy prices are the usual candidates for exclusion owing to their extreme volatility. The CPI-U minus food and energy is commonly referred to as the "core" rate of inflation.

Some analysts watch the CPI minus housing and medical costs. Economists have raised doubts about the way in which the BLS measures prices in both these sectors.

What is its impact on financial markets?

Financial market participants anxiously await the Consumer Price Index because it drives much activity in the market place. The fixed income market and a great deal of the equity market react adversely to sharp increases in inflation. Interest rates will rise, stock prices will fall; and the value of the dollar will rise. This is due to the fact that the rise in interest rates is due to price increases, not economic expansion. Market participants, in a similar fashion to their approach with the Producer Price Indexes, discount increases in food and energy prices to some degree. A sharp increase in the Consumer Price Index excluding food and energy prices will bring about a more negative reaction than an increase in the total CPI.

Markets do consider the total CPI as well as the index excluding food and energy prices. They will ignore an increase in food and energy prices when they are certain that prices will reverse in coming months. Food and energy constitute about 25 percent of consumer expenditure.

It would be unwise to ignore big price changes in those categories because they could potentially have important ramifications with respect to inflation, economic activity and Federal Reserve Policy (*see* Box 6.7).

Box 6.7: Market reaction to an unexpected change in Consumer Price Index (CPI)

Degree of market sensitivity:
High ✓
Medium
Low

Consumer Price Index	↑	↓
Bond market	↓	↑
Equity market	↓	↑
US dollar	↑	↓

AVERAGE HOURLY EARNINGS

Definition

Average hourly and weekly earnings measure the level of wages and salaries for workers on private non-farm payrolls. These monthly payroll figures from the Establishment Survey (discussed further in Chapter 7) are reported before deductions for taxes, social insurance and fringe benefits. They include pay for overtime, holidays, vacation, and sick leave but *exclude* retroactive pay or bonuses unless they are earned and paid regularly each pay period. The figures are seasonally adjusted.

Who publishes it and when?

Average hourly and weekly earnings data are published with the monthly Employment Report from the BLS. This is normally released on the third Friday after the week containing the 12th, with data for the month earlier.

Real average weekly earnings are published in a press release from the Labor Department on the day of release of the consumer price index. As illustrated earlier, the CPI is usually published in the second week of each month with data for the month earlier.

How do you interpret them?

Average hourly earnings for workers in private industry are derived by dividing total non-farm payrolls by total hours reported for each industry, with the exception of government employees. The hourly earnings figures reflect changes in basic hourly rates as well as increases in premium pay because of overtime hours worked. For example, if employees worked a 40-hour work week, no premium would be paid for overtime, but if they worked 42 hours in a given week, they would be paid a higher rate for the extra 2 hours. However, the true hourly wage rate would remain unchanged, a fact not evident from the statistics. The calculated figure for average hourly earnings is misleading because hourly wages did not increase on the whole. Changes in the number of employees in low-paid work versus high-paid work also affect the hourly earnings figures.

The markets will concentrate on the monthly and year-on-year percentage changes in seasonally adjusted average hourly and weekly earnings. Analysts smooth the figures by looking at the 3- and 6-month averages for a better gauge of the underlying trend.

Because of the inconsistency in the series from changes in employment or overtime, you should not place a lot of weight on average hourly earnings. They do not represent labor costs to the employer. But just as other measures of inflation tend to move in tandem, so do the measures of wage inflation. This is the only monthly indicator of wage inflation, so it is a good proxy for other measures that are calculated quarterly.

What is its impact on financial markets?

Average hourly earnings are the earliest available indicator of underlying trends in industry's wage and salary costs and are closely monitored by the Federal Reserve and has received the acclaim of being mentioned by Fed Chairman Alan Greenspan as being an indicator he closely follows.

Their main disadvantage from the point of view of financial markets is that they exclude non-wage costs such as insurance, retirement, savings and other benefits. The Employment Cost Index (ECI), described below, includes these items and is a better measure of total labor costs.

Despite its volatility and limitations, financial market participants pounce on the average hourly earnings data – it is the first inflation news for the month. A rapid rise in hourly wages is negative for the stock and fixed-income market because it signals inflationary pressures. This is good news for the dollar if it is expected to provoke a rise in interest rates (*see* Box 6.8).

Box 6.8: Market reaction to an unexpected change in average earnings

Degree of market sensitivity:
High   ✓
Medium
Low

Average earnings	↑	↓
Bond market	↓	↑
Equity market	↓	↑
US dollar	↑	↓

EMPLOYMENT COST INDEX (ECI)

Definition

Wage pressures can be measured in two ways: average wages and the employment cost index. Average earnings measure the level of wages and salaries for employees on non-farm payrolls. The Employment Cost Index (ECI) tracks all civilian employee compensation. Apart from wages and salaries it also includes many of the other benefits that employees receive. These include paid leave (vacations, holidays, sick leave); supplemental pay (for overtime and shift differentials, and non-production bonuses); insurance benefits (life, health, sickness, and accident); retirement and savings benefits (pension, savings, and thrift plans); legally required benefits (social security, railroad retirement and supplemental retirement, federal and state unemployment insurance, workers' compensation, and other legally required benefits); and other benefits such as severance pay and supplemental unemployment plans.

Who publishes it and when?

The ECI is published quarterly by the Bureau of Labor statistics. The survey is conducted quarterly for the pay period including the 12th day of the four months: March, June, September and December. Data is released on the fourth Tuesday in the month following the survey.

How do you interpret it?

The Labor Department, which designed and conducts the survey, cautions users to the limitations of this index. The Employment Cost Index is not a measure of change in the total cost of employing labor. For example, it does not include training costs. Also, it does not report retroactive pay. The index does not cover all employers and employees in the US, although it does cover nearly all workers in the civilian non-farm economy. The main group not covered are the self-employed.

What is its impact on financial markets?

Financial market participants react to the Employment Cost Index as they would to any other inflation measure. Because it is a quarterly release, and a more stable series than most, the market impact is often muted. Financial markets focus on the quarterly percentage change in the seasonally adjusted ECI compared with the previous quarter and the same quarter of the year before.

Its advantage over average earnings is that it includes non-wage costs which can add 30 percent to total labor costs.

It is known to be watched closely by Alan Greenspan, the Chairman of the Federal Reserve, giving it extra impetus should the outcome be significantly different from market expectations (*see* Box 6.9).

Box 6.9: Market reaction to an unexpected change in the Employment Cost Index (ECI)

Degree of market sensitivity:
High
Medium ✓
Low

Employment Cost Index	▲	▼
Bond market	▼	▲
Equity market	▼	▲
US dollar	▲	▼

INDEX OF LEADING INDICATORS (LEI)

Definition

The Index of Leading Indicators is a weighted average of the economic variables that lead the business cycle. It is part of the family of indicators designed to provide information on the current stage of the business cycle.

As discussed in Chapter 3, the direction of a variable relative to the business cycle can be procyclical, countercyclical, or acyclical. A procyclical variable moves in the same direction as aggregate economic activity, rising in booms and falling in recessions. A countercyclical variable moves oppositely to aggregate economic activity, falling in booms and rising in recessions. An acyclical variable has no clear cyclical pattern.

The timing of a variable relative to the business cycle may be coincident, leading, or lagging. A coincident variable's peaks and troughs occur at about the same time as peaks and troughs in aggregate economic activity. Peaks and troughs in a leading variable come before, and peaks and troughs in a lagging variable come after, the corresponding peaks and troughs in aggregate economic activity.

The ten variables that make up the index are listed below. They were chosen because each has a tendency to predict (lead) economic activity and because data on them are frequently and promptly reported. This second characteristic is essential because a variable cannot be of much help in forecasting if accurate data on the variable arrive only after a long delay.

Leading economic indicators, constituents of the index

- Average work week in manufacturing measured by hours worked.
- Average weekly initial jobless measured by claims for unemployment insurance.
- Manufacturers' new orders for consumer goods and materials – $, 1982.
- Vendor performance – percentage experiencing slower deliveries to their factories. NAPM.
- Plant and equipment contracts and orders – $, 1982.
- New private sector building permits 1967=100.
- M2 – $, 1982.
- S&P 500 and dividend yields. S&P Corporate Composite.
- Michigan Index of Consumer Sentiment. This consists of two parts:
  (a) consumers assessment of current economic conditions – not included in LEI
  (b) expected economic changes, *included* in LEI
- Yield spread.

Who publishes it and when?

The indices are published in a monthly press release by the Bureau of Economic Analysis within the Commerce Department. The data are released about one month after the end of the reference month. The BEA lists the components from the largest negative/positive contributor to the smallest. The preliminary data are subject to revision in each of the following five months as new source data become available.

How do you interpret it?

The interpretation of the index of leading indicators was discussed in detail in Chapter 3. Although the components of the index are varied, there are good economic reasons why each component helps predict economic activity. For example, new orders for plant and equipment, and new building permits are all direct measures of the amount of future production being planned in the economy. The index of stock prices reflects the optimism or pessimism of stock market participants about the economy's future. However, the index is not without problems, and some of these are discussed below.

Despite the emphasis on the use of data that are promptly available, the data on the ten components of the index and thus the index of leading indicators itself are usually revised during the first two months after their initial releases. As a result, an early signal of recession or recovery may be reversed when the revised data become available.

On several occasions, the index has given false warnings, predicting a recession when in fact no recession occurred in the several months following the drop in the index. A recent example of this was when the index fell in five successive months early in 1995 but the economy kept moving briskly forward.

Although it may forecast that a recession is coming, the index does not provide much information about how far in the future the recession is or how severe it will be when it arrives.

Changes in the structure of the economy over time may cause some variables to become better predictors of the economy and others to become worse. For this reason, the index of leading indicators must be revised periodically, either to change the list of component indicators or to change the weights of the components.

It is essential to determine whether increases or decreases in the index are broadly based. If six indicators rise and four indicators fall it is difficult to generalize about the trend. The LEI is particularly useful in forecasting business cycle turning points.

What is its impact on financial markets?

The percentage change in the index of leading indicators is reported monthly, with two or three consecutive monthly declines being regarded by financial markets as the warning sign that a recession is on the way (but see Chapter 3 for serious caveats regarding this general rule). The index tends to turn down in advance of cyclical peaks. On the whole, the index is a valuable and much-watched forecasting device, correctly predicting a large majority of economic turning points during the post-World War II period.

Consequently the financial markets will certainly react violently to large shifts in the index. Large rises in the LEI will boost equities and the dollar, with adverse effects on bonds. The markets will react in the opposite direction to large falls in the LEI.

Even small changes in the LEI will be seized upon by market participants in order to prove their point when market sentiment is particularly negative or positive. This is particularly true around business cycle turning points (*see* Box 6.10).

Box 6.10: Market reaction to an unexpected change in Leading Economic Indicators (LEI)

Degree of market sensitivity:
High ✓
Medium
Low

Leading Economic Indicators	↑	↓
Bond market	↓	↑
Equity market	↑	↓
US dollar	↑	↓

VENDOR DELIVERIES INDEX

Definition

The index is a diffusion index, a concept discussed in detail in Appendix 3.1 and in Chapter 9. The National Association of Purchasing Managers are asked how the overall delivery performance from vendors compared with the month before, is changing. The index is calculated by dividing the percentage who said "the same" by two. The answer is then added to the percentage who said deliveries were "slower." The outcome is then multiplied by a seasonal adjustment factor.

Who publishes it and when?

This index is one of the indices published in the index of the National Association of Purchasing Managers, and is published monthly.

How do you interpret it?

The index is benchmarked at 50. An index greater than 50 indicates that more manufacturers are reporting slower deliveries rather than faster deliveries. So if, to take an example, the index was 65 then this can be interpreted that 65 percent are reporting slower deliveries with 35 percent reporting faster deliveries. This would be seen by the financial markets as evidence of an acceleration of economic activity and with it the possibility of price increases.

An index less than 50 indicates that more manufacturers reported faster deliveries than slower deliveries. So, again to take an example, an index of 35 would be interpreted as 35 percent reporting slower delivery with 65 percent reporting faster delivery. This would be interpreted by the financial markets as evidence of an economic slowdown and with it less pressure for price increases.

What is its impact on financial markets?

If manufacturers are reporting prompter deliveries, this is seen as evidence of slackness in the economy, taking pressures off price increases. Slower deliveries provide evidence that capacity constraints are being hit provoking fears of inflationary pressure. Again this is an index that Alan Greenspan has, at times, drawn attention to, making it at those times very market sensitive.

A major limitation of the index is that it is centered on the manufacturing sector, which represents only 20 percent of the economy and gives us no information about pressures to raise wages in the service sector (*see* Box 6.11).

Box 6.11: Market reaction to an unexpected change in the Vendor Deliveries Index

Degree of market sensitivity:
High
Medium ✓
Low

Vendor Deliveries Index	▲	▼
Bond market	▼	▲
Equity market	▼	▲
US dollar	▲	▼

Computation of price indexes

This Appendix provides additional details about the GNP deflator and the consumer price index. Knowing how the indexes are actually put together makes it easier to understand the differences between the two and how to best interpret them.

The GNP deflator for a simplified economy

A much simpler economy than that of the US will serve to illustrate the computation of price indexes. Table 6.1.1 shows price and quantity data for two years for an economy in which only three goods are produced: movies, apples and shirts. The table indicates that nominal GNP grew from $400 in 1982 to $1,000 in 1992. But how are these figures to be interpreted? Do they mean that people really had more of the things they wanted in 1992 than in 1982? More exactly, do they mean that people had 2.5 times as much? These questions are not easy to answer from an inspection of the table as it stands.

Table 6.1.1 ● Nominal GNP in selected years for a simple economy

1982	Quantity	Price ($)	Value ($)
Movies	50	2.00	100
Apples	1,000	0.20	200
Shirts	10	10.00	100
1982 Nominal GNP			400
1992			
Movies	100	4.00	400
Apples	500	0.60	300
Shirts	20	15.00	300
1992 Nominal GNP			$1,000

In this simple economy, where only three goods are produced, nominal national income grew from $400 in 1982 to $1,000 in 1992. Prices also went up in that time, though, so people did not really have 2.5 times as many goods as in 1982.

A line-by-line comparison of the two years shows that the figures on nominal income do not tell the whole story. Clearly, prices went up sharply between 1982 and 1992. Movies cost twice what they used to, apples three times as much, and shirts half again as much.

We notice also that the quantities of goods produced have changed. Twice as many movies and shirts were produced in 1992 as 1982, but only half as many apples.

If we want to know how much better off people were in 1992 than in 1982, we need a way to separate the quantity changes that have taken place from the price changes. One way to do this is to ask how much the total value of output would have changed from 1982 to 1992 if prices had not changed. This approach gives the results shown in Table 6.1.2. There, we see that the 1992 output of 100 movies, 500 apples, and 20 shirts, which had a value of $1,000 in terms of the prices at which the goods were actually sold, would have had a value of only $500 in terms of the prices that prevailed in 1982. The $500 is thus a measure of real GNP for 1992. It is this measure that should be compared to the 1982 GNP of $400 if we want to know what really happened to output between the two years. Instead of having 250 percent more output in 1992 than in 1982, as indicated by the change in nominal GNP from $400 to $1,000, the people in this simple economy really had only about 25 percent more, indicated by the change in real GNP from $400 to $500.

Table 6.1.2 shows how the figures from Table 6.1.1 can be adjusted to take changing prices into account. The 1992 quantities are multiplied by 1982 prices to get the value of 1992 GNP as it would have been if prices had not changed. The total of 1992 quantities valued at 1982 prices is a measure of real GNP for 1992, stated in constant 1982 dollars. The implicit GNP deflator for 1992, calculated as the ratio of 1992 nominal GNP to 1992 real GNP, has a value of 200.

Table 6.1.2 ● Nominal and real GNP in 1992 for a simple economy

	1992 quantity	1992 price ($)	Value at 1992 price ($)	1982 price ($)	Value of 1992 Output at 1982 price ($)
Movies	100	4.00	400	2.00	200
Apples	500	0.60	300	0.20	100
Shirts	20	15.00	300	10.00	200
Totals		1992 nominal GNP = 1,000		1992 real GNP = 500	

We have now seen how to compute real and nominal GNP for 1992 directly from price and quantity data, without using a price index to convert nominal to real values. But although we have not explicitly used a price index, we have created one implicitly. This implicit index, or implicit GNP deflator, is the ratio of current-year nominal GNP to current-year real GNP times 100, as expressed by the formula

$$\text{GNP deflator} = \frac{\text{Current year output valued at current year prices}}{\text{Current year output valued at base year prices}} \times 100$$

Applying the formula to the data in Tables 6.1.1 and 6.1.2 gives a value of 200 for the deflator.

THE CONSUMER PRICE INDEX FOR THE SIMPLE ECONOMY

The consumer price index differs from the GNP deflator in two ways. First, as mentioned earlier in the the chapter, it takes into account only the prices of goods and services typically consumed by urban households. Second, it is calculated according to a formula that uses base-year quantities rather than current-year quantities. The first difference does not matter for this simple economy in which all goods are consumer goods, but the second difference does matter, as Table 6.1.3 demonstrates.

The consumer price index can be calculated as the base-year market basket of goods valued at current-year prices divided by the base-year market basket valued at base-year prices, multiplied by 100. This exhibit shows how such an index can be calculated for the simple economy used in Tables 6.1.1 and 6.1.2. The 1982 output cost $400 at the prices at which it was actually sold. If it had been sold at 1992 prices, it would have cost $950. The CPI for 1992 is thus 237.5.

Table 6.1.3 ● Calculation of a consumer price index for a simplified economy

Good	1982 quantity	1982 price ($)	Value of 1982 quantity at 1982 price ($)	1992 price ($)	Value of 1982 Output at 1992 price ($)
Movies	50	2.00	100	4.00	200
Apples	100	0.20	200	0.60	600
Shirts	10	10.00	100	15.00	150
Totals			400		950

$$CPI = \frac{\$950}{\$400} \times 100 = 237.5$$

To calculate the CPI for this economy, instead of asking how much current-year output would have cost at base-year prices, we begin by asking how much base-year quantity would have cost at current-year prices. The index is then calculated as the ratio of the two different valuations of base-year quantities.

$$\text{Consumer price index} = \frac{\text{Base-year market basket valued at current-year prices}}{\text{Base-year market basket valued at base-year prices}} \times 100$$

The CPI is calculated using base-year quantities in part because current price data are easier to collect than are current output data. This index can thus be announced each month with a minimum of delay.

COMPARING THE CPI AND GNP DEFLATOR

As Table 6.1.3 shows, the CPI for 1992 in our simple economy had a value of 237.5, whereas the GNP deflator for 1992 was only 200. Both indexes were calculated using the same underlying data, and both used 1982 as a base year. Which, if either, is the true measure of the change in the price level between the two years?

The reply is that neither the CPI nor the GNP deflator is the only correct measure of change in the price level. Instead, each is the answer to a different question. The GNP deflator is the answer to the question: How much more did the 1992 output cost at the prices at which it was actually sold than it would have cost if it had been sold at 1982 prices instead? The CPI, in contrast, is the answer to the question: How much more would the 1982 output have cost if it had been sold at 1992 prices instead of its actual 1982 prices?

Careful inspection of the data shows why the answers to the two questions are not the same. In 1982, lots of apples and not very many shirts were produced in comparison to 1992. Yet, between the two years, the price of apples increased 200 percent while the price of shirts increased only 50 percent. Because the CPI uses base-year quantities, it gives a heavy weight to apples, which experienced relatively the greatest price increase, and not much weight to shirts, which experienced only a modest price increase. In contrast, the GNP deflator uses current-year quantities, thereby down-playing the importance of apples and emphasizing that of shirts.

The above discussion explains why it is often claimed that the CPI tends to have an upward substitution bias relative to the GNP deflator. But that does not make the GNP deflator a true measure of change in the cost of living. It could just as well be said that the GNP deflator has a downward substitution bias relative to the CPI or that each has an opposite bias from some "true" price index lying between them.

Macroeconomic announcements

Announcement time, title, and reporting entities for 18 monthly macroeconomic announcements and one weekly (initial jobless claims) macroeconomic announcements. All times are Eastern Time (ET).

Time	Short title	Full title	Reporting entity
08.30	Consumer Price Index (CPI)	Consumer Price Index	Bureau of Labor Statistics
08.30	Durable Goods Orders	Advance Report on Durable Goods Manufacturers' Shipments and Orders	Bureau of the Census
08.30	Employment	The Employment Situation	Bureau of Labor Statistics
08.30	Gross Domestic Product (GDP)	Gross Domestic Product	Bureau of Economic Analysis
08.30	Housing Starts	Housing Starts and Building Permits	Bureau of the Census
08.30	Initial Jobless Claims	Initial Jobless Claims	Bureau of Labor Statistics
08.30	Leading Indicators	Composite Indexes of Leading, Coincident, and Lagging Indicators	Bureau of Economic Analysis
08.30	Personal Income	Personal Income and Outlays	Bureau of Economic Analysis
08.30	Producer Price Index (PPI)	Producer Price Indexes	Bureau of Labor Statistics
08.30	Retail Sales	Advance Retail Sales	Bureau of the Census
08.30	Trade Balance	U.S. International Trade in Goods and Services	Bureau of the Census. Bureau of Economic Analysis
09.15	Industrial Production and Capacity Utilization	Industrial Production and Capacity Utilization	Federal Reserve Board
10:00	Business Inventories	Manufacturing and Trade: Inventories and Sales	Bureau of the Census
10:00	Consumer Confidence	Consumer Confidence Index	Conference Board
10:00	Construction Spending	Value of New Construction Put in Place	Bureau of the Census
10:00	Factory Inventories	Manufacturers' Shipments, Inventories, and Orders	Bureau of the Census
10:00	NAPM Survey	National Association of Purchasing Management Index	National Association of Purchasing Management
10:00	New Single-Family Home Sales	New One-Family Houses Sold and For Sale	Bureau of the Census
14:00	Federal Budget	Treasury Statement (The Monthly "Budget")	Department of the Treasury

CHAPTER 7

Consumer expenditure

- Introduction
- Auto sales
- The Employment Report
- Quit rate
- Retail sales
- Personal income and consumer expenditure
- Consumer installment credit

INTRODUCTION

Consumer expenditure accounts for two-thirds of GDP. Consequently, it is the major component of nominal GNP and its behavior is of great interest to the financial markets. A strong consumer sector signals a healthy economy which can lead to inflation and higher interest rates.

Consumer indicators that point to increased spending are bearish for the fixed-income market; bullish for the stock market; and favor a strong dollar. Consumer indicators that point to sluggish spending are bullish for the fixed income market; bearish for the stock market and negative with respect to the dollar.

The majority of the consumer sector indicators are reported monthly although a couple are available more often. The more frequently the indicator is reported, the more it is followed by financial market participants, but the more careful they must be in interpreting it. The equity, fixed income, and foreign exchange markets are constantly moving, as traders revise their expectations of economic activity based on economists' forecasts, market rumors, or actual economic reports. As a result, the more frequent the economic data, the more readily the market can incorporate new economic information in line with the discussion in Chapter 1.

The key indicators affecting consumer expenditure are listed in Figure 7.1.

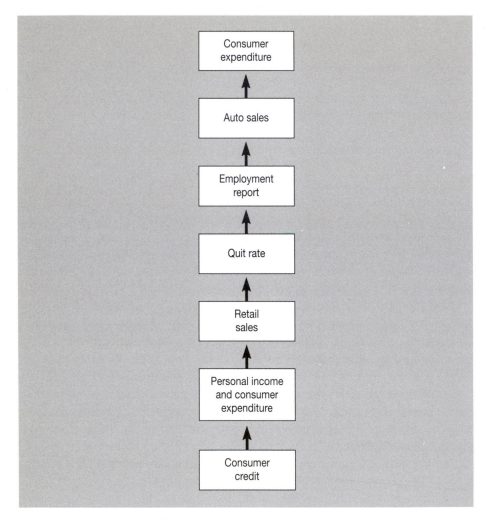

Fig 7.1 ● Key indicators affecting consumer expenditure

AUTO SALES

Definition

The most frequently reported indicator of consumer spending is ten-day unit auto sales. Unit auto sales tell us the number of autos that were sold during that particular ten-day period. It is officially called unit sales for autos and light trucks.

Who publishes them and when?

The major auto manufacturers of domestically produced autos report their sales for the first ten days, the middle ten days, and the last ten days of each month. These sales figures are available on the third business day following each ten-day period. Sales for the first ten days of any month are usually reported on the 13th of the month; sales for the middle ten days, on about the 23rd; and for the last ten days, on the 3rd business day of the subsequent month.

The American Automobile Manufacturers Association (AAMA) report their raw sales data for the ten-day period compared with the same period in the previous year. This means that the preceding year's sales figures are just as important to the calculation as the current year's sales figures.

How do you interpret them?

Most importantly they provide the very *first* piece of information concerning the strength or weakness of the economy in the monthly cycle. No other indicator is as timely because none is released during the course of that same month.

Auto sales have a second great strength. They can provide us with an important clue concerning the retail sales and personal consumption expenditures (PCE) data to be released later in the month, both of which can be big market movers. Auto sales represent about 25 percent of retail sales and about 8 percent of consumption.

Auto sales have a third important feature. They can give us an early warning signal of an impending recession, and tell us when we can begin to expect a recovery. The underlying reason is that auto sales are very sensitive to changes in interest rates and consumer psychology. If consumers get nervous about the economic outlook, or are concerned by rising interest rates, one of the first things they do is cancel plans to buy a new auto. This makes sense because autos and housing are the largest expenditures in the family budget. If you are going to cut costs, this is the place to start!

Historically, the auto and housing sectors of the economy are the first to dip into recession when times are bad. They are also the first to experience a recovery. Thus, auto sales tend to be a leading indicator of economic activity, and can provide some clues concerning when the economy is about to change direction. This is why auto sales data are followed closely by the financial markets.

The raw sales figures reported by auto makers are volatile from period to period, and there is a general trend toward higher sales as the month progresses, possibly because sales people and dealers may be given greater incentives to sell autos toward the end of the month if auto sales are flat. So if you were to compare each ten-day period of most months, sales would increase as the month progresses with the highest sales level occurring in the final ten-day period.

As a result, the Bureau of Economic Analysis (BEA), a division of the US Department of Commerce, releases seasonal adjustment factors for ten-day auto sales. Thus, we can divide the raw auto sales data for the ten-day period by a seasonal factor and yield a *seasonally adjusted annual rate* (SAAR). The seasonal adjustment factor blows up the current level of sales to an annual rate and takes account of normal seasonal behavior at the same time.

The BEA use these data to estimate portions of GDP components – notably durables, personal consumption expenditures, producer durable equipment and government consumption expenditures and gross investment.

What is their impact on financial markets?

Participants in the fixed income or bond market prefer to see weak auto sales in turn signalling an economic slowdown. Participants in the stock and foreign exchange markets would prefer to see a rise in auto sales. In the case of the stock market, strong auto sales signal a healthy economy and good earnings in auto and related industries. Any factor which boosts earnings and dividends is good for the stock market. A strong economy followed by rising interest rates increases the demand for dollars. However, if the market share of foreign-produced autos increases at the expense of domestically produced autos, the demand for foreign currencies will go up and the exchange value of the dollar will decline. Strong auto sales, if they provoke the Fed to push up interest rates, would thereby push down bond prices (*see* Box 7.1).

Box 7.1: Market reaction to an unexpected change in auto sales

Degree of market sensitivity:
High
Medium ✓
Low

Auto sales	↑	↓
Bond market	↓	↑
Equity market	↑	↓
US dollar	↑	↓

THE EMPLOYMENT REPORT

Definition

The Employment Report consists of employment related data which in turn comes from two separate surveys, the *Establishment Survey* and the *Household Survey*. The Establishment Survey provides information on non-farm payroll employment, the average hourly workweek and the aggregate hours index. The household survey provides information on the labor force, household employment and the unemployment rate (*see* Figure 7.2). The establishment survey, used to compile non-farm payrolls, is based on a much larger sample than the household survey used to compile unemployment figures.

Non-farm payroll employment measures the number of people in gainful employment in all non-farm industries, such as manufacturing and services. The financial markets focus on the seasonally adjusted monthly change in the number of payroll jobs.

The average hourly workweek represents the length of the working week in private non-agricultural industries. It is based on reports of paid hours for production, construction and non-supervisory workers.

The aggregate hours index is derived by dividing total hours paid for by the number of employees during the pay period. Pay periods longer than a week are adjusted to represent a week. The average weekly hours derived from the total hours reflect the effect of factors such as absenteeism, labor turnover, part-time work and strikes. The effect of strikes can be significant as was seen from the effects of the General Motors strike in 1998.

The headline civilian unemployment rate, based on the household survey, is the number of unemployed people as a percentage of the total civilian labor force (which includes unemployed and employed people in the US).

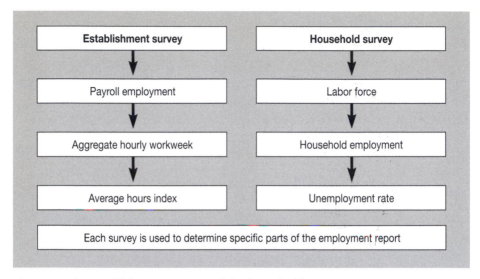

Fig 7.2 ● The establishment survey and the household survey

The employed include non-farm and farm workers aged 16 and above, with the exception of those in institutions (such as a prison or mental hospital). It includes people who:

● did any work at all as paid civilians, including full and part-time and temporary employees;

● were self-employed in their own business or profession or on their own farm;

● worked 15 hours or more in a family business, even if the work was unpaid.

The employment measures based on the household survey count people rather than jobs (unlike the establishment survey which does the opposite – see below) so a person holding more than one job is only counted as employed in the job in which he or she works the most hours.

People are classified as unemployed, regardless of their eligibility for unemployment benefit or public assistance, if they meet all the criteria. These are that they had no employment during the survey week, were available for work at that time (except for temporary illness), and had made specific efforts to find work in the previous four weeks. People laid off from their jobs and awaiting recall and those expecting to report to a job within 30 days need not be looking for work to be counted as unemployed.

The unemployed include both people collecting unemployment benefits or public assistance and those who are not eligible, for example, because they have exhausted their unemployment insurance or are former students who have not accumulated unemployment benefits. Students (including those aged 16 and above who are still at school) are counted as unemployed if they have looked for a job and are available for at least a part-time position.

People without a job and not actively looking for work are not in the labor force and, therefore, are not counted as unemployed.

Once we know the number of people who are employed along with the number of people who are unemployed, it is a simple process to calculate the unemployment rate. The labor force is the sum of employed plus unemployed individuals. The unemployment rate is equal to the number of unemployed people divided by the total number of people in the labor force.

$$\frac{\text{Unemployed}}{\text{Employed} + \text{Unemployed}} = \text{Unemployment Rate}$$

Either the numerator (number of employed) or denominator (number in the labor force) can cause changes in the unemployment rate. The unemployment rate will increase whenever the labor force increases (barring an equal increase in the number of employed people) and whenever the number of unemployed people increases (barring any change in the labor force). Conversely, either a drop in the labor force, or a decline in the number of unemployed people, will cause the jobless rate to decrease.

The headline unemployment rate does not include the military as part of the labor force and so is always about 0.1 of a percentage point higher than the unemployment rate including the military.

Employment figures based on the establishment survey are restricted to wage and salary employees in the non-farm sector and government civilian workers. All paid people are counted whether they are at work or absent.

The survey excludes agriculture, the self-employed, unpaid family workers, private household workers, members of the armed forces and people on unpaid leave. It counts as employed both workers on paid sick leave (when pay is received directly from the employer) and those on paid holiday. People are considered employed if they receive pay for any part of the specified pay period, but not if they receive no pay at all for the pay period.

Who publishes it and when?

As already mentioned, the employment information comes from two separate surveys, the establishment survey and the household survey. Both surveys are conducted by the Bureau of Labor Statistics (BLS) for the calendar week that includes the 12th of the month. The data are generally released the first Friday of the following month.

The household survey is carried out for the BLS by the Census Bureau. It is based on a sample of about 60,000 households, out of a total of more than 95 million. Information is obtained each month for only about 144,000 people,

75,000 of whom are actually in the labor force.

The data for a given month actually relate to a particular week. A special group of 1,600 Census Bureau interviewers visit or telephone households in the calendar week including the 19th of the month and ask about their employment status during the week including the 12th of the month, which is called the survey week. The number of weeks from survey to survey can be easily calculated – about every third month, it is five weeks instead of four.

The non-farm payroll data are compiled from the monthly establishment survey of employer payroll records. They refer to people who worked during, or received pay for, any part of the pay period that includes the 12th of the month. The number of weeks from survey to survey will depend on the individual firm's pay policy; in most cases, the interval between the reference period for each survey will be the same.

The data are obtained from a postal survey of employers. The survey sample covers about 360,000 employers who employ more than 40 million people, or about 40 percent of non-farm employment. The likelihood of an establishment being selected depends on its employment level. While all establishments with 250 or more employees are included in the survey, smaller establishments are represented by a sample.

Since this survey simply asks respondents to provide the number of workers currently on their payroll, double counting occurs when individuals hold more than one job.

How do you interpret it?

It is essential to concentrate on the seasonally adjusted monthly unemployment rate and the change in non-farm payrolls. Since monthly payroll changes can be volatile, use the three- and six-month average changes in non-farm payrolls to gauge the underlying trend.

The unemployment rate and non-farm payrolls can move in opposite directions, rendering labor market activity unclear. The establishment survey, which generates the non-farm payroll data, generally has much smaller movements on a monthly basis and offers a smoother short-term trend than the household survey used in calculating the unemployment rate. This is because the establishment survey has a much larger sample, adjusts for new companies (which reduces the likelihood of a fall in the payroll) and aims to maintain its sample base while trying to ensure that the companies in the sample respond to the survey.

Interpretation of the employment data is affected by layoffs and strikes. Striking workers reduce non-farm payrolls until they return to work, at which stage they boost the payrolls total. In months where the employment data have been affected by strikes, economists estimate the number on strike and forecast the payrolls change both including and excluding strikers to give a better picture of the underlying trend. The 1998 General Motors strike resulted in the need for considerable adjustments.

The average hourly work week reflects the demand for labor since employers typically increase or reduce hours worked before hiring or laying off workers in response to changes in demand. Aggregate weekly hours, published as an index, are the product of employment and the average working week. A rise in the average working week can offset a fall in employment, and vice versa. The average working week falls relatively less quickly in the early stages of an economic slowdown because employees with shorter working hours (particularly in industries with many part-time workers, such as the retail trade) tend to be dismissed first.

Weekly reports of jobless figures contain two useful pieces of information for forecasters: initial claims for unemployment benefits and the number of insured unemployed.

When workers are laid off they can apply for unemployment benefits. These applications, called *initial claims for state unemployment benefits*, are one of the most closely watched pointers to employment trends and a good indicator of the pace of layoffs. Initial claims are available two and a half weeks after applications are recorded.

Economists use a four-week seasonally adjusted moving average of initial (new) unemployment insurance claims to gauge by how much non-farm payrolls may rise or fall in the main employment release. If the average number of new weekly claims in the period leading up to the main employment release is rising, then the increase in non-farm payrolls should be lower (or the fall higher) and vice versa.

As discussed in the next section, the employment report provides future information on industrial production, wage and salary disbursements in the personal income report of the BEA, and is a component of the index of current indicators, published by the Conference Board.

What is its impact on financial markets?

The Employment Report has frequently been referred to as the "jewel in the crown" of all the economic indicators to which financial markets will react. It is the most market sensitive monthly economic indicator. Financial market participants can extract a wealth of market sensitive information from the fine details of this report (*see* Figure 7.3) which is where its sensitivity comes from.

Participants in the fixed income market favor small increases or outright declines in non-farm payrolls because they signal economic weakness. Economic weakness usually signal lower interest rates through decreased market demand for loans or for an easing of monetary policy.

Conversely, robust increases in non-farm payrolls could indicate a healthy economy and signal higher interest rates as credit demands pick up or the

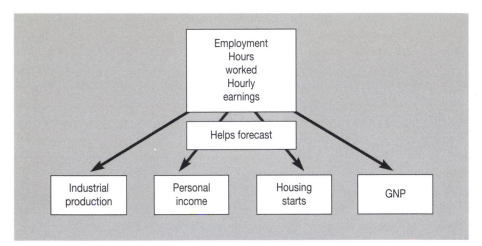

Fig 7.3 ● Why the employment report is so market sensitive

Federal Reserve tightens to prevent inflationary pressures. The potential for higher interest rates makes foreign exchange market participants eager for robust gains in non-farm payrolls, as they will push up the value of the dollar. Participants in the equity market also will favor healthy employment gains because a strong economy means healthy corporate profits, which gives a boost to stock prices.

Special factors in the payroll employment number must be watched carefully. For example the totally unexpected rise of 35,000 when the expected outcome was for some 300,000 in September 1997 provoked an unexpected move in the bond market (*see* Box 7.2).

Box 7.2: Market reaction to an unexpected change in non-farm payroll employment

Degree of market sensitivity:
High ✓
Medium
Low

Non-farm payroll employment	↑	↓
Bond market	↓	↑
Equity market	↑	↓
US dollar	↑	↓

Stock prices and the value of the dollar rise when the unemployment rate falls. A rising unemployment rate is associated with a weak or contracting economy and declining interest rates. Conversely, a decreasing unemployment rate is associated with an expanding economy and potentially rising interest rates. This is bad news for the bond market.

QUIT RATE

Definition

The quit rate, published monthly in the BLS's employment report, is officially defined as: job leavers as a percentage of the total unemployed. It is essentially the share of unemployed people who have chosen to leave their jobs. Job leavers are not workers who were fired or laid off. They are those who leave voluntarily, i.e., they quit.

Who publishes it and when?

It is published in the BLS Employment Report.

How do you interpret it?

Presumably most people who quit their jobs do so because they have better, higher-paying jobs lined up. This view is certainly supported by the empirical evidence. A higher quit rate is not a leading indicator of wage pressure; it is the *result* of it.

What is its impact on financial markets?

The quit rate acquired the status in 1997, 1998 and 1999 of being one of the indicators that the Federal Reserve Chairman, Alan Greenspan, follows when setting the course of monetary policy. The empirical evidence shows that if the quit rate rises above 12 percent pressure for wages and prices to rise takes place. If the quit rate falls to 10–12 percent, then there are pressures for wages and prices to fall (*see* Box 7.3).

Box 7.3: Market reaction to an unexpected change in the quit rate

Degree of market sensitivity:
High ✓
Medium
Low

Quit rate	↑	↓
Bond market	↓	↑
Equity market	↑	↓
US dollar	↑	↓

RETAIL SALES

Definition

Retail sales include:

- all merchandise sold for cash or credit by establishments primarily engaged in retail trade;
- new motor vehicles except those sold to rental fleets (e.g. Hertz, Avis);
- used auto sales;
- leasing of vehicles and rental and leasing of equipment, instruments, and tools, etc.;
- delivery, installation, maintenance, repair, alteration, storage and other services;
- excise taxes on gasoline, liquor, tobacco, etc., which are levied on manufacturers but passed on to retailers;
- trade-in allowances and manufacturers' rebates (i.e., these are not deducted from total sales).

Retail sales exclude:

- retailers' rebates;
- sales and excise taxes collected directly from customers whether it be by a local, state or federal tax agency.

Who publishes them and when?

Sales of non-durable and durable consumer goods are reported between 11th and 15th of each month for the previous month. This series is published by the

Commerce Department's Bureau of the Census and is derived from a sample of establishments of all sizes and types across the country. Because the sales figures come from a sample they are subject to substantial revision for several months after the initial report.

Three components make up the sample for retail sales estimates. Companies whose 1982 sales were greater than a certain cut-off were chosen to report their sales figures every month. These 2,000 stores account for roughly 40 percent of total retail sales. The second component of retail sales comes from about 30,000 establishments that are separated into three panels and are asked to report their sales only once every three months. This group makes up about 56 percent of total retail sales. The remaining 4 percent come from retailers who represent areas not covered by the other two components. Participation in the retail sales survey is voluntary.

How do you interpret them?

Retail sales are reported in current, or nominal, dollars; that is, they are not adjusted for inflation. Auto sales constitute the largest single component of retail sales, about 25 percent of the total. Although monthly auto sales are not as volatile as 10-day auto sales, they still jump around from month to month, and the wild fluctuations can obscure the underlying trend. The dollar value of auto sales reflects the quantity of autos sold as well as the price of the auto. The changing mix of expensive versus less expensive autos needs to be taken account of. Even when the quantity of auto sales increases, the auto price can be low if consumers buy cheap autos rather than expensive autos. As a result, the price times quantity equals a low dollar value and holds down the growth in retail auto sales. Conversely, fewer autos may be sold, but if consumers purchase expensive autos, this puts upward pressure on the dollar value of sales.

For this reason, financial market participants talk about *retail sales excluding autos*. By removing the volatile component of the series, you can assess the underlying spending behavior of consumers. The auto sales portion of retail sales also includes truck sales.

Statisticians at the Bureau of the Census say that a single month's retail sales figures can only give a hint of a new trend – they cannot confirm a change in the pattern of sales. There is a tendency for any sharp rise or fall in the monthly report to be reversed the next month. For this reason, some financial market analysts take a two-month average of the retail sales figures. Bureau statisticians reckon that a three- or four-month moving average is better still.

Many financial market analysts focus on the year-on-year change in retail sales and look at how this has changed over, say, the past three months rather than constructing any moving average. However, this approach is likely to be slow in capturing a change in trend, and, with seasonally adjusted data available, there is a strong case to be made for concentrating on the three-monthly comparison.

Because of the volatile nature of auto sales, as suggested above, most analysts base their work on the retail sales total minus autos. All the big auto manufacturers (except Chrysler) issue sales figures every ten days, so analysts already have an extremely good idea of what auto sales are doing.

There is a good correlation between personal consumer expenditure and the retail sales data. The monthly personal income and spending data comes out after retail sales but can be used as a confirmation signal.

Financial market analysts believe that when the Federal Reserve looks at the retail sales data it is not so much concerned with the trend in the total but in that of discretionary spending which is taken to be retail sales minus energy, food and drug store sales. This represents a better picture of consumer confidence.

The retail sales figures provide information on the durable and non-durable personal consumption expenditures in the personal income report.

What is their impact on financial markets?

Participants in the fixed income market favor a drop in retail sales, or at least weakness in the figures because that points to a weakening economy. There is then pressure for the Federal Reserve to cut interest rates which is good for bond prices. If retail sales rise sharply, bond market participants will push up interest rates and push down bond prices.

Equity market professionals favor rising retail sales. Strong consumer spending figures indicate a healthy economy and that augurs well for corporate profits. Stock prices, especially those directly related to the retail sector, are likely to rise on this news. If retail sales decline, or show only a small rise, stock prices will fall or at best not show any upward momentum.

Foreign exchange participants also favor a healthy rise in retail sales because it points to a strong US economy and suggests that the Federal Reserve may force up interest rates. Rising interest rates relative to the rest of the world lead to a rise in demand for the dollar. If retail sales decline, however, interest rates are likely to drop, and the softer demand will then cause the dollar to fall (*see* Box 7.4).

Box 7.4: Market reaction to an unexpected change in retail sales

Degree of market sensitivity:
High ✓
Medium
Low

Retail sales	↑	↓
Bond market	↓	↑
Equity market	↑	↓
US dollar	↑	↓

LJR Johnson Redbook

The Johnson Redbook series is compiled by a unit of Lynch, Jones and Ryan, a New York brokerage firm. Johnson conducts a weekly survey of 25 retailers across the country including chain stores, discounters and department stores. This weekly indicator of retail sales is reported every Tuesday afternoon and provides information on sales for the previous week. The Johnson Redbook figures are faxed to customers, but as is the case with all economic indicators, the data are picked up by the media. Note that the Redbook survey's coverage is much narrower than the official retail sales data and the two may diverge. The Redbook is a useful predictor of department store sales in the retail sales report.

Bond traders do react to the Johnson Redbook data, so it is worth following the series. The market reaction will be similar to auto sales: if retailers post higher sales, suggesting healthy or improving economic growth, bond prices will fall and cause yields to rise. A weak report signals economic sluggishness and suggests interest rates will fall. The market reaction to the Johnson Redbook series affects the bond market and is ignored by the equity and currency markets.

PERSONAL INCOME AND CONSUMER EXPENDITURE

Definition

Personal income represents the compensation that individuals receive from all sources. That includes wages and salaries, proprietor's income, income from rents, dividends and transfer payments such as social security, unemployment and welfare benefits. Personal income is important for financial markets as it clearly holds the key to future spending and hence economic activity.

Consumer expenditure data also involves data collection from many different sources. Personal consumption expenditures include durable goods, non-durable goods and services. Motor vehicles, furniture, appliances, boats and pleasure craft, jewellery, watches and books would be durable goods. Food, clothing, shoes, gasoline and fuel oil would be non-durable goods.

The services sector represents roughly half of consumer spending. This would include electricity, gas, telephone, domestic services, motor vehicle repairs, insurance, medical care, investment services, beauty parlors, etc.

Who publishes it and when?

The income and consumption data are prepared monthly by the Commerce Department's Bureau of Economic Analysis. Given the many different types of income, there is a wide variety of source data. For example, wage estimates are prepared primarily from the payroll employment data that is submitted by the Bureau of Labor Statistics. Data on transfer payments come from information collected by the Social Security Administration, the Veterans Administration, and the monthly statement of receipts and outlays published by the Treasury Department. Dividend income is estimated from a sample of corporate dividend payments. Interest income is derived by applying interest rates to household asset data that is collected by the Federal Reserve Board.

Similarly, the monthly estimates of consumption expenditures involve data collection from many different sources. The Commerce Department relies heavily upon trends shown in the Census Bureau's retail sales report. In addition, the Commerce Department uses the unit auto sales data that are reported by each of the manufacturers. They also have some price data for autos, gasoline and tobacco because prices for these items tend to be quite volatile. It should be noted that the personal consumption data are presented in both nominal and "real" or inflation-adjusted terms. This latter series *is* the consumption portion of the GNP estimate. If you average the figures for the three months of the quarter, you will have the Personal Consumer Expenditure (PCE) component of Gross National Product.

The income and expenditure figures are compiled, edited and eventually released one day after the GNP report – which generally appears in the third week of the month.

How do you interpret it?

Personal consumer expenditures (PCE) are the "C" portion of the GDP equation $C+I+G+(X–IM)$ discussed in Chapter 5.

Since consumer spending is two-thirds of GDP the financial markets have thus two-thirds of their forecast. The data tend to be relatively stable, given that the service sector spending has traditionally been less volatile than spending on durable and non-durable goods. See Chapter 3 for further discussion of recent changes in the service sector.

Personal income has to be adjusted for inflation, giving a figure for real income, a more accurate barometer of spending power. The personal income figures also provide information on savings behavior. A sharp drop in the savings rate indicates that the consumer is dipping into savings to finance purchases. This is not a sustainable situation, and one should expect to see slower consumption and GNP growth in the months ahead. Special factors which can skew growth in personal income come mainly from two government-related sources. Every January, government workers and Social Security recipients receive cost-of-living adjustments. Economists and financial market participants have learned to anticipate these annual adjustments.

Farm income can spurt or plunge in any given month depending on the amount of subsidy payments made by the Commodity Credit Corporation. Commerce Department economists know in advance when subsidy payments are allocated. Thus, business economists who regularly forecast economic indicators have a sense about movements in farm income. But surprises can still occur. Always look at farm income as a main source of volatility in total personal income.

What is its impact on financial markets?

The financial market participants rarely find this indicator very market sensitive. Increases in personal income generally point to increases in consumer spending and gains in economic activity overall. That is bad news for the fixed-income market because bond traders fear that economic expansions are inflationary. Consequently, bonds are likely to fall in price and rise in yield. Decelerating or falling personal income growth indicating signs of economic weakness in consumer spending is favorable news to bond traders because it suggests recession and a deceleration of inflationary pressures or potential Federal Reserve easing. This would cause bond prices to rise and yields to decline.

Stock market participants view personal income as well as personal consumption expenditure growth favorably. Strong consumer spending points to healthy corporate profits and thereby dividends. Thus, stock prices are likely to rise when personal income growth increases and fall when personal income growth declines.

The foreign exchange markets will take the same perspective as the equity trader. Rising personal income growth augers well for the economy pointing to higher interest rates and therefore an increase in the demand for dollars. This will raise the value of the dollar. Sluggish gains in personal income or outright declines (which are unusual) clearly suggest economic weakness. Consequently, interest rates would fall and lead to a drop in the demand for the dollar.

Financial market participants (either in the fixed income, equity, or foreign exchange markets) do not tend to react forcibly to monthly data on personal consumption expenditures due to the fact that it is highly predictable and consequently is normally "expected" news (*see* Box 7.5).

Box 7.5: Market reaction to an unexpected change in personal income and consumer expenditure

Degree of market sensitivity:
High
Medium ✓
Low

Personal income and consumer expenditure	↑	↓
Bond market	↓	↑
Equity market	↑	↓
US dollar	↑	↓

CONSUMER INSTALLMENT CREDIT

Definition

Consumer installment credit covers loans to households, scheduled to be repaid in two or more monthly payments, for purchases of goods and services. The main categories of consumer installment credit are:

- automobile credit – passenger autos and station wagons;
- revolving credit – credit cards used for sales transactions or cash advances and check credit plans that allow overdrafts up to certain amounts on personal accounts;
- other credit – consumer bank loans other than mortgages, including those for home improvements, recreational vehicles, mobile homes, vans and pick-up trucks, and student loans.

Secured and unsecured loans, except those secured with real estate which are defined as mortgage loans, are included. Securitized consumer loans, which are those made by finance companies, banks and retailers and sold as securities, are also included.

Who publishes it and when?

The net change in consumer installment credit is reported by the Federal Reserve Board between five and six weeks after the end of the month. This series is based on data from monthly surveys from several sources: monthly surveys of commercial banks, monthly surveys of consumer finance companies, monthly surveys of savings and loan associations, and monthly surveys of retail sales.

How do you interpret it?

The financial markets focus on the seasonally adjusted net credit advanced, which takes into account both extensions (loans) and repayments.

For the most part, when consumer credit increases, it suggests gains in consumer spending and a sense of optimism about the economy. This will happen during economic expansions. When consumer credit decreases, it suggests decreased consumer spending, possibly coupled with a sense of pessimism about future economic activity. This often happens during recessions.

Consumer credit outstanding usually rises, but the rate of increase is quicker during expansions than recessions. The rare monthly falls in consumer credit show up during recessions. Consumer credit therefore magnifies cyclical changes in consumer spending, particularly for durable goods.

Another measure that can be helpful in interpreting changes in credit outstanding is the ratio of consumer instalment credit to disposable income, more commonly known as the debt-to-income ratio. (The terms *consumer credit* and *consumer debt* are, somewhat confusingly, used interchangeably.) The debt-to-income ratio will rise during an expansion as consumers feel comfortable about their future financial obligations and increase their spending on credit. The debt-to-income ratio will stabilize or decline during recessions as consumer spending, especially on durable goods, falls sharply.

What is its impact on financial markets?

Consumer credit data is difficult to interpret on its own. Financial markets, as ever, include this along with the other indicators in order to gain a clearer picture of the economy. For example, increases in consumer credit coupled with increases in auto sales and retail sales clearly point to consumer optimism and a strong economy. Conversely, if retail sales and auto sales decline, but consumer credit increases, consumers may not be repaying their debt as rapidly. They are simply using the debt to finance their weaker personal financial situation. This could signal lackluster economic activity along with some cautious consumer behavior. Finally, declines in consumer credit coupled with increases in retail sales or auto sales, suggest that consumers are repaying their loans more rapidly than they are undertaking new loans. This would also indicate worries about the prospects for the economy.

In practice, financial market participants do not usually react to consumer credit data. It is "expected news," by the time it is reported, having followed all the other consumer indicators. Other economic indicators would have already revealed whether the economy was in an expansionary or contractionary phase during the month. Also, the indicator is usually reported late in the afternoon and generally goes unnoticed by market participants (*see* Box 7.6).

Box 7.6: Market reaction to an unexpected change in consumer installment credit

Degree of market sensitivity:
High
Medium
Low   ✓

Consumer installment credit	↑	↓
Bond market	↓	↑
Equity market	↓	↑
US dollar	↑	↓

CHAPTER 8

Investment spending, government spending and foreign trade

- Introduction
- Residential fixed investment – housing starts and permits
- Residential fixed investment – construction spending
- Residential fixed investment – new home sales
- Non-residential fixed investment – advance durable goods orders: manufacturers' shipments, inventories and orders release
- Non-residential fixed investment – construction spending
- Inventory investment – manufacturing inventories, business inventories and sales
- Government spending
- Budget deficits and financial markets
- Foreign trade – net exports, trade and current accounts

INTRODUCTION

Investment spending refers to the creation of capital: the purchase or putting into place buildings, equipment, roads, houses and the like. Sound investment in capital results in future benefits that are more valuable than the present cost. Capital is also able to generate future benefits in excess of cost by increasing the productivity of labor. A person who has to dig a hole can dig a bigger hole with an excavator than with a shovel. A computer can do in several seconds what it took bookkeepers hours to do only a few years ago. This increase in productivity makes it less costly to produce products.

While many factors influence business peoples desire to invest, the state of business confidence, which in turn depends on expectations about the future, is very important. While difficult to measure it does seem obvious that businesses will build more factories and purchase more machines when their expectations are optimistic. Conversely, their investment plans will be very cautious if the economic outlook appears bleak.

High levels of sales relative to current capacity and expectations of rapid economic growth create an atmosphere favorable to investment. On the other hand, low levels of sales and slow anticipated growth are likely to discourage investment. Economists discuss this relationship with a concept known as the output gap, which relates the level of actual output in the economy to its potential level. Potential output or GDP is the total amount of goods and services which could be produced if the economy operated at full capacity. This capacity depends on the resources available: the total quantity of labor and capital – in other words, the factors of production.

The amount that businesses will want to invest will also be affected by the real interest rate they have to pay on their borrowings. The lower the real interest rate the more investment spending there will be, and vice versa.

There are fewer indicators of investment spending than there are of consumer spending because investment spending accounts for only about one-fifth of gross domestic product. Despite its smaller contribution to GDP, investment spending is significant because the volatility inherent in investment spending exacerbates the business cycle. Growth in investment expenditure outpaces GDP growth during a cyclical upswing but also declines more sharply during recessions. In general, most of the investment indicators discussed below are not followed as intimately as the consumer indicators.

It is useful to break down investment spending into the major components, these being residential fixed investment, non-residential fixed investment and inventory investment, and then to examine the individual subcomponents. The format we will follow is outlined in Figure 8.1.

The importance of investment spending to the economy can be also seen by examining some of the categories of spending in Figure 8.2.

In theoretical discussions, it is common to lump all the components of investment together, which is very misleading because the investment components of GNP consist of several distinct categories which vary considerably over the business cycle.

Whereas all three investment categories – residential fixed investment, non-residential fixed investment (often called business fixed investment), and changes in business inventories – are substantially more volatile than the remaining GNP components, their individual behavior can vary widely. They differ with respect to both the magnitude of changes and the timing of changes over a business cycle.

In recent recessions, the dollar decline in real investment expenditure was larger than the total decline in real GNP. Furthermore, a large portion of the total decline in investment was owing to the swing in inventory accumulation from positive values at the start of the recession to large negative values at the end of the recession. It is clear that investment is the most volatile part of GNP. Even though it represents less than one-fifth of total GNP it is responsible for much of the cyclical change that takes place.

There are also important differences in cyclical timing among the investment components. In particular, the specific cycle in housing leads both the peaks and troughs of the business cycle, often by several quarters. That is, residential investment expenditures begin to decline well before the onset of a recession and begin to increase before the recovery begins. Non-residential fixed investment, on the other hand, tends to coincide with or lag the turning points. The large differences in the amplitude and timing of cyclical changes among the investment categories are the reason why they should be examined separately when analyzing their impact on financial markets.

RESIDENTIAL FIXED INVESTMENT – HOUSING STARTS AND PERMITS

Definition

The level of activity in the US housing market is measured monthly at each stage of construction; the number of permits issued authorizing a new house to be built; the number of houses actually started; the number of houses completed; and the number of houses sold. For the purposes of these statistics, a house includes single family homes, town houses and apartments.

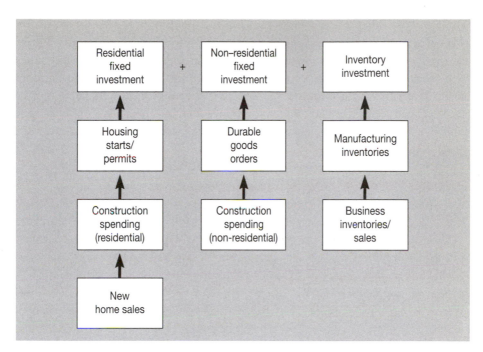

Fig 8.1 ● Investment spending

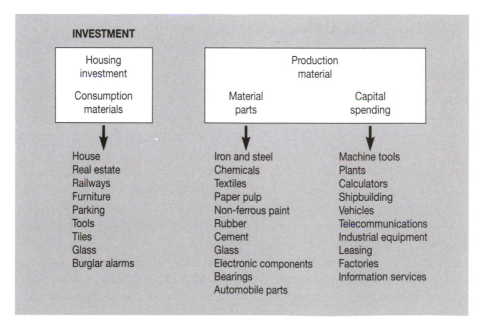

Fig 8.2 ● Investment spending categories

The Bureau of the Census equates the granting of a building permit with authorizations to build. A housing unit is considered started when excavation begins for the footings or foundations. Very approximately, there is a one-month delay between gaining a building permit and starting work on single-home developments, one-and-a-half-months for two to four-unit developments and two months for developments of 5 units or more. (It then takes another six to nine months to complete the housing – the bigger the development, the longer the completion time.)

The housing data are based on a set of monthly surveys, as outlined below.

Number of permits. For permit issuing areas (which cover 95 percent of US land space) a postal survey of approximately half the 17,000 permit issuing offices establishes the number of new permits issued each month.

Number of housing starts in permit issuing areas. For 840 of the permit issuing offices, monthly on-site visits are made to establish how soon after the permit was issued construction actually started. This gives the crude number of housing starts.

Housing starts in non-permit-issuing areas. Because 5 percent of the US is not covered by permit issuing offices, a separate survey is made of this area. Approximately 130 representative areas are scanned each month by the Bureau of the Census field representatives for signs of housing starts.

Who publishes them and when?

The Bureau of the Census, within the Department of Commerce, reports housing starts and permits about two to three weeks after the end of the month.

How do you interpret them?

Housing construction plays a critical role in the economy. Increases in housing starts raise construction employment, and recent homebuyers often purchase other consumer durables leading, through a multiplier effect, to increased employment. Construction is especially important for the business cycle, because changes in residential construction tend to lead recessions and recoveries. In addition, the supply of new housing is a determinant of movements in house prices, which affect both housing affordability and the wealth position of homeowners.

The numbers are expressed at an annual rate and the financial markets concentrate on the number of monthly housing starts.

It is useful to focus on the seasonally adjusted figures for housing starts and new permits. Completions and sales are interesting, but the value of the housing statistics lies in their forward-looking nature. Starts and permits are statistics that say something about what construction companies think of future prospects and, thus, their likely demand for other products.

Concentrate on permits and starts for single family units as the total figures include apartments, which tend to be more volatile.

Seasonal adjustment is a nightmare. It is for this reason that some economists prefer to use new permits issued rather than housing starts as the basis for analyzing prospects for the housing sector. Application for authorization to build a new house is far less likely to be postponed due to unseasonable weather than is the start of construction.

The Bureau of the Census warns that monthly changes in seasonally adjusted housing permits and starts can show irregular movements and says that it may take three months to establish a change in trend.

Building permits is a pointer to *housing starts*, which is a pointer to *completions* and, ultimately, *sales*. There is no pointer to *building permits*, which is regarded as a forward indicator for the US economy. *Building permits* are included in the leading, coincident and lagging indicators of US economic activity.

What is their impact on financial markets?

Participants in the fixed-income market view a rise in housing starts unfavorably because it signifies strong economic growth. They will sell bonds which force down bond prices and cause yields to rise. When housing starts decline, bond and money market traders will view this favorably, pushing up prices, and causing bond yields to fall.

In contrast, an increase in housing starts will be good news for equity markets. A healthy economy provides potentially robust corporate earnings. Although rising interest rates are unfavorable for bond market professionals, they are a positive factor for the foreign exchange markets because they increase the likelihood of interest rates rising and thus the potential value of the dollar. A drop in housing starts has negative implications for stock prices and for the dollar because it signals weak domestic growth.

Financial market reaction to housing starts data is not as strong as the reaction to some other figures, but it can move the markets when the changes are significant and in line with market psychology. As already mentioned housing starts typically lead the economy out of recession, so they are closely monitored at turning points of the business cycle. They are particularly watched at the early stages of recovery, when market participants assess the magnitude of strength of the recovery; and at expansion peaks, when market participants anticipate declines in housing activity. In the middle of an expansion or recession, housing starts are virtually ignored (*see* Box 8.1).

Box 8.1: Market reaction to an unexpected change in housing starts and permits

Degree of market sensitivity:
High
Medium ✓
Low

Housing starts and permits	↑	↓
Bond market	↓	↑
Equity market	↑	↓
US dollar	↑	↓

RESIDENTIAL FIXED INVESTMENT – CONSTRUCTION SPENDING

Definition

The definition includes residential buildings and new housing. New housing is broken down into single units and new units.

Who publishes it and when?

This is included in all construction expenditures and it is published by the Bureau of Census about five weeks after the end of the month.

How do you interpret it?

Residential construction provides information about the residential component of investment. Together with non-residential construction and state and local government spending on construction they account for 20 percent of GNP, a number too large to be ignored. Residential spending accounts for around 5 percent of GNP.

Construction industries, together with automobiles, are typically the first two sectors to go into recession when the bad times arrive and the first two sectors to recover when conditions improve. Analysts track home and automobile sales for hints about when these changes are beginning to occur, and they revise their forecasts accordingly. However other indicators report the same information as to where the economy is in the business cycle in a more timely fashion. Housing starts, for instance, come out roughly three weeks earlier.

The residential outlay figure is used to forecast residential investment in GDP by the BEA.

What is its impact on financial markets?

Unfortunately there are two problems with the monthly report on construction spending. This includes residential construction spending as well as other construction spending. First, it is not very timely. It is released on the first business day of the month for two months prior. That makes it one of the *last* pieces of information we receive about the state of the economy for any given month. Since we have already seen at least 14 reports on various sectors of the economy, we basically know what has happened during that month. The incremental value of the 15th report is quite small.

Second, the report tends to be quite volatile and revisions can be sizable. With any of these volatile reports, economists are forced to work with year-over-year statistics, or three-month moving averages, in order to detect changes in trends. Thus, it takes three or four months before one can conclude that a trend rate of growth has been broken (*see* Box 8.2).

Box 8.2: Market reaction to an unexpected change in construction spending

Degree of market sensitivity:
High
Medium
Low   ✓

Construction spending	↑	↓
Bond market	↓	↑
Equity market	↓	↑
US dollar	↑	↓

RESIDENTIAL FIXED INVESTMENT – NEW HOME SALES

Definition

Sales of new and existing single family houses are another indicator of housing demand. Figures are issued on the number of houses sold, homes for sale, and the month's supply of unsold homes.

Who publishes them and when?

The statistics on sales of new and existing single family homes are reported about four to five weeks after the end of the month, although new and existing home sales are not reported on the same day. New single-family home sales are published by the Bureau of the Census; existing single-family home sales are compiled by the National Association of Realtors. Both new and existing home sales are reported on a seasonally adjusted basis at an annualized rate.

How do you interpret them?

New home sales are an important indicator of the degree of strength of the housing market. As discussed earlier, large changes in consumer spending first appear in housing and automobiles.

The problem with the home sales data is that they tend to be quite volatile. This obviously limits the data's usefulness. As with construction spending it is usually best to look at a three month moving average when trying to interpret changes in the growth rate trend of this series.

For the most part, sales of new and existing homes move together. Home sales, like housing starts, tend to be more meaningful during turning points of the economy. For example, new home sales will recover before other economic sectors when interest rates are low and near the trough of the business cycle.

It is important to check for unexpectedly large changes. New home sales tend to follow the same seasonal pattern as housing starts. As a result, unusually warm weather during winter months can cause a temporary spurt in home sales, especially in the Midwest or Northeast. Similarly, unusually rainy seasons in the spring or summer months can hold down home sales temporarily. In addition, it can be useful to put the home sales data together with the housing starts figures as well as the current level of mortgage rates to gain a feel for turning points.

What is their impact on financial markets?

Since they are so volatile, new home sales are difficult to predict. Volatility always adds the potential for surprise; the unexpected news referred to in Chapter 1. When surprises occur, the home sales data may have a moderate impact on the fixed-income markets. However traders and sales people are aware of the volatility and tend to view these data cautiously.

Nevertheless, if home sales rise unexpectedly and market participants conclude that this is the beginning of a new trend, the participants react adversely and push interest rates higher. An unanticipated decline prompts the opposite response.

The stock market and the foreign exchange market do not appear to attach a great deal of importance to this report and, as a result, it is rare to find a reaction in either market, but if there is one it will be in line with Box 8.3.

Box 8.3: Market reaction to an unexpected change in new home sales

Degree of market sensitivity:
High
Medium
Low   ✓

New home sales	↑	↓
Bond market	↓	↑
Equity market	↑	↓
US dollar	↑	↓

NON-RESIDENTIAL FIXED INVESTMENT – ADVANCE DURABLE GOODS ORDERS: MANUFACTURERS' SHIPMENTS, INVENTORIES AND ORDERS RELEASE

Definition

Durable goods are goods designed to last for three years or more. The report when published is referred to as "advance" because it is an early release of the manufacturers' shipments, inventories and orders. New orders are leading indicators of production three to six months in the future. Shipments, which are the same as sales, are indicators of current production and sales of manufactured goods. Shipments tend to be more stable than orders. Companies can order multiple products, but producers make them one at a time. Remember these are substantial items, not easily made using conveyor belt production systems. Inventories, often referred to as *unfilled orders*, are also part of this report.

The durable goods report is divided into broad categories such as defence and non-defence capital goods, including such diverse items as blast furnaces and computers. They are an indicator of capital spending. Non capital goods are generally of the household variety, such as automobiles, refrigerators, and other appliances.

Who publishes it and when?

The Bureau of Census, within the Department of Commerce, produces an advance report of manufacturers' shipments, new orders, and unfilled orders of durable goods about three weeks after the end of the month.

About one week after the advance (and partial) report on durable goods, the

Census Bureau releases the entire report on manufacturers' goods. The monthly survey of manufacturers has a response rate of roughly 55 percent. This complete report includes figures on non-durable goods as well as durable goods. Non-durable goods, which make up roughly half the total, tend not to be as unstable as durable goods. New orders and unfilled orders of detailed non-durable goods are not officially published.

The data on durable goods orders, shipments, and the order backlog are compiled by the Census Bureau of the Department of Commerce from a monthly survey of approximately 5,000 manufacturers. These sample data are used to estimate a universe of some 70,000 establishments. Thus, the Census Bureau is sampling less than 10 percent of the existing manufacturing firms.

The reported data are supposed to represent firm orders for immediate or future delivery. These orders must be legally binding – supported by a signed contract, a letter of intent, or some similar document. Options to place additional orders at some future date are *not* included.

The shipments data represent the sum total of sales for that month whether for domestic use or export.

How do you interpret them?

Durable goods orders have the potential to provide market participants with hard information. Orders are generally believed to be a front runner for activity in the manufacturing sector because a manufacturer must have an order before contemplating an increase in production. Conversely, a drop-off in orders eventually causes production to be scaled back; otherwise the manufacturer accumulates inventories which must be financed.

Unfortunately the orders report has two major drawbacks. The first problem with the orders data is that they are extremely volatile. This is because they include civilian aircraft and defence orders. Include an aircraft carrier or two in one month's figures and they will dwarf the other components.

The second problem with the orders data is that they are notable for sizable revisions once more data becomes available one week later. The revised data, as discussed above, are contained in the report on manufacturing orders, shipments and inventories.

To interpret durable goods data it is essential to:

● exclude defence orders
● exclude transportation orders
● calculate a three-month moving average
● calculate a year to year percentage change.

What is their impact on financial markets?

Fixed-income market participants will consider a rise in orders and shipments indicative of economic strength; a decline in durable orders and shipments signals weakness. As a result, strong orders and shipments lead to rising interest rates, whereas weak orders and shipments signal lower interest rates. Shipments are much less relevant to the markets than orders, however, because shipments represent present conditions and orders represent future conditions. The financial markets continuously try to anticipate the future.

Equity markets, along with foreign exchange markets, prefer economic strength over weakness and would favor strong durable orders over declines in the series. The stock market looks for growth in corporate profits, whereas the foreign exchange market looks to push up the value of the dollar based on rising interest rates. A decline in orders could lower the value of the dollar if interest rates fall.

Economic growth is unfavorable to fixed-income market professionals because it either signals inflationary pressures (during economic expansions) or the end of Federal Reserve easing (during recoveries). Neither foreign exchange or equity market participants want to see economic growth accompanied by inflation. But, foreign exchange participants tend to prefer high interest rates, so they would be relieved to see the end of a period of Federal Reserve easing (*see* Box 8.4).

Box 8.4: Market reaction to an unexpected change in durable goods orders

Degree of market sensitivity:
High
Medium ✓
Low

Durable goods orders	↑	↓
Bond market	↓	↑
Equity market	↑	↓
US dollar	↑	↓

NON-RESIDENTIAL FIXED INVESTMENT – CONSTRUCTION SPENDING

Definition

Non-residential construction spending includes spending on buildings, industrial, offices, hotels/motels, religious, educational buildings and hospitals.

Who publishes it and when?

It is published at the same time as residential construction spending.

How do you interpret it?

The statistics are incorporated directly into GDP by the Bureau of Economic Analysis. If you follow the pattern you can develop a feel for GDP revisions.

What is its impact on financial markets?

As with residential construction spending these statistics contain little new information on the state of the economy and are largely ignored.

INVENTORY INVESTMENT – MANUFACTURING INVENTORIES, BUSINESS INVENTORIES AND SALES

Definition

Total business inventories can be broken down into:

- manufacturing inventions
- wholesale inventories
- retail inventories.

In addition to a more complete and detailed report of shipments, new orders, and unfilled orders, the manufacturers' release on factory orders also includes data on manufacturing inventories.

Who publishes them and when?

Data on manufacturing inventories is published as part of the factory orders report, by the Bureau of the Census of the Department of Commerce. It is published in the first week of the month and refers to the two months prior.

How do you interpret them?

Inventories are stocks of goods on hand which may be raw materials, goods in process or finished products. They are generally thought of as being a necessary evil, providing a cushion against unexpected orders. Businesses are anxious to keep inventories at low levels in order to minimize the funds tied up in working capital. Their role tends to aggravate both the upswing and the downswing of the business cycle. It is essential to follow both the business upswing and the downswing.

Business upswing

If demand rises businesses must increase production. If this is not done speedily enough sales grow quicker than production and this results in an unplanned draw down of inventories. This is known as involuntary inventory depletion. If a business has too few inventories sales could be jeopardized. Consequently an expected rise in demand means businesses will increase output, increase capacity utilization, productivity decreases unit labor costs rise and this forces up the rate of inflation. Consequently, inventory accumulation adds to the inflationary cycle, aggravating the upswing.

Business downswing

As sales weaken, inventories build up and businesses will cut back production. This will then provoke attempts to liquidate inventories by price cutting in an attempt to reduce money tied up in working capital. As goods are sold from inventories, production and employment are reduced by more than sales since orders can be filled from inventories rather than current production. Consequently, inventory liquidation aggravates the downswing.

Desired versus undesired inventories

As mentioned earlier, inventories are a necessary evil. If these are produced in order to face an expected increase in demand then this is a signal that economic growth is happening and that prices are rising with the possibility that interest rates may be rising. Similarly, an expected drop in sales and a consequent reduction in inventories will be a natural forerunner to falling prices and a reduction in interest rates. Consequently, falls in desired inventories suggest interest rate falls. Rises in desired inventories indicate pressures for interest rate rises.

In order to know whether inventories are desired or not it is essential to compare them with sales. If the ratio of inventories to sales rises then there are pressures for interest rates to fall, and vice versa. *See* Figure 8.3.

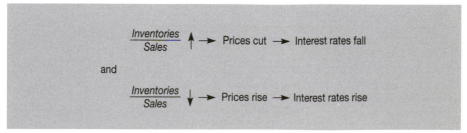

Fig 8.3 ● Inventories and sales

Manufacturing inventories represent about half of total business inventories. To this manufacturing inventory figure it is necessary to add inventories at the wholesale and retail levels to obtain overall business inventories, available about two weeks later.

What is their impact on financial markets?

The report on business inventories and sales comes out on the back of several previously published reports. The durable goods data (which contains information on the sales of durable goods by manufacturers), the report on factory orders, shipments and inventories, the retail sales report, and the wholesale inventories and sales data have all been published.

Given that so much of this inventory and sales information is published throughout the month, by the time business inventories/sales information is published most of the information is already "expected" news. Consequently it has a very limited effect on the financial markets.

However at business cycle turning points, the markets will react to business inventories. Undesired inventory accumulation during a sluggish economic period suggests producers will have to unload unwanted inventories and production will suffer. Declines in production are favorable news for the bond market participants because they indicate possible recession and lower interest rates. See Figure 8.3. Production declines are not favorable news to stock market participants nor to foreign exchange players looking for a strong dollar. A weak economy means lacklustre earnings. Low interest rates indicate capital flows to the US will be reduced and a drop in demand for the dollar will ensue.

Desired inventory liquidation suggests future rebuilding of inventories and increases in production. Bond market participants will anticipate yields rising. In contrast, stock market players will view the potential rise in production favorably as corporate earnings move upward. Similarly, foreign exchange participants would anticipate economic growth and a rise in the dollar (see Box 8.5).

Box 8.5: Market reaction to an unexpected change in business inventories/sales

Degree of market sensitivity:
High
Medium
Low   ✓

Business inventories/sales	↑	↓
Bond market	↓	↑
Equity market	↓	↑
US dollar	↑	↓

GOVERNMENT SPENDING

In January of each year, the President of the US sends his budget message to Congress. For over a decade now the event has set off an annual debate over how best to reduce the budget deficit, the amount by which the government expenditures exceed its receipts during a specified period of time, usually one year. These debates have been acrimonious, time consuming, and highly political. But they also have an important economic aspect, for the two sides are arguing over the government's fiscal policy, i.e., the overall balance of government spending and taxation.

Government purchases of goods and services (G) are a direct component of total spending. As we discussed in Chapter 5, they are to be added to Investment (I), Consumption (C) and Net Exports (X – IM) if we are to foresee the likely trend in GNP.

The interpretation of budget deficits and surpluses can be ambiguous. Since a falling GNP means higher expenditures and lower tax receipts: the deficit rises in a recession and falls in a boom, even with no change in fiscal policy.

Figure 8.4 depicts the relationship between GNP and the budget deficit. The government's fiscal program is summarized by the two black lines. The horizontal line labeled G indicates that federal purchases of goods and services are approximately unaffected by GNP. The rising line labeled "Taxes minus Transfers" indicates that taxes rise and transfer payments fall as GNP rises. Notice that the *same* fiscal policy (that is the same two black lines) can lead to a large deficit if GNP is Y_1, a small deficit if GNP is Y_2, a balanced budget if GNP is Y_3, or even

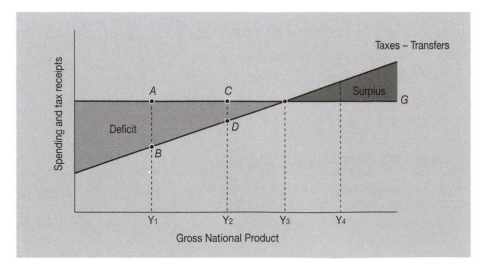

Fig 8.4 ● The effect of the economy on the budget

a surplus if GNP is as high as Y_4. The deficit itself cannot be a good measure of the government's fiscal policy as it clearly depends on what is happening to GNP. For this reason, many economists pay less attention to the *actual* deficit or surplus and more attention to what is called the *structural deficit* or surplus. This is a hypothetical construct that replaces both the spending and taxes in the *actual* budget by estimates of how much the government *would be* spending and receiving, given current tax rates and expenditure rates, if the economy were operating at some fixed high-employment level. For example, if the high-employment benchmark in Figure 8.4 was Y2, while actual GNP was only Y1, the actual deficit would be AB while the structural deficit would be only CD.

Because it is based on the spending and taxing the government would be undertaking at some fixed level of GNP, rather than on actual expenditures and receipts, the structural deficit is insensitive to the state of the economy. It changes only when policy changes. That is why most economists view it as a better measure of the thrust of fiscal policy than the actual deficit.

Active macroeconomic stabilization policy can be carried out either by means that tend to expand the size of government (by raising either G or taxes when appropriate) or by means that hold back the size of government (by reducing either G or taxes when appropriate). Expansionary fiscal policy can cure recessions, but it normally exacts a cost in terms of higher inflation. This dilemma has led to a great deal of interest in "supply-side" tax cuts designed to stimulate the output of the economy, known as aggregate supply.

Supply-side tax cuts aim to push the economy's aggregate supply curve higher. If successful, they can expand the economy and reduce inflation at the same time – a highly desirable outcome. But critics point out five problems of supply-side tax cuts:

- they also stimulate aggregate demand;
- the beneficial effects on aggregate supply may be small;
- the demand-side effects occur before the supply-side effects;
- they make the income distribution more unequal;
- large tax cuts lead to large budget deficits.

How do you interpret the budget deficit?

In interpreting the budget deficit it is essential to distinguish between the structural deficit or surplus and the actual deficit and surplus. The structural deficit is sometimes known as the full employment deficit and the actual deficit as the cyclical deficit.

As discussed earlier, the same fiscal program can lead to a large or small deficit, depending on the state of the economy (e.g. Y_1 versus Y_2 and Y_3). Failure to appreciate this point has led many people to assume that a larger deficit always signifies a more expansionary fiscal policy. But that is not always true.

Think, for example, about what happens to the budget when the economy experiences a recession and GNP falls. The government's most important sources of tax revenue – income taxes, corporate taxes and payroll taxes – all shrink because firms and people pay lower taxes when they earn less. Similarly, some types of government spending, notably transfer payments like unemployment benefits, rise when GNP falls because more people are out of work.

Remember that the deficit is the difference between government expenditures and tax receipts and that it is important to consider all the items.

$$\text{Budget deficit} = \text{Government spending} + \text{Transfers} - \text{Taxes}$$

BUDGET DEFICITS AND FINANCIAL MARKETS

Financial markets distrust budget deficits under most circumstances, as they fear that they are inflationary. The reasoning behind this is that when government policy pushes up aggregate demand, firms may find themselves unwilling or unable to produce the higher quantities that are being demanded at the going prices. Prices will therefore have to rise. Deficit spending will not cause much inflation if the economy has lots of slack. But deficit spending is likely to be highly inflationary in a fully employed economy. Remember that budget deficits involve the government issuing bonds to finance the difference between revenues and taxation, and do not simply involve the government printing dollars.

The monetization issue

Deficit spending normally drives up real GNP and the price level. The increased transactions demand for money associated with rising GNP, discussed in Chapter 4, tends to force up interest rates. Suppose now that the Federal Reserve does not want interest rates to rise. What can it do? To prevent the initial rise in interest rates, it must engage in expansionary monetary policies. Expansionary monetary policies normally take the form of open market purchases of government bonds. So deficit spending might induce the Federal Reserve to increase its purchases of government bonds, that is, to buy up some of the newly issued government debt.

But why is this called monetizing the debt? Open market purchases of bonds by the Federal Reserve initially give banks more reserves, which leads, eventually, to an increase in the money supply. So a monetized deficit results in an increase in the money supply which increases inflationary pressures and forces up real interest rates.

Financial markets, particularly bond markets and currency markets are very wary of inflation, and see budget deficits as sources of this inflation. They worry more about structural deficits which appear permanent, and thus potentially inflationary, but are more happy with cyclical deficits which are likely to be temporary (*see* Box 8.6).

Budget deficits: a historical curiosity?

In November 1995, the US Congress passed the Balanced Budget Act. The bill provided a fiscal package that would, according to Congressional Budget Office projections, balance the federal budget by fiscal year 2002. On 20 November 1995, President Clinton signed into law a Continuing Resolution for fiscal year 1996 that provided short-term financing for most federal government operations. It also heralded an agreement between the President and Congress on the goal of producing a long-term budget plan that would eliminate the federal deficit on the seven-year schedule proposed in the Balanced Budget Act.

On 6 December 1995, the President vetoed the Balanced Budget Act, at the same time proposing the Administration's own seven-year plan. Consistent with the November Continuing Resolution, the President's plan undertook to eliminate the government deficit by 2002.

The arithmetic of Clinton's plan is impressive. As can be seen from Figure 8.5 the budget forecasts are for the fiscal year, which begins in October 1999. In 1992, the year of his election as President, the deficit in the $1.3 trillion budget was $290 billion. In the 1998 fiscal year the $1.7 trillion budget has a predicted budget deficit of $22 billion.

This has largely taken the US budget deficit out of the picture as a factor influencing financial markets, for the first time in 40 years.

Box 8.6: Market reaction to an unexpected change in the budget deficit

Degree of market sensitivity:
High
Medium
Low ✓

Budget deficit	↑	↓
Bond market	↓	↑
Equity market	↑	↓
US dollar	↑	↓

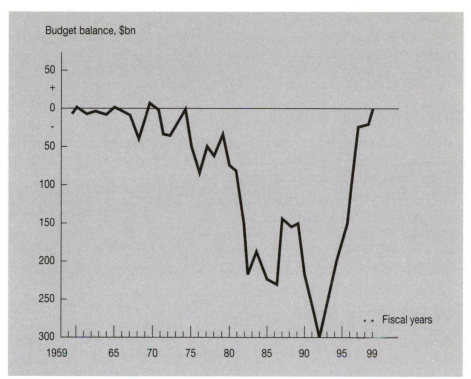

Fig 8.5 ● US budget 1959–99

* Forecast
Sources: Congressional Budget Office; Department of Commerce; OMB

FOREIGN TRADE – NET EXPORTS, TRADE AND CURRENT ACCOUNTS

Definition

The *balance of payments* is the collective term for the accounts of US transactions with the rest of the world.

Merchandise trade

This is the raw balance on trade in visible goods, published monthly. The financial markets focus on the seasonally adjusted monthly trade data on an f.a.s./c.i.f. basis (see *How do you interpret them?* below).

Current account

This is the balance of trade plus services (passenger and freight transportation, insurance, telecommunications, construction, engineering and income from royalties, patents, etc.) plus defence transactions (transfers under foreign military sales programs, defence purchases) plus remittances and government grants.

Statistical discrepancy

This is the difference between total credits (exports of goods and services, unilateral transfers to the US, and capital inflows) and total debits (imports of goods and services, unilateral transfers overseas, and capital outflows) in the balance of payments.

Who publishes them and when?

There are two sources for US trade data. The bureau of the Census in the Department of Commerce provides monthly trade figures about 45 days after the month to which they refer.

The Bureau of Economic Analysis (BEA) provides monthly figures about 55 days after the relevant month. There are revisions to the Census figures to take account of "balance of payments" measurement conventions.

The BEA publishes quarterly current account figures including services and capital account estimates approximately 75 days after the quarter to which they refer.

How do you interpret them?

Focus on the seasonally adjusted trade numbers. A single month's trade figures are not regarded as a reliable guide to the underlying trend, so take a three-month moving average at the very least. If the three-monthly comparison suggests a change of trend, check to see whether the six- and nine-monthly averages fit in with that picture.

Once evidence of a change in trend has been established, find out whether it is import- or export-driven by looking at the way total imports and total exports have moved. Look for corroborative evidence from other economic releases. If imports are depressed, does this tally with readings of domestic demand from retail sales? If exports are booming, how does that fit in with the data on factory orders, or industrial production?

When the price of oil has been moving sharply, look at the trade balance minus oil for an underlying picture of trade trends since this is regarded as a better guide to competitiveness.

Occasionally, other categories are excluded (airplanes when there is a bunching of export deliveries, non-monetary gold when the Japanese were importing a large volume in 1988 for a medal struck in honour of Emperor Hirohito), the reason being to identify lasting trends and to refrain from extrapolating on non-recurring events. However, the full deficit does have to be financed and most economists say such exclusions should be used with care and to focus on special issues only.

Factory orders include *goods shipments* which, given some assumptions about the strength of domestic demand, can offer clues on export performance.

The *National Association of Purchasing Management's* (NAPM) *export orders index* points to the trend in exports. However, as discussed in Appendix 3.1 this is a "diffusion index" based on the percentage of respondents reporting higher/lower/unchanged export orders and, as such, gives no quantitative guide.

What is their impact on financial markets?

The impact of the trade deficit on financial markets has been subject to violent changes of fashion. Currently its impact is less significant than it was in the 1970s and 1980s.

A decline in the trade deficit is usually good news for the US dollar, as one must buy dollars to purchase US exports and sell dollars to buy imports. However generally speaking if the dollar has been trading within a well-defined range, the monthly trade figures tend to be ignored beyond a few hours. Conversely if the dollar has just broken out of its recent trading range, data on trade flows have a greater impact.

The case for bond investors is a little subtler. Suppose the trade deficit comes in less than expected. Bond investors are torn between two factors. First, a smaller deficit triggers a dollar rally – good news for bond market participants. But, if the trade deficit is shrinking, it simultaneously adds to GNP growth. A faster pace of economic activity is negative for bonds. What should an investor do? It is not always clear – the market reaction seems to be determined by the mood of the moment.

The stock market response depends on whether the trade deficit is deemed a "problem" at the time. Currently it is not and the stock market would, in most circumstances, ignore the trade numbers (*see* Box 8.7).

Box 8.7: Market reaction to an unexpected change in the trade deficit

Degree of market sensitivity:
High
Medium
Low   ✓

Trade deficit	↑	↓
Bond market	↓	↑
Equity market	↓	↑
US dollar	↑	↓

CHAPTER 9

The effect of consumer confidence and consumer sentiment on financial markets

- Introduction
- National Association of Purchasing Managers Index (NAPM)
- Business Outlook Survey of the Philadelphia Federal Reserve
- Help-Wanted Advertising Index
- Sindlinger Household Liquidity Index

INTRODUCTION

As well as relying on "hard" economic data financial market analysts also pay a great deal of attention to non-economic factors such as consumer attitudes towards spending. While such data is, by its nature, more qualitative rather than quantitative it is no less important in providing valuable information as to the future behavior of the economy. Household sentiment which turned adverse in early 1990 has frequently been cited as a major cause of the 1990/91 recession. Attitudes, expectations and sentiment are terms that are frequently used when people refer to the psychological mood of consumers. These are distinct concepts. Attitudes reflect the feelings that consumers have about current conditions, and expectations are attitudes which have been projected to some point in the future. Both attitudes and expectations are subsumed into the larger category called consumer sentiment or consumer confidence.

Intuitively, it is clear that confidence or sentiment is an important causal factor in any one person's spending. If, for example, people feel that the government is mismanaging the economy and that this will lead to a recession and possibly cause them to be laid off, they will be less likely to purchase a new auto than if they are optimistic about the future.

Definition

Two organizations provide indicators of US consumer attitudes. They focus on consumer perceptions of general business conditions and of their personal financial well being, plus their attitudes toward purchasing big-ticket items, purchases that last a relatively long time – homes, autos, furniture and major household appliances.

Who publishes them and when?

These attitude indicators are the *Consumer Sentiment Index* of the University of Michigan and the *Consumer Confidence Index* of the Conference Board. Both indexes measure similar phenomena but, because the methodologies differ and the concepts are not identical, there are periods when their movements differ.

Michigan Index of Consumer Sentiments (ICS)

Each month, the University of Michigan conducts a representative cross-section sampling of 700 respondent households by telephone. In general, the sampling for a given month takes about four weeks. The interviewers are paid employees who ask the five questions which comprise the index along with other questions which are designed for the business clients who pay for the survey. While these other questions (which could, for example, ask about the respondent's attitude toward a tax cut) do vary; the five questions comprising the ICS never change and these are listed below.

Index of consumer sentiment questions

1. We are interested in how people are getting along financially these days. Would you say that you and your family are better off or worse off financially than you were a year ago?

2. Now – looking ahead – do you think that a year from now you people will be financially better off or worse off or just about the same as now?

3. Now turning to business conditions in the country as a whole – do you think that during the next 12 months we'll have good times financially or bad times or what?

4. Looking ahead, which you would say is more likely – that in the country as a whole, we'll have continuous good times during the next five years or so, or that we will have periods of widespread unemployment or depression, or what?

5. About the big things people buy for their homes – such as furniture, house furnishings, refrigerator, stove, television, and things like that – for people in general – do you think that now is a good or bad time to buy major household items?

Questions 1 and 5 highlight attitudes, while questions 2, 3 and 4 emphasize expectations. Although question 4 asks about the next five years, the time horizon in the other questions in general is 12 months. The survey also asks whether this is a "good" or a "bad" time to make a purchase. It does *not* query about the actual intention to buy. Each question is equally weighted in the ICS. All positive replies are given a weight of 2, a neutral response receives a 1 and a negative reply, 0. Therefore, if all respondents in the survey sample gave positive responses to all questions, the ICS would have a value of 200. Alternatively, the index level can be calculated by subtracting the number of negative responses from the number of positive and adding the constant 100.

The Index of Consumer sentiment is recognized by the National Bureau of Economic Research and is included as one of the components of the Index of Leading Economic Indicators, discussed in Chapter 6.

Conference Board Consumer Confidence Index

The Conference Board survey is ten times larger than the University of Michigan's Survey covering a representative sample of 5,000 households. The survey is conducted by NFO Research, Inc., of Connecticut, which mails a questionnaire to an entirely different sample of individuals each month, representing all geographic regions, age groups and income levels.

The consumer confidence index is calculated from the responses to the questions posed below. These questions are divided into two categories: the *present situation* (questions 1 and 2) and *consumer expectations* (remaining questions). The survey questionnaire also asks about actual intentions to purchase a home, auto, and other durable goods. These data are used to calculate a buying plans index.

Consumer confidence index questions

1. How would you rate the present general business conditions in your area:
   ☐ Good?   ☐ Normal?   ☐ Bad?

   a. SIX MONTHS from now, do you think they will be:
   ☐ Better?   ☐ Same?   ☐ Worse?

2. What would you say about available jobs in your area right now?
   ☐ Plenty   ☐ Not so many   ☐ Hard to get

   a. SIX MONTHS from now do you think there will be:
   ☐ More?   ☐ Same?   ☐ Fewer?

3. How would you guess your total family income to be SIX MONTHS from now?
   ☐ Higher   ☐ Same   ☐ Lower

For each question, the respondent is given a choice of three reply options. To compute the CCI, neutral responses are discarded, while the positive and negative replies are added together. The positive responses are then expressed as a percentage of this total for each question. Each series, or question, is then adjusted for seasonal variation.

The logic of asking consumers whether they will buy durable goods is that these are infrequent purchases and presumably would not be made unless consumers were reasonably confident about their economic prospects.

How do you interpret them?

Consumer spending and consumer confidence indices rarely move in tandem. It is essential to look at the trend in the index rather than a one-month picture.

Moreover, both the Index of Consumer Sentiment (Michigan Survey) as well as the Consumer Confidence Index (Conference Board) tend to move in similar directions over time but may diverge in any one month. The Conference Board series tends to increase more rapidly at business cycle peaks when employment prospects improve. Also, the Conference Board surveys an entirely different group of individuals each month. The consistency would not be the same as in the Michigan Survey, which talks to the same group each month.

While both indices measure consumer confidence, it is important to understand the respective methodologies in order to interpret them properly. The most basic issue is how to interpret level versus change. On the Conference Board Index, it is useful to examine the *present* and *expectations* components separately – the former as a proxy for economic activity, the latter as a proxy for growth. On the Michigan Index, this distinction is less clear, as both components mix level and growth measures. One must also be careful in comparing moves in the Michigan Index and Conference Board indices. Due to differences in methodology and base years, monthly changes should not be compared in absolute terms but rather on a standardized basis (adjusting for range of movement) – a 1-point change in the Michigan Index is roughly comparable to a 2-point change in that of the Conference Board. There is no basis at all for comparing index levels.

One advantage of the Michigan Index is its earlier availability. However one should bear in mind that the Michigan Index's preliminary figures, as against its final figures, are based on a much smaller sample size (about 250) than the Conference Board Index (about 2,500), and are thus subject to somewhat greater measurement error. Finally, because the two questionnaires focus on different issues, the indices sometimes give mixed signals. During such periods, having both indices is particularly useful, because their contrasting signals may offer some insight on how various segments of the economy are performing.

What is their impact on financial markets?

Consumer confidence is a coincident indicator of the economy. Typically, consumers feel confident about the economy during an expansion and pessimistic about the economy during a recession.

The consumer confidence series were very fashionable in the financial markets in 1990 and 1991. Most likely, this was because the Federal Reserve Chairman cited them once or twice as indicators that he monitors. When a Federal Reserve chairman talks, market participants listen.

In the past few years, the markets have also reacted strongly to consumer confidence surveys. The reaction is similar to that of actual consumer spending. Bond traders would anticipate a drop in consumer confidence signaling a weaker economy and thereby pointing to lower bond yields (but higher bond prices). Conversely, the bond prices will drop (and yields will rise) if consumer confidence increases.

Participants in the stock market do not favor a drop in consumer confidence because that means lower corporate profits. Lower corporate earnings should lead to a dip in the stock market.

Economic pessimism signals a weak economy and low interest rates, leading to a drop in the value of the dollar. An optimistic consumer is favorable to the prospects for the dollar in that interest rates will rise and the demand for dollars will rise, pushing up the value of the dollar (*see* Box 9.1).

Box 9.1: Market reaction to an unexpected change in Michigan Index of Consumer Sentiments/Conference Board Consumer Confidence Index

Degree of market sensitivity:
High
Medium ✓
Low

ICS and CCI	↑	↓
Bond market	↓	↑
Equity market	↑	↓
US dollar	↑	↓

NATIONAL ASSOCIATION OF PURCHASING MANAGERS INDEX (NAPM)

Definition

The NAPM is a composite index of five series:

- new orders
- production
- supplier deliveries (also known as vendor deliveries or vendor performance, discussed in Chapter 6)
- inventories
- employment.

The NAPM is derived from the *Report on Business*. This is based on data compiled from monthly replies to questions asked of purchasing executives in more than 300 industrial companies.

The purchasing executives are asked eight questions which then make up the Index. Separate seasonally adjusted diffusion indexes (*see* Appendix 3.1) are created for the responses to each question. Five of these indexes, listed above, are weighted together to produce the composite Purchasing Managers Index (PMI).

The indexes and their weights are:

- new orders (30 percent);
- production (25 percent);
- employment (20 percent);
- supplier deliveries (15 percent);
- inventories (10 percent).

The *Report on Business* survey is designed to measure the change (i.e., whether there has been an improvement or deterioration), if any, in the current month compared to the previous month for the answers to the eight questions which produce the indexes.

The NAPM derives these figures based on answers to rather straightforward questions. Purchasing managers are asked if their business situation is "better," "same," or "worse" than the previous month. Sometimes, the terms "higher" or "faster" are substituted for "better"; sometimes, "slower" is substituted for "worse." In any case, the questionnaire is not asking for actual levels, just a subjective assessment of the company's business prospects. The results are compiled into a diffusion index.

Diffusion indices, which fluctuate between 0 percent and 100 percent, include the percentage of positive responses plus half of those responding the same (considered positive). They have the properties of leading indicators and are convenient summary measures showing the prevailing direction and scope of change. (*See* Appendix 8.1 for further discussion of diffusion indices.)

The most important indicators, in terms of economic activity, receive most weight. New orders, which tends to be the most leading indicator and drives the others, has greatest weight (30 percent), while inventories, which tends to lag in the economic cycle, has least weight (10 percent).

Membership of the Business Survey Committee, from which the companies surveyed are drawn, is composed of 20 industries in 50 states. The composition of the committee membership is designed to parallel closely each manufacturing industry's contribution to gross domestic product (GDP). The responses from each member, or company, are treated as having equal weight regardless of the size of the company.

Who publishes it and when?

The NAPM is a purchasing, education and research organization in the US with over 35,000 members. The data are reported on the first day of the subsequent month (May figures are reported 1 June), making this the most timely of all monthly indicators – its appearance could predate the employment situation by as much as a week. The figures are available on a seasonally adjusted basis (as well as unadjusted). Unlike most other economic data, these figures are never revised from month to month.

The NAPM family

The NAPM is divided into ten regions, some of which issue their own reports (*see* Table 9.1). There are also cities within the regions which issue separate reports. As the level of disaggregation grows, however, these reports may be a more useful indicator of local conditions (which are reflective of particular industries or the weather) than of the national economy.

Table 9.1 ●

Purchasing Managers' Regions

Arizona
Austin, Texas
Buffalo, New York
Chicago, Illinois
Cleveland, Ohio
Detroit, Michigan
Grand Rapids, Michigan
Toledo, Ohio
Oregon
Rochester, New York

Financial markets do give attention to the Chicago area's *Purchasing Managers Index (Chicago PMI)*. Chicago is considered the industrial heartland and its PMI release also precedes the NAPM index.

How do you interpret it?

The NAPM indexes are different from most other indexes. Instead of setting a base year equal to 100, and measuring growth from there, the NAPM series are set at a trigger rate of 50 percent. According to the NAPM, an index level of 50 percent or more indicates that the economy as well as the manufacturing sector is expanding; an index level less than 50 percent but greater than 45 percent suggests that the manufacturing sector has stopped growing, but the economy is still expanding; a level less than 45 percent signals a recession both in the economy and in the manufacturing sector.

The farther the index is away from 50 percent, the stronger the economy when the index value is more than 50, and the weaker the economy is when the index value is less than 50. A reading of 50, the so-called boom–bust line is consistent with flat manufacturing growth and 2¼ percent GDP growth, about the long run trend GDP growth. So the further the index is away from 50 percent the more evidence is provided for a recession or a boom taking place.

The basis for using the 50 percent level as the point at which the economy is neither expanding nor declining is a function of diffusion indices. Basically, it eliminates the need to use a plus or minus with an index that uses zero as the dividing point between expansions and contraction. The evidence that a reading above 50 percent generally indicates an expanding economy, and below 50 percent a declining one, is based on analysis by the Commerce Department.

The rationale for incorporating the five components in the NAPM is clearly straightforward. *New orders* are a leading indicator of economic activity. Manufacturers' orders lead to increases in production. *Production* reflects the current state of affairs and is a coincident indicator of the economy. As output expands, producers hire additional workers to meet the increased demands. *Employment* is also a coincident indicator. *Inventories* are typically a lagging indicator of economic activity. Inventory build-ups usually continue into a cyclical downturn as manufacturers are not sure whether the decline in demand is temporary or permanent. Inventories may continue to decline early in a recovery as producers unload stocks that were built up during the recession. *Supplier deliveries*, also known as vendor performance, work in much the same way as unfilled orders. When producers slow down their deliveries, it means they are busy and cannot fill all the orders quickly. Slower deliveries mean rapid economic growth. In contrast, faster deliveries suggest a moderating economy. When orders can be filled rapidly, it means producers aren't as busy. Vendor performance, as discussed in Chapter 6, is included in the Commerce Department's Index of Leading Indicators.

It is important to look at the monthly seasonally adjusted NAPM. Use a three-month average of the index to better assess the underlying trend. The NAPM individual indices are closely correlated with comparable official figures in manufacturing activity, a key component of GDP.

The number 45 on this index is important. In the past, whenever the Purchasing Managers Index has dropped below 45, a recession has occurred. (Note that recessions have also occurred without the index falling below the 45 level.) The first oil shock in 1974, for example, precipitated a recession before the index fell below 50. The 1969 recession began before the index actually dropped below 45. However, whenever the index did fall below 45, a recession did unfold. There is one exception: the "growth recession" of 1966/67. After two years of real GDP growth near 6 percent, growth fell to 2.6 percent and the unemployment rate rose. An actual recession, however, never developed, and the Purchasing Manager Index rebounded quickly to the mid-50s range.

Statistical analysis suggests that the rule of thumb based around the reading of 50, mentioned earlier, was justified for the period 1960–89. But the relationship has altered in the so-called "new paradigm" 1990s. The new paradigm was discussed in detail in Chapter 3. For the 1990s the correlation between the trend growth of GDP and the NAPM has become less reliable with GDP surging in several quarters in the 1990s despite NAPM readings below 50 for a majority of the time. Indeed some commentators are now suggesting that the NAPM would now have to drop to 41 to signal recession.

Limitations to the NAPM

There are a number of drawbacks associated with the compilation of the NAPM.

● It is concentrated on the industrial sector because that is the one that changes direction most quickly and is therefore of most interest to economists. The service sector, representing over 50 percent of GDP is thereby excluded.

● The purchasing managers' survey does not use a scientific sample (unlike official surveys). Instead, responses are taken from handpicked, established firms.

● There is no attempt to take into account the growing importance of some industries by increasing the number of firms in that sector. Newer, fast-growing firms are added to the sample only after they have become established in the business, while contracting firms stay in the sample until they fold.

● The sample covers less than 1 percent of the NAPM's membership. The response rate varies from month to month (though the NAPM says it is "exceptionally high") and, compared with the entry and exit of members, firms answering the survey questionnaire can vary between samples.

What is its impact on financial markets?

Financial market participants have anxiously anticipated the NAPM ever since Federal Reserve Chairman, Alan Greenspan, once claimed that he placed great emphasis on this report. As usual, equity and foreign exchange market players look forward to healthy figures, whereas the fixed income professionals prefer weakness. As the NAPM moves in an upward direction, signalling future economic strength, bond market participants will anticipate inflationary pressures or the end of a favorable environment for Federal Reserve easing conditions. Conversely, a declining trend in the NAPM will lead to a bond market rally (*see* Box 9.2).

Box 9.2: Market reaction to an unexpected change in the NAPM

Degree of market sensitivity:
High   ✓
Medium
Low

NAPM	↑	↓
Bond market	↓	↑
Equity market	↑	↓
US dollar	↑	↓

BUSINESS OUTLOOK SURVEY OF THE PHILADELPHIA FEDERAL RESERVE

The Federal Reserve Bank of Philadelphia began to conduct monthly surveys of manufacturers in May 1968 to monitor business conditions in its district. The Business Outlook Survey (BOS) was based on the premise that surveying businesses about recent activity is one of the least costly methods of gathering economic data. Recent activity is available before other indicators reported by the government or private agencies. The trade-off is that most other economic data is quantitative whereas this survey is qualitative. Therefore, it is helpful in indicating "where we are and whither we are tending" in the Philadelphia Federal Reserve region as well as the country.

This survey is limited to manufacturing firms with plants in the area that employ at least 350 workers. It covers durable and non-durable industries. About 100 of the 550 eligible establishments agreed to participate in the monthly survey. Each month, the managers of the plants receive the survey questionnaire in the mail. On average, the response rate is just better than 50 percent each month.

The survey produces a seasonally adjusted diffusion index which represents the percentage of respondents indicating an increase in general business activity minus the percentage indicating a decrease. The survey also compiles data on a broad spectrum of questions meant to parallel the items in the NAPM including orders, shipments, delivery time, inventories, employment, and prices. Since the Philadelphia Survey includes questions about the workweek and capital expenditures, but not production, it cannot be used to duplicate the NAPM precisely. But forecasters do use it to refine their NAPM estimates. For an indicator of its market sensitivity *see* Box 9.3.

Box 9.3: Market reaction to an unexpected change in the Philadelphia Survey

Degree of market sensitivity:
High
Medium ✓
Low

Philadelphia Survey	▲	▼
Bond market	▼	▲
Equity market	▲	▼
US dollar	▲	▼

HELP-WANTED ADVERTISING INDEX

Definition

The help-wanted advertising index tracks employers' advertisements for job openings in the classified section of newspapers in 51 labor market areas. The index represents job vacancies resulting from turnover in existing positions such as workers changing jobs or retiring, and from the creation of new jobs. It excludes non-advertised job vacancies and jobs advertised in non-classified sections. Many analysts believe it provides the most reliable long-term measure of pressures in the labor market.

The help-wanted advertising figures cover jobs in many fields – professional, technical, crafts, office, sales, farm, custodial, etc. They include a higher proportion of all junior and middle level vacancies than managerial, executive, or unskilled levels. In addition to the national help-wanted index, local indexes for 51 labor markets are provided.

The help-wanted advertising figures are obtained from classified advertisements in one daily (including Sunday) newspaper in each of 51 labor markets (51 cities including their suburbs). Newspapers are selected according to how well their advertisements represent jobs in the local labor market area.

The index reflects the number of job advertisements. Each advertisement is weighted equally regardless of whether it is an ad for one job or for multiple positions or whether for full time or part time work. Advertisements of both employers and employment agencies and advertisements for the same job on successive days are included in the count.

Index weights for the 51 labor markets are based on the proportion of non-agricultural employment accounted for by each of the labor markets. These weights are updated every two years. Within each market area, help-wanted advertisements in the Sunday newspaper are weighted according to the ratio of the average Sunday advertising volume to average daily advertising volume.

Who publishes it and when?

Measures of the help-wanted advertising index are provided monthly by the Conference Board. The figures are published in a press release and in the Conference Board's monthly *Statistical Bulletin*. Secondary sources include *Business Conditions Digest*.

The Conference Board publishes the Index of Help Wanted Advertising Index about four weeks after the end of the month.

How do you interpret it?

The help-wanted advertising index indicates the direction of employers' hiring plans. In theory, it provides an advance signal of future changes in employment and cyclical turning points. In practice, the help-wanted index leads the downturn from the expansion peak to a recession, but it lags the turning point in moving from recession to expansion, based on analyses conducted as part of the leading, coincident and lagging indexes. The lag in timing as the economy is in recovery from a recession results from the tendency of employers to increase average weekly hours of existing workers when business improves or call back workers on layoff before advertising for new workers. Consequently it lags average weekly hours worked as an indicator of the economy moving from recession to expansion.

The help-wanted index is inversely related to unemployment. When help-wanted advertisements increase, unemployment declines, while a decline in help-wanted advertisements is accompanied by a rise in unemployment. The help-wanted movements sometimes are sharper than the unemployment movements because of changing advertising practices. For example, during periods of low unemployment, employers may rely more heavily on help-wanted advertisements than on alternative means of finding workers. During high unemployment, employers may find workers easily through alternative means such as through workers initiating the contact on their own or on the advice of friends.

Some advertised jobs may not be filled, because employers are not satisfied with the applicants, there is an overall shortage of applicants, or employers decide not to fill the jobs.

What is its impact on financial markets?

Most economic releases are reported when the financial markets are open. The help-wanted index is released after markets have already closed. Usually, the financial press will bury the story in a corner and the local press may not even carry it. As a result, financial market participants traditionally did not react to this indicator. However, as Fed Chairman, Alan Greenspan, has frequently referred to labor market pressures this indicator has become much more market sensitive (*see* Box 9.4).

Box 9.4: Market reaction to an unexpected change in the Help-Wanted Advertising Index

Degree of market sensitivity:
High
Medium ✓
Low

Help-Wanted Advertising Index	⬆	⬇
Bond market	⬇	⬆
Equity market	⬆	⬇
US dollar	⬆	⬇

SINDLINGER HOUSEHOLD LIQUIDITY INDEX

Definition

Sindlinger's Household Liquidity Index is constructed from findings on current income, expected income, expected employment and expected business. These are combined to derive the index. Data are gathered through a continuous nationwide telephone survey of the US's household heads.

Who publishes it and when?

A widely watched indicator of potential spending power is provided by the privately produced Sindlinger Household Liquidity Index, published bi-weekly each Tuesday and Friday.

How do you interpret it?

Significant changes in consumer attitudes are apt to show up first in expectations for future employment conditions. Virtually all working Americans are sensitive to changing working conditions and information about changes in the local labor market is quickly transmitted through formal channels or by word of mouth.

This component of confidence in future employment prospects tends to be sensitive to production, export sales, and stock market performance.

Expectations for local business conditions generally tend to follow the same pattern as expectations for employment. Declines in this component will show up in the early stages of an economic downturn. As household current income or expected income starts to diminish, expectations of local business conditions driven by consumer demand eventually falter. Changes in this component are less pronounced than the changes which occur in job and income expectations due to the fact that fewer people (in the total population) have a genuine awareness of business conditions.

The component which deals with expected household income is very sensitive to interest rates, US Federal monetary policy, US fiscal policy, as well as foreign monetary and fiscal policies. If tighter monetary policy is implemented to slow the economy, or a looser monetary policy is implemented, this influences the direction of expected income. In turn, the stock market is highly influential in determining whether there will be a tighter or looser monetary policy. If consumers perceive the trend in stock market prices, this directly affects the "wealth effect" which in turn significantly changes expectations of income. By and large, American household heads expect their income to be the "same" or "higher," except for those persons engaged in seasonal employment or those who are leaving the labor market. On the negative side, a sustained decline in expected income will signify the economy is in an advanced phase of contraction and on the positive side an acceleration in expected income will signify an expansion in the pace of economic activity.

All household liquidity indicators are derived from responses to four questions which are asked of thousands of household heads each week. The four questions deal with the following.

Current household income compared to the level of household income six months ago. Responses are recorded as "up," "down," "same," or "don't know."

Expected household income in six months. Responses also are recorded as "up," "down," "same," and "no opinion."

Expected local employment situation in six months. Responses are recorded as "more jobs," "fewer jobs," "same," or "no opinion."

Expected local business condition in six months. Categories of response are "better," "worse," "same," and "no opinion."

Total Household Liquidity is expressed as a percentage and as a numerical projection of all US household heads. As a percentage, it represents the proportion of household heads in the US sample who provide either a positive or neutral answer to all four component questions. Respondents who provided a negative answer to any of the four questions are not included in the Household Liquidity Index sample percentage.

Because the sample size is sufficiently large and is representative of all US household heads, the Household Liquidity Index percentage provides a broad trend as to consumers' spending patterns.

What is its impact on financial markets?

Household liquidity is an important determinant of future economic activity. When household liquidity is high consumer's willingness to spend or preparation to spend provides a stimulus to the economy. Low levels of household liquidity signal household decisions to cut back on spending and to increase saving. Although not a highly sensitive market indicator its main value is in reinforcing consumer confidence indicators at times when market sentiment is changing rapidly (*see* Box 9.5).

Box 9.5: Market reaction to an unexpected change in the Sindlinger Household Liquidity Index

Degree of market sensitivity:
High
Medium
Low ✓

Sindlinger Household Liquidity Index	↑	↓
Bond market	↓	↑
Equity market	↑	↓
US dollar	↑	↓

ADDRESSES AND WEB SITES

Board of Governors of the Federal Reserve System
Publications Services
Division of Administrative Services
Washington, D.C. 20551
202-452-3244
http://www.bog.frb.fed.us

Federal Reserve Bank of Atlanta
Publications Unit
Public Affairs Department
104 Marietta Street, N.W.
Atlanta, Georgia 30303
404-521-8020
http://www.frbatlanta.org

Federal Reserve Bank of Boston
Public and Community Affairs Department
P.O. Box 2076
Boston, Massachusetts 02106-2076
617-973-3459
http://www.bos.frb.org

Federal Reserve Bank of Chicago
Public Information Department
230 LaSalle Street
Chicago, Illinois 60690
312-322-5112
http://www.frbchi.org

Federal Reserve Bank of Cleveland
Public Information Center
P.O. Box 6387
Cleveland, Ohio 44101-1387
216-579-3079
http://www.clev.frb.org

Federal Reserve Bank of Dallas
Public Information Department
2200 North Pearl Street
Dallas, Texas 75201
214-922-5270
http://www.dallasfed.org

Federal Reserve Bank of Kansas City
Public Affairs Department
925 Grand Boulevard
Kansas City, Missouri 64198
816-881-2683
http://www.kc.frb.org

Federal Reserve Bank of Minneapolis
Public Affairs Department
250 Marquette Avenue
Minneapolis, Minnesota 55401-2171
612-340-2446
http://woodrow.mpls.frb.fed.us

Federal Reserve Bank of New York
Public Information Department
33 Liberty Street
New York, New York 10045
212-720-6134
http://www.ny.frb.org

Federal Reserve Bank of Philadelphia
Public Affairs Department
P.O. Box 66
Philadelphia, Pennsylvania 19105
215-574-6115
http://www.libertynet.org/~fedresrv/fedpage.html

Federal Reserve Bank of Richmond
Public Services Department
P.O. Box 27622
Richmond, Virginia 23261
804-697-8109
http://www.rich.frb.org

Federal Reserve Bank of St. Louis
Public Affairs Department
Box 442
St. Louis, Missouri 63166
314-444-8809
http://www.stls.frb.org

Federal Reserve Bank of San Francisco
Public Information Department
P.O. Box 7702
San Francisco, California 94120
415-974-2163
415-974-2246
http://www.frbsf.org

TRAINING IN FINANCIAL MARKETS

The author runs training courses on financial markets for banks, financial institutions, investment banks and for institutional and retail investors.

The courses are taught in-house and can be modified according to the needs of the client. Courses currently being taught range from graduate trainee programmes to courses on specific instruments and markets.

Among the courses offered are:

- Graduate training programme for newcomers to financial markets
- Financial markets for dealers/fund managers/investors
- Foreign exchange market fundamentals for dealers/fund managers/investors
- Portfolio management and investment analysis: the basics
- Fed-Watching for dealers/fund managers/investors
- Economics of financial markets – what lies behind all this volatility?
- Finance for Non-Financial Managers
- Statistics and mathematics for financial markets: what you really need to know.

For further information on in-house training please contact
Brian Kettell
Managing Director
9A South End Road
Hampstead
London NW3 2PT
United Kingdom
Telephone 020 7435 4487
Fax 020 7431 8410
E mail: brian@bkettell.com
Web site: www.bkettell.com/b.kettell

INDEX